Flowering Shrubs

Flowering Shrubs

by

JAMES UNDERWOOD CROCKETT

and

the Editors of TIME-LIFE BOOKS

Watercolor Illustrations by

Allianora Rosse

An Owl Book

HENRY HOLT AND COMPANY

NEW YORK

THE TIME-LIFE ENCYCLOPEDIA OF GARDENING
EDITOR: Robert M. Jones
EDITORIAL STAFF FOR FLOWERING SHRUBS:
EDITOR: Ogden Tanner
Text Editor: Jay Brennan
Picture Editor: Adrian Condon
Designer: Leonard Wolfe
Staff Writers: Marian Gordon Goldman, Lee Greene,
Gerry Schremp, Timberlake Wertenbaker
Researchers: Barbara Ensrud, Helen Fennell,
Rhea Finkelstein, Gail Hansberry, Mary Leverty
Lyn Stallworth, Sandra Streepey, Gretchen Wessels

Copyright © 1972 by Time-Life Books Inc.
All rights reserved, including the right to reproduce
this book or portions thereof in any form.
Published by Henry Holt and Company, Inc.,
521 Fifth Avenue, New York, New York 10175.

Library of Congress Cataloging-in-Publication Data
Crockett, James Underwood.
Flowering shrubs.
(The Time-Life encyclopedia of gardening)
"An Owl book."
Reprint. Originally published: New York: Time-Life Books, 1972.
Bibliography: p.
Includes index.
1. Flowering shrubs.   I. Time-Life Books.
II. Title.   III. Series.
SB435.C83 1987   635.9'76   86–33580
ISBN 0-8050-0353-3 (pbk.)

First published by Time-Life Books in 1972.
First Owl Book Edition—1987
Printed in the United States of America
10 9 8 7 6 5 4 3 2 1

ISBN 0-8050-0353-3

THE AUTHOR: The late James Underwood Crockett, author of 13 of the volumes in the Encyclopedia, co-author of two additional volumes and consultant on other books in the series, was a lover of the earth and its good things. He graduated from the Stockbridge School of Agriculture at the University of Massachusetts and worked all his life in horticulture. A perennial contributor to gardening magazines, he also wrote a monthly bulletin, "Flowery Talks," distributed through retail florists. His television program, *Crockett's Victory Garden,* shown all over the United States, won countless converts to his approach to growing things.

THE ILLUSTRATOR: Allianora Rosse, who provided the 98 delicate, precise watercolors of flowering shrubs beginning on page 92, is a specialist in flower painting. Trained at the Art Academy of The Hague in The Netherlands, Miss Rosse worked for 16 years as staff artist for *Flower Grower* magazine. Her illustrations of shrubs, trees and flowers have appeared in many gardening books.

GENERAL CONSULTANTS: Dr. C. Gustav Hard, Professor, University of Minnesota, St. Paul, Minn. Albert P. Nordheden, Morganville, New Jersey. Staff of the Brooklyn Botanic Garden: Elizabeth Scholtz, Director; Robert S. Tomson, Assistant Director; George A. Kalmbacher, Plant Taxonomist; Edmund O. Moulin, Horticulturist.

THE COVER: A flowering shrub that puts on a show of color from early spring through fall is redvein enkianthus. Tiny bell-shaped blossoms appear even before the leaves and last about three weeks, bringing a subdued loveliness to spring gardens; the foliage, a rich green all summer, blazes brilliant orange and scarlet in fall.

CONTENTS

1 Bargains in beauty
7

Picture essay: A CALENDAR OF COLOR
18

2 Choosing, planting and caring for shrubs
35

Picture essay: A PRETTY WAY TO SOLVE A PROBLEM
64

3 Six ways to multiply your plants
81

4 An illustrated encyclopedia of flowering shrubs
93

APPENDIX

Characteristics of 274 flowering shrubs
146

A guide to pests and diseases
152

Where and when flowering shrubs bloom
154

Credits and acknowledgments
155

Bibliography
155

Index
156

Bargains in beauty 1

When I was a small boy in New England, my sister and I watched in fascination one May while a pair of hummingbirds built their tiny nest in a Japanese barberry bush beneath the dining-room window of our house. That was a long time ago—I was about 12 years old when we moved away to another house—but I treasure the memory because that barberry sums up so many of the merits of flowering shrubs. It offered red-tinged yellow flowers in spring, scarlet foliage in fall and bright red berries through the winter—and, these attractions aside, it brought the hummingbirds. Gardens rich in flowering shrubs seem to attract more birds than do other gardens *(pages 42-47)*. Just the other day a friend told me about a couple of cardinals that return every year to a beautifully flowered withe rod that grows beside his back door; the birds come to raise their broods and long ago became so accustomed to household noise they stopped flying off the nest every time the door opened. They feel secure in the profusion of flowers and foliage, and the plant's berries provide a feast—as do those of other flowering shrubs.

Even if you are not especially fond of birds, there are compelling reasons for incorporating flowering shrubs in your garden. First, of course, is the brilliant display of the flowers themselves; from early spring to fall, and even into winter in mild climates, there are various species in flower, and during spring and summer scores of them seem to compete to outshine one another. Such shrubs yield armfuls of bouquets for the house during their normal blooming period—and before they bloom outdoors as well, for stems or branches can be cut and induced to flower indoors. Even when they are not in bloom they make unique contributions to the garden—you would have to see the red stems of a Siberian dogwood glowing in the sunlight across a snow-blanketed lawn to appreciate fully how flowering shrubs serve in all seasons (for a review of shrubs' year-round usefulness, see pages 18-33).

From a practical point of view, most flowering shrubs have the additional virtue of fast growth, generally maturing within five

A big-leaved hydrangea, each of its flower clusters a foot across, blooms in late summer outside a Southampton, Long Island, house near the Atlantic Ocean. A popular flowering shrub, it flourishes in seaside locations.

years. And they seem to flourish forever. In Concord, Massachusetts, where I live, some of the lilacs, flowering quinces and bottle-brush buckeyes that adorn the town's historic homes have been growing for a century or more.

Flowering shrubs not only live for many years, they get along during their extended life spans with a minimum of care—some, in fact, require none. And they are generally inexpensive. I have a magnificent Persian lilac whose 8-foot height and 10-foot spread bow under great clusters of sweet-scented blooms each May. I am almost embarrassed to admit that it cost me 14 cents when I bought it as a small plant some years ago. Nurserymen can afford to sell flowering shrubs at reasonable prices because they grow so fast in the nursery, and because many of them can be moved without a heavy ball of soil around their roots. The light weight of such bare-rooted plants reduces the nurseryman's labor costs and keeps postage down on plants shipped by mail-order garden suppliers.

SHRUBS VERSUS TREES When shrubs reach a size like that of my lilac, people sometimes refer to them as trees. Although this is understandable, there is a distinction. Both shrubs and trees are woody plants, which means that their stems and branches survive from year to year in areas where they are resistant to winter cold. But a shrub, as the majority of people—nurserymen included—think of one, is a plant that has multiple trunks or stems and does not grow more than 20 feet high; a tree generally has a single trunk and may attain great height.

The distinction between shrubs and trees is a semantic one, devised by man rather than by nature. In this country, a mature Chinese redbud grows as a strikingly beautiful shrub from 6 to 8 feet high, but in the climate of central China, where it is native, it becomes a 40-foot tree. Flowering dogwoods are usually small trees, but if they are cut back after their first year in the garden, they will produce several stems rather than one and develop as shrubs. Occasionally gardeners train shrubs to grow in tree form—the technical term for such a shrub form is a "standard"—by eliminating all but one stem and all side branches until the plant is 4 or 5 feet tall; when branches develop above that point, the shrub assumes the appearance of a small tree. Shrubs include both evergreens and deciduous plants, that is, those that drop their leaves seasonally. But when a nurseryman says "flowering shrubs," he generally means deciduous flowering shrubs, which are the subject of this book.

WHERE SHRUBS GROW Flowering shrubs can be grown almost everywhere in the United States and Canada, although the heat of the Gulf Coast and the aridity of much of the Southwest limit the gardener's choices in those areas, and even the most rugged shrubs will not survive where winter temperatures drop to 50° below zero. Some are native plants, as the first European explorers discovered: red chokeberry, serviceberry, witch hazel, summer sweet, bayberry, sumac, blueberry, cranberry bush and certain deciduous azaleas. Yet most of the favorites of American gardeners—notably forsythia, lilac, flowering quince, spirea, hydrangea and honeysuckle—originally came from China, Japan, Korea or Siberia. For plants that, like the flowering shrubs, thrive in temperate climates, Asia is the treasure trove —China alone counts some 15,000 species of flora, of which at least half are not native elsewhere. Yet many of the most beautiful varieties common in American gardens today are not the original imported species but hybrids, the results of complex crossbreeding. The modern hybrids far surpass their ancestors in beauty, hardiness and variety of colors and flower shapes.

Among modern hybrid flowering shrubs that are great favorites today in northern areas are cold-resistant species and hybrids of lilacs, bridal wreaths, pussy willows and Japanese roses. Forsythias, deutzias, mock oranges and deciduous azaleas, not quite so hardy, adorn gardens in more temperate areas. Crape myrtles, butterfly bushes and winter jasmines, seldom seen in the North, flourish in the South. Perhaps the shrub with the widest distribution is the flowering quince. Handsome and adaptable, it opens its appleblossom-like pink, white or red flowers as early as January in the Deep South, and as late as early April in Maine.

The varied shapes and sizes of flowering shrubs, the beauty of their blossoms, and the colors of their fruits, berries, foliage and bark provide the landscape gardener with a broad palette. There is a type to fill almost any need in the garden, as the pictures on pages 65-79 show. Some, such as witch hazel, daphne, mock orange and snowberry, tolerate light shade and will flourish under trees or on the north side of a house. Others, such as five-leaved aralia, Japanese barberry, forsythia, rose of Sharon and crape myrtle, withstand the polluted air of cities and grow well in backyards and doorways close to the street. Sweet shrubs, summer sweets, spicebushes, pussy willows and azaleas thrive in moist soil and can be used in low-lying ground or beside a pond or stream. Sweet fern, broom, beauty bush and sumac stand dry soil and do well on slopes or banks or at the tops of garden walls. Beach plum, groundsel bush, cotoneaster, broom, bayberry and lilac stand up to seaside conditions and are ideal for gardens at the beach. So are certain roses, which are not often thought of as shrubs but are, since like others of this class they are bushy, woody flowering plants. Some species, such as the cabbage rose, are particularly useful as shrubs because they require little care compared to the garden varieties grown for show.

A SHRUB FOR EVERY PURPOSE

When it comes to choosing and locating specific shrubs on your own property, it pays to study both the nature of the plants and the functions you want them to perform. Some flowering shrubs, such as the flowering quince, are handsome enough to merit positions as showpieces, standing alone in a spot where they can grow to their full size and beauty unhindered by competition from other plants. But almost all shrubs can perform several functions and the smaller the garden, the more important it becomes that they do double or even triple duty. One of these functions, the production of flowers, may occupy only two or three weeks of the year, but during the rest of the time that the plants are in leaf, and even when they are not, they can provide edible or decorative berries, act as screens to blot out unpleasant views, serve as windbreaks to deflect annoying winds, form hedges that define property lines and areas within a garden, or soften the lines of a house and its foundations. One of the most versatile shrubs I know is the high-bush blueberry in my own backyard—it bears masses of bell-shaped white flowers in spring, yields 8 quarts of delicious fruit in late summer and adds vivid hues to the landscape when its leathery dark green foliage turns scarlet in fall; it also serves to separate my vegetable garden visually from the sitting area on my back lawn.

SHRUBS NEAR THE HOUSE One of the most common uses for flowering shrubs is next to a house, to accent a doorway, to hide unsightly aboveground foundation walls or to make the house blend into its site. Probably the most important consideration in choosing shrubs for this purpose is size and shape. The plants should complement the lines of the house and should be of kinds that will not soon outgrow their locations.

(continued on page 15)

The shrub hunters

Many flowering shrubs that adorn American gardens today look so much at home, it is hard to realize they were originally brought back from the Far East by professional plant hunters who went on long and often hazardous journeys to find them. Plant hunting probably started 5,000 years ago when the Pharaohs of Egypt sent ships down the Red Sea in search of cinnamon and cassia; its golden age, however, began in the 18th Century when European naturalists stumbled upon such then-exotic species as honeysuckle, azalea and kerria and made them instant favorites back home. The botanist-explorers who followed probed deep into China, where so many new species were found that one man called that country "the central flowery land." In this century Americans, sent by the Department of Agriculture as well as American arboretums, have become leaders in plant exploration as the search for new species goes on.

Collecting for future gardens

One of the first important collectors the U.S. Department of Agriculture sent to Asia was Frank Meyer, who in the years between 1905 and 1918 brought back several new species of euonymus, viburnum and lilac. Meyer had a passion for walking—on one expedition in Manchuria alone he covered 1,800 miles on foot. It was during a trek through the high Wu-tai-shan mountains of northeastern China that he came across a species of lilac that was smaller than most of the ones previously known; later named *Syringa meyeri (page 140)*, it blossoms even as a very young plant and is especially treasured in today's smaller gardens.

LILAC

Frank Meyer shows off native garb —furry hat, coat and boots—that he wore while hunting hardy plants in the mountains of China in 1908.

At the top of a pass in northeastern China in 1913, Meyer paused with the mule caravan that carried his supplies and his plant finds.

"Tact and a sound physique"

FORSYTHIA

Ernest Wilson once summarized the traits that his profession demanded: "An eminently sane mind [and] an optimistic temperament . . . above all else tact and a sound physique." Such attributes sustained "Chinese" Wilson through 20 years of plant hunting. He survived an avalanche and malaria, traveled with assurance among head-hunters (below)—and smuggled seeds through his own country's quarantine process to avoid precautionary treatments that might harm them. He brought back new species of buddleia and hydrangea as well as Forsythia ovata, the forsythia that is the hardiest and the earliest to bloom.

A crude hut (top)—shared with pigs and cockroaches—was Wilson's lodging in the high country of China in 1906.

Faring better afloat than ashore, Wilson sailed the Yangtze on another trip in a houseboat he called "my Chinese home."

In 1918 Wilson posed among his porters—Formosan head-hunters who worked for wine and the privilege of carrying a gun.

From lepers to lamas

Joseph Rock was first sent to the Orient by the U.S. Department of Agriculture in 1920 to search for the chaulmoogra tree, whose oil was used to treat leprosy. He found his trees—in Burma—then proceeded to China, where he remained, on and off, for the next 27 years, much of it plant hunting for the Arnold Arboretum. He sent back several new species, among them the seeds of a tree peony he had seen growing only in the courtyard of a Tibetan lamasery. Several years later, the lamasery burned down and its unique peonies were destroyed, but by that time Rock was able to send the lamas new seeds of their own shrub.

TREE PEONY

With an escort of Yunnan tribesmen, Joseph Rock crossed the Koko Nor Mountains in Tibet in 1925, during a search for new species of azaleas.

A shrub for every garden

Among the most active of modern shrub hunters is John L. Creech, chief of plant exploration for the U.S.D.A. Creech has traveled extensively through Asia, seeking to extend the range of cultivation of already familiar species. He looks for plants growing at the limits of their natural habitat, where they exhibit resistance to climatic extremes. Among the most welcome of such discoveries was one Creech made in 1971 in Yakutsk, Siberia, where severe conditions resemble those of the North Central States and Canada: a lovely pink Japanese rose that promises colorful blossoms for areas lacking a variety of flowering shrubs.

Standing at the base of the Nepalese Himalayas before an expedition in 1962, John L. Creech leans on the long pole he uses to inspect high branches.

A forsythia that normally grows 6 feet tall and arches out an equal distance, for example, would be a poor choice close to a front door or window; it would have to be sheared back constantly to keep it from getting in the way, destroying its natural beauty as well as causing a great deal of unnecessary work and annoyance. Such locations generally demand a more compact species—for example, one that will never become more than 3 feet or so tall; you might as well face that requirement first and save yourself frustration later. You will find many 3-foot shrubs in the encyclopedia section starting on page 93 and the charts on pages 146-151—barberries, spireas, brooms, cotoneasters, daphnes, viburnums. The choice is wider than you might think at first, for among the species that normally grow much taller than 3 feet are many special compact types. Once you have decided on the size and shape you need, you can go on to select the flower color and other characteristics you like best from a number of plants that will fit near your house.

An equally common use for flowering shrubs is in hedges, either low ones to define an area without shutting off the view and breeze, or higher ones to do just that. I must confess I cannot become very enthusiastic about most of the hedges I have seen, mainly because of the lack of imagination shown by those who have recommended such a small variety of plants for this purpose. In many nurseries even today the common privet is simply called hedge, as though no other plant were suitable.

SHRUBS FOR HEDGES

When you mention the word hedge to most people, they generally think of plants like the privet, laid out in a long line and neatly trimmed into a boxy shape. And to most gardeners this kind of hedge means hard work—the never-ending chore of keeping it trimmed, for which a special tool of torture, the hedge shears, was invented. Actually a hedge can be any row of shrubs used to define an area or separate one area from another and, if desired, act as a privacy screen, a windbreak or a background for flower beds. It can be sheared and formal or unsheared and informal. I much prefer the latter kind, in which plants grow in their own natural, graceful shapes, do not exhibit stubby stems and mutilated leaves from repeated cuttings and, because their buds are not sheared off, produce their full complement of lovely flowers and fruit.

Up-to-date nurserymen offer a wide variety of plants that make fine informal hedges, requiring virtually no pruning yet staying attractive year after year. Even though they lose their leaves during the winter, these shrubs give abundant privacy to a patio or garden during the summer months, the time when these areas are most used. When the leaves are gone the branches still afford partial screening while they continue to define the garden's shape.

Informal hedges, however, generally require more space than formal ones because they are allowed to spread naturally, and unless you have ground to spare, I suggest you first consider shrubs that will form a relatively narrow hedge without need for trimming back. Among the best of these are the barberry known as truehedge columnberry, which grows 3 to 4 feet tall and 2½ feet wide; the Mentor barberry, which reaches 6 to 7 feet in height and 4 feet in width; and the variety of alder buckthorn called New Tallhedge, which may become 12 to 15 feet tall yet only about 4 feet wide.

Despite my personal preference for informal hedges, I must admit there are instances when sheared hedges are the best solution to privacy. They respond to shearing by putting forth great numbers of twigs that produce a very dense screen, and they can be trimmed to take up an even narrower space than the informal varieties mentioned above—as little as 2 feet. Some of the shrubs most suitable for formal clipped hedges are Japanese barberry, five-leaved aralia, dwarf winged euonymus, Amur privet and Regel privet; for an extremely narrow hedge, use the truehedge columnberry (the same one that makes a fine informal hedge). None of these plants are noted for their flowers, so they can be clipped any time; the flower buds removed will hardly be missed.

SHRUBS IN BORDERS Flowering shrubs can be both practical and beautiful in house plantings and hedges, but to my mind their most striking use is in what, for lack of a better term, are called borders. A border is any grouping of plants, generally of different kinds, designed primarily to please the eye. A border composed of shrubs can also act, like a hedge, as boundary marker, privacy screen or windbreak, but it transcends these functions by becoming a major decorative element of the garden. The most successful borders, in fact, are intricate and carefully planned gardens in themselves, made up of a variety of shrubs that in turn can be used as a foreground for taller trees and a background for lower flowers.

When I plan a border for a backyard, I try to visualize myself in a boat, floating on a pond, for the wild plants that surround a pond are nature's own border for the pond. In my mind the lawn I must frame is the surface of the water, and as I recall how woodland plants fringe an open area like a pond, I imagine how this shrub or that one would look in a given location. In this way it is possible to create a very natural assemblage of plants that look as though they belong together in their site. If the border is at some distance from the house, and particularly if it is in a rural or semirural setting, it will look more natural if many of the plants chosen are native to the area in which you live. These are also the plants that are most apt to be tolerant of the climate, soil and light conditions of your garden, as well as the most resistant to local diseases and pests.

I plan a shrub border from the back, starting with the tallest-growing shrubs. First of all, make sure your tallest plants will not be too tall for your garden; in most suburban gardens the maximum height should not exceed 6 or 8 feet, just high enough to give you privacy and screen you from a neighbor's yard, but not so tall as to cut off welcome breezes and sunlight. Shrubs that will eventually grow 15 to 18 feet tall may make an effective screen if you are trying to blot out a two-story house across the way, but they may also dwarf your backyard, making it seem smaller than it really is. Second, think also of varying the appearance—heights, foliage textures and colors—so that you can achieve a more interesting effect. Plants toward the back of a border are often set relatively close to one another. Massed in this way, they grow together to form a more or less solid green background for the bright flowers of shorter plants in front and they also make a better privacy screen, windbreak and shelter for birds.

Once you have established a pattern in your mind for the tallest background plants, you can begin to fill in with somewhat smaller shrubs in front. The most interesting borders are not straight as a string, but are designed with bays and nooks and curves that can be planted with displays of flowers lower than the medium-sized shrubs. These medium-sized shrubs, like the taller ones in back, should be clustered in groups rather than used singly to avoid a spotty, disorganized appearance, and if they are chosen to bloom at different times, they give a changing display of color from spring through fall. For example, one of the groups could be made up of a number of plants of slender deutzia, which grows 2 to 4 feet tall and bears snow-white flowers in late spring. Another group could be alpine Japanese spirea, which grows about a foot tall and produces pink flowers most of the summer. Still another cluster could be composed of a blending of soft yellow and white varieties of dwarf bush cinquefoil, which vary in height from 6 inches to 2½ feet and blossom from early summer until fall.

Finally, in the bays and nooks created by these groups, you can find some excellent wind-protected spots for early-flowering bulbs, for massive displays of perennials and for the summer-long color of annuals. Be bold with these foreground plantings lest they be overpowered by the larger shrubs behind and around them. Use dozens of daffodils; take advantage of the mighty summertime display of garden phlox and day lilies; plant bright marigolds, zinnias or petunias to bring ample drifts of color to the border's front. Many gardeners vary such plantings from year to year; the permanent background of flowering shrubs remains as a frame and a source of pleasure whatever they do.

A PLANT-BREEDER'S DREAM

The Exbury azaleas, among the most spectacular of modern flowering shrubs, are the result of a remarkable crossbreeding program started in the 1920s by Lionel de Rothschild, an English member of the banking family, at Exbury, his country estate. An avid plant fancier, he maintained 250 acres of gardens, complete with 30 greenhouses and a staff of 225 men including 75 professional gardeners. Rothschild was no idle dabbler; every Friday he rushed out from London in his Rolls-Royce, distributing cigars to his senior gardeners along with detailed instructions for the weekend's work. He did most of the hand-pollinating of flowers himself and personally chose the site for each new plant by marking the ground with the tip of his cane. Rothschild eventually crossed more than 50 different types of azaleas—including species from Japan, China, Russia's Black Sea region and North America—to produce hundreds of thousands of seedlings. By 1934 he was able to exhibit the first varieties of an entirely new strain of plants, which soon were prized for their vigor as well as their large, vividly colored blooms (page 129; photograph, page 80). The Exbury Strain is so lovely that gardeners in the lands of its ancestors, notably Japan, import specimens of it from Britain and America to grow themselves.

A calendar of color

Sometimes the last patches of winter snow still fleck the ground when the flowering shrubs burst into activity, starting a year-round calendar of color: vivid flowers in spring and summer, followed by berries, bright foliage in fall, more fruit and handsome bark in winter. Shrubs alone can keep a garden aglow season after season. The bright yellow pollen-bearing stamens of the goat willow *(right)* appear early, braving the chill of spring on branches still bare of foliage. They are followed through spring and summer by the varied blooms of more than a thousand different types of flowering shrubs, from the golden sprays of forsythia and the fragrant pyramids of lavender lilacs to the graceful blossoms of pink and white azaleas. Long before the last blooms begin to fade and fall, other flowering shrubs offer new delights to the gardener. From the seed receptacles left behind by departed flowers comes an assortment of berries that are not only red but yellow, blue and black as well. Some, like the delicious blueberry, soon fall prey to the appetites of men and birds. Others, like the bright red Japanese barberry, are inedible and remain all winter long, adding a bit of gaiety to the winter garden.

Yet even before winter comes, autumn's shortening days and cool nights trigger another outburst of color as the green foliage of many shrubs turns scarlet, orange, purple or bronze. And finally, when the leaves wither and most of the berries are gone, the stark and graceful branches stand revealed, enhanced in many cases by bright bark of handsome hues.

You can find a few shrubs, like the Westonbirt dogwood, that put on a good show in every season; not only do they bear desirable flowers but their berries, autumn leaves and bark are noteworthy as well. Most gardeners, however, seek a succession of display by selecting species to suit each part of the year. To assist in such a selection, lists on the following pages match 121 shrubs to the seasons in which they are particularly attractive. An accompanying guide specifies the seasons in months for the U.S. and Canadian climate areas shown on the zone map on page 154.

One of the first shrubs to bloom is the goat willow, whose buds burst open as early as January in the Deep South.

GOAT WILLOW

SEASON

Zone 2: Late April through May

Zone 3: Mid-April to mid-May

Zone 4: Late March to mid-May

Zone 5: Mid-March to mid-May

Zone 6: Late February to mid-April

Zone 7: Mid-February to mid-April

Zone 8: February to mid-March

Zone 9: Mid-January to mid-March

Zone 10: January to mid-February

The shrubs that flower earliest, like the Chinese witch hazel shown below, begin producing flowers when the first warm days of spring awaken dormant buds formed during the previous year. As the days grow warmer and longer other shrubs come into bloom. In virtually an ordered sequence *(opposite, top left to bottom right),* the cornelian cherry is followed by spicebush, forsythia, quince and rhododendron —all forerunners of the still later springtime display shown overleaf, which marks the height of the flowering season.

Early spring

Shrub and zones in which it can be grown (see chart above for dates of flowering in your zone).

Early season

CHINESE WITCH HAZEL (Zones 5-9)

GOAT WILLOW (Zones 4-9)

Midseason

BORDER FORSYTHIA (Zones 5-9)

CORNELIAN CHERRY (Zones 4-8)

FEBRUARY DAPHNE (Zones 4-9)

KOREAN ABELIALEAF (Zones 5-8)

SPICEBUSH (Zones 4-9)

SPIKE WINTER HAZEL (Zones 6-9)

WINTER HONEYSUCKLE (Zones 5-9)

WINTER JASMINE (Zones 6-9)

Late season

BRIDAL WREATH (Zones 4-10)

HYBRID FLOWERING QUINCE (Zones 6-10)

KOREAN RHODODENDRON (Zones 4-8)

LILAC DAPHNE (Zones 6-9)

CHINESE WITCH HAZEL

CORNELIAN CHERRY   SPICEBUSH   BEATRIX FARRAND FORSYTHIA

FLOWERING QUINCE   KOREAN RHODODENDRON

	SEASON
Zone 2:	Late May to mid-June
Zone 3:	Mid-May to mid-June
Zone 4:	May to mid-June
Zone 5:	May to mid-June
Zone 6:	Mid-April to mid-June
Zone 7:	April through May
Zone 8:	Mid-March to mid-May
Zone 9:	March to mid-May
Zone 10:	Mid-February to mid-April

Late spring

LORBERG'S PEA TREE   LARGE FOTHERGILLA

Shrub and zones in which it can be grown (see chart above for dates of flowering in your zone).

Early season

DWARF FLOWERING ALMOND (Zones 4-9)

THE BRIDE PEARLBUSH (Zones 5-9)

Midseason

CHINESE REDBUD (Zones 6-9)

COMMON LILAC (Zones 3-7)

DOUBLEFILE VIBURNUM (Zones 4-9)

FRAGRANT SNOWBALL (Zones 5-9)

JAPANESE BARBERRY (Zones 4-10)

JETBEAD (Zones 5-8)

KERRIA (Zones 4-9)

KEW BROOM (Zones 6-10)

LARGE FOTHERGILLA (Zones 5-9)

PINKSHELL AZALEA (Zones 3-8)

REDVEIN ENKIANTHUS (Zones 4-9)

ROYAL AZALEA (Zones 4-8)

SIBERIAN PEA TREE (Zones 2-9)

SWEET SHRUB (Zones 4-10)

TATARIAN HONEYSUCKLE (Zones 3-9)

Late season

AMUR HONEYSUCKLE (Zones 2-9)

BRILLIANT CHOKEBERRY (Zones 4-10)

EXBURY AZALEA (Zones 5-8)

FATHER HUGO'S ROSE (Zones 5-10)

FOUNTAIN BUTTERFLY BUSH (Zones 5-10)

HYBRID WEIGELA (Zones 5-9)

LEMOINE DEUTZIA (Zones 4-9)

MARIE'S DOUBLEFILE VIBURNUM (Zones 4-9)

MOLLIS HYBRID AZALEA (Zones 5-8)

ORIENTAL PHOTINIA (Zones 4-8)

PERSIAN LILAC (Zones 5-9)

ROSE ACACIA (Zones 5-9)

TATARIAN DOGWOOD (Zones 5-10)

TREE PEONY (Zones 5-8)

VANHOUTTE SPIREA (Zones 4-10)

WARMINSTER BROOM (Zones 5-10)

CONGO LILAC   DOUBLEFILE VIBURNUM

AMUR HONEYSUCKLE MOLLIS HYBRID AZALEA

FATHER HUGO'S ROSE   VANHOUTTE SPIREA   WESTONBIRT DOGWOOD

SEASON

Zone 2: Mid-June to mid-July

Zone 3: Mid-June to mid-July

Zone 4: Mid-June to mid-July

Zone 5: June to mid-July

Zone 6: June to mid-July

Zone 7: Late May to mid-July

Zone 8: Mid-May to mid-July

Zone 9: May to mid-July

Zone 10: April to mid-July

Among the most pleasing characteristics of many summer-flowering shrubs like Ural false spirea *(below)* and five-stamened tamarisk *(overleaf)* are their long blooming periods, brightening the midsummer season when few other plants are in flower. Some shrubs blossom in early summer and continue until first frost—as does the bush cinquefoil *(below)*. Summer also ushers in the berry season as some of the early-flowering shrubs begin to bear their fruit—the first of a colorful harvest that reaches its peak in the fall.

Early summer

Shrub and zones in which it can be grown (see chart above for dates of flowering or berrying in your zone).

Early season

BEAUTY BUSH (Zones 4-9)

*FEBRUARY DAPHNE (Zones 4-9)

FLAME AZALEA (Zones 5-8)

HYBRID WEIGELA (Zones 5-9)

JAPANESE ROSE (Zones 2-10)

LEMOINE MOCK ORANGE (Zones 5-9)

SMOKE TREE (Zones 5-10)

*WINTER HONEYSUCKLE (Zones 5-9)

Midseason

AMERICAN ELDER (Zones 3-9)

BUSH CINQUEFOIL (Zones 2-9)

BUMALDA SPIREA (Zones 5-10)

CABBAGE ROSE (Zones 5-10)

*CHERRY ELAEAGNUS (Zones 4-10)

CUT-LEAVED STEPHANANDRA (Zones 5-8)

FUZZY DEUTZIA (Zones 5-9)

KIRILOW INDIGO (Zones 4-8)

MAGELLAN FUCHSIA (Zones 6-8)

*TATARIAN DOGWOOD (Zones 5-10)

URAL FALSE SPIREA (Zones 2-8)

VIRGINALIS MOCK ORANGE (Zones 5-9)

Late season

BOTTLE-BRUSH BUCKEYE (Zones 4-10)

GOLDEN ST.-JOHN'S-WORT (Zones 5-9)

HILLS-OF-SNOW HYDRANGEA (Zones 4-10)

KALM ST.-JOHN'S-WORT (Zones 4-8)

LEAD PLANT (Zones 2-10)

OAK-LEAVED HYDRANGEA (Zones 5-9)

ODESSA TAMARISK (Zones 4-10)

SHOWY STEWARTIA (Zones 5-9)

SPIKE BROOM (Zones 5-10)

*TATARIAN HONEYSUCKLE (Zones 3-9)

Early summer berries

LEMOINE MOCK ORANGE   STYRIACA WEIGELA

BUSH CINQUEFOIL   URAL FALSE SPIREA

ANTHONY WATERER SPIREA

AMERICAN ELDER

OAK-LEAVED HYDRANGEA

SEASON

Zone 2: Mid-July to early August

Zone 3: Mid-July to early August

Zone 4: Mid-July to mid-August

Zone 5: Mid-July through August

Zone 6: Mid-July to early September

Zone 7: Mid-July to mid-September

Zone 8: Mid-July to mid-September

Zone 9: Mid-July through September

Zone 10: Mid-July through September

Late summer

Shrub and zones in which it can be grown (see chart above for dates of flowering or berrying in your zone).

Early Season
BIG-LEAVED HYDRANGEA (Zones 6-10)

*BLUE-LEAVED HONEYSUCKLE (Zones 5-9)

BUTTONBUSH (Zones 4-10)

*CORNELIAN CHERRY (Zones 4-8)

FIVE-STAMENED TAMARISK (Zones 2-10)

*MARIE'S DOUBLEFILE VIBURNUM (Zones 4-9)

*RUNNING SERVICEBERRY (Zones 4-8)

SHRUB BUSH CLOVER (Zones 4-8)

SUMMER SWEET (Zones 3-10)

Midseason
CHASTE TREE (Zones 6-10)

CRAPE MYRTLE (Zones 7-10)

ORANGE-EYED BUTTERFLY BUSH (Zones 5-10)

PEEGEE HYDRANGEA (Zones 4-9)

ROSE OF SHARON (Zones 5-9)

SHINING SUMAC (Zones 4-9)

Late season
BLUEBEARD (Zones 5-9)

FRANKLINIA (Zones 6-9)

HARLEQUIN GLORY BOWER (Zones 6-10)

*SHINING SUMAC (Zones 4-9)

Late summer berries

PINK CASCADE FIVE-STAMENED TAMARISK

CHASTE TREE

ROSE OF SHARON   SHINING SUMAC

By early fall berries dot the branches of many shrubs, and soon these colors are joined by a blaze of changing leaves. The fall berry season comes first to the Southern zones and moves northward as the fruits reach maturity after a summer of sun. At the same time, the fall foliage season begins in the North as the days grow shorter and the nights grow cooler; the colors move slowly south, stopping short of the warm, sunny climates of the southernmost zones, where it hardly ever gets cold enough to trigger the color change.

Early fall

Shrub and zones in which it can be grown (see chart above for dates of berrying or fall color in your zone).

Early season

*ALDENHAM SPINDLE TREE (Zones 3-9)

*AMERICAN ELDER (Zones 3-9)

*CRANBERRY COTONEASTER (Zones 4-10)

*HARLEQUIN GLORY BOWER (Zones 6-10)

*HIGH-BUSH BLUEBERRY (Zones 3-8)

*SNOWBERRY (Zones 3-9)

*WINTERBERRY (Zones 3-8)

Late season

*AMERICAN CRANBERRY BUSH (Zones 2-9)

ARROWWOOD (Zones 2-9)

*BAYBERRY (Zones 2-8)

*BRILLIANT CHOKEBERRY (Zones 4-10)

CORNELIAN CHERRY (Zones 4-8)

CUT-LEAVED STEPHANANDRA (Zones 5-8)

JAPANESE BARBERRY (Zones 4-10)

*JAPANESE BARBERRY (Zones 4-10)

*JAPANESE ROSE (Zones 2-10)

RUNNING SERVICEBERRY (Zones 4-8)

SHINING SUMAC (Zones 4-9)

SMOOTH SUMAC (Zones 2-8)

*SPICEBUSH (Zones 4-9)

SPREADING COTONEASTER (Zones 5-10)

STAGHORN SUMAC (Zones 3-8)

*STRAWBERRY BUSH (Zones 6-9)

* Early fall berries

WINTERBERRY

STAGHORN SUMAC

SNOWBERRY

CUT-LEAVED SMOOTH SUMAC

AMERICAN CRANBERRY BUSH

ARROWWOOD

SEASON

Zone 2: Late August to mid-September

Zone 3: Late August to mid-September

Zone 4: September to mid-October

Zone 5: Mid-September to mid-October

Zone 6: Late September through October

Zone 7: October to mid-November

Zone 8: Mid-October to mid-November

Zone 9: November to mid-December

Zone 10: Mid-November through December

Late fall

OAK-LEAVED HYDRANGEA   SAPPHIREBERRY

Shrub and zones in which it can be grown (see chart above for dates of berrying or fall color in your zone).

Early season

AMERICAN CRANBERRY BUSH (Zones 2-9)

BRIDAL WREATH (Zones 4-10)

BRILLIANT CHOKEBERRY (Zones 4-10)

*CHENAULT CORALBERRY (Zones 4-9)

CHINESE REDBUD (Zones 6-9)

CHINESE WITCH HAZEL (Zones 5-9)

CRANBERRY COTONEASTER (Zones 4-10)

FIVE-LEAVED ARALIA (Zones 4-9)

FRAGRANT SNOWBALL (Zones 5-9)

HIGH-BUSH BLUEBERRY (Zones 3-8)

LARGE FOTHERGILLA (Zones 5-9)

*NANNYBERRY (Zones 2-9)

OAK-LEAVED HYDRANGEA (Zones 5-9)

PINKSHELL AZALEA (Zones 3-8)

*PURPLE BEAUTY-BERRY (Zones 5-8)

REDVEIN ENKIANTHUS (Zones 4-9)

*SEA BUCKTHORN (Zones 3-7)

*SPREADING COTONEASTER (Zones 5-10)

*STRAWBERRY BUSH (Zones 6-9)

*SUNGARI COTONEASTER (Zones 3-10)

WINGED EUONYMUS (Zones 3-9)

Late season

*AUTUMN ELAEAGNUS (Zones 3-8)

DOUBLEFILE VIBURNUM (Zones 4-9)

*JAPANESE BEAUTY-BERRY (Zones 5-8)

JAPANESE ROSE (Zones 2-10)

*ORIENTAL PHOTINIA (Zones 4-8)

ROYAL AZALEA (Zones 4-8)

*SAPPHIREBERRY (Zones 5-8)

SHOWY STEWARTIA (Zones 5-9)

SPICEBUSH (Zones 4-9)

Late fall berries

STRAWBERRY BUSH   LARGE FOTHERGILLA

PURPLE BEAUTY-BERRY

WINGED EUONYMUS

DOUBLEFILE VIBURNUM

Even in winter, when snow covers lifeless gardens in much of the U.S., the flowering shrubs continue to lend color to the drab scene. On some the brightly hued berries that appeared earlier remain on the branches, while others have bark in unusual shades like the red and yellow of the dogwoods shown at right. Because bark color is brightest on the youngest twigs, some gardeners intensify the display by heavily pruning their dogwood plants each spring. The new growth splashes additional color over the winter garden.

Winter

Shrub and zones in which it can be grown (see chart above for dates of winter in your zone).

BERRIES

Black

AMUR PRIVET (Zones 3-9)

IBOLIUM PRIVET (Zones 4-9)

JETBEAD (Zones 5-8)

Gray

BAYBERRY (Zones 2-8)

Red

BRILLIANT CHOKEBERRY (Zones 4-10)

EUROPEAN CRANBERRY BUSH (Zones 3-9)

JAPANESE BARBERRY (Zones 4-10)

KOREAN BARBERRY (Zones 4-10)

SEA BUCKTHORN (Zones 3-7)

SHINING SUMAC (Zones 4-9)

STAGHORN SUMAC (Zones 3-8)

Yellow

YELLOW-FRUITED EUROPEAN CRANBERRY BUSH (Zones 3-9)

BARK

Gray

AMERICAN CRANBERRY BUSH (Zones 2-9)

MORROW HONEYSUCKLE (Zones 4-9)

Green

KERRIA (Zones 4-9)

GREEN-STEMMED FORSYTHIA (Zones 5-9)

SCOTCH BROOM (Zones 5-10)

WINTER JASMINE (Zones 6-9)

Red

DWARF EUROPEAN CRANBERRY BUSH (Zones 3-9)

HIGH-BUSH BLUEBERRY (Zones 3-8)

KELSEY DOGWOOD (Zones 2-9)

TATARIAN DOGWOOD (Zones 5-10)

Yellow

AUREO-VITTATA KERRIA (Zones 4-9)

YELLOW-TWIGGED DOGWOOD (Zones 2-9)

JAPANESE BARBERRY

SIBERIAN DOGWOOD   BRILLIANT CHOKEBERRY

AMUR PRIVET   YELLOW-TWIGGED DOGWOOD

Choosing, planting and caring for shrubs 2

Choosing the right plants for the right places and purchasing them knowledgeably are essential to success with flowering shrubs—perhaps even more important than the care you give them once they are in the ground. Even the most experienced gardeners make mistakes. George Washington, no novice at gardening, once ordered for his Mount Vernon estate shrubs and seeds of crape myrtle, the lovely "lilac of the South" that has long adorned plantation houses and city streets. But he had them sent from the East Indies, which has a tropical climate, and got a variety of crape myrtle that could not survive even the mild winters of Virginia. Crape myrtle does grow at Mount Vernon now, but it was planted by later caretakers and is not the variety that disappointed the General.

The first President was a great admirer of fine landscaping—between 1785 and 1788 he had as many as 150 plantings set out at Mount Vernon, including such flowering shrubs as mock orange and lilac, and some of them lived well into the 20th Century. But when choosing his crape myrtle he failed to follow the first of a few rules the wise gardener observes:

• Never choose a plant unless you are absolutely sure that it is resistant to winter cold—hardy, in nurserymen's jargon—in the area where you live.

• Avoid choosing a sun-loving shrub for a shady place (it will blossom sparsely, if at all), or a shade-loving shrub for a spot that gets hot sun virtually all day long (it will not do its best and its leaves will almost surely turn brown around the edges or actually suffer sunburn, which destroys the leaf tissue).

• Do not buy for an exposed site a shrub that needs shelter from winter winds; chances are it will dry out and die of thirst, leaving a gap in the planting.

• Compare the space available to the size of the shrub when it matures, not to the size when you buy it. One that will grow tall and broad may fit well enough while it is young, but will be much too constricted later; to keep such a shrub to manageable size, it must

The billowing "smoke" of a smoke tree
—feathery hairs formed on flower stems
after the blooms have faded—creates tawny
clouds in a Lancaster, Pennsylvania, yard.
The shrub is planted to get maximum sun.

be pruned year after year at great cost to its natural beauty and its production of flowers.

• Consider the entire span of a shrub's usefulness. How long can you wait before the new plant bears flowers and fruit? And how long will your need for the plant last?

Applying these rules calls for close study not only of the shrub, but also of your yard and the way you intend to use it. Sometimes you cannot even be sure a shrub meets the first requirement, hardiness, just by checking its description. Plant catalogues sometimes describe shrubs as hardy but fail to specify just where they are hardy, and a plant that is hardy in Delaware may not be hardy in Maine. The encyclopedia section gives this information by geographical zones *(map, page 154)*. But a plant that is hardy a mile or 2 from where you live may not be so in your yard and, conversely, you may be able to grow a shrub that gardeners a mile away cannot; every climate zone has pockets of microclimates created by special conditions. A friend of mine who lives 20 miles north of New York City has a lovely winter jasmine that ordinarily is not found north of Maryland; his gets along fine because his yard sits beside the Hudson River and is guarded on three sides by mountains—the water moderates the air temperature, and the mountains fend off cold winds. To determine whether a shrub actually will prove hardy in your situation, scout your immediate neighboorhood for similar plants and ask their owners how they are doing. Visit, if you can, the nearest botanical garden and seek out expert advice there. Consult a local nurseryman, who will be as anxious as you that your plantings succeed. The best time to ask for his advice is a quiet weekday, when he has fewer customers than on a busy spring weekend. Some large nurseries will even send an expert to your property without charge to guide you in choosing plants.

Expert guidance can also help you find shrubs that suit the particular requirements of your family and yourself. Because your needs change over the years, the ways a shrub changes during its lifetime become an important consideration. It is not farfetched to compare the growth of a shrub to that of a human being. Like people, shrubs have their formative years, during which they spend most of their energy just growing up; their productive years, when they bloom superbly; and their declining years, in which they lose vigor and slow down. The last stage can be delayed by proper care, as with human beings, but it will inevitably arrive. These facts of plant life should weigh in your choice, for they relate to the facts of your own life. A young couple, if they are fixing up a home in which they expect to live a long time, might be advised to set out plants like honeysuckle, lilac, rose of Sharon or mock orange; those shrubs produce few blooms during their first three or four years, but then

MAKING BAYBERRY CANDLES

If you have female bayberry shrubs in your garden—and a male one near enough to pollinate them to produce berries (encyclopedia)—you can enjoy the fresh scent of traditional hand-dipped bayberry candles. They are easy to make from the tiny wax-bearing berries, although it takes about 5 pounds of berries—the crop of several large bushes—to make a good-sized candle. Collect the berries when they are ripe and put them in a pot of cold water. Simmer for about three hours (do not boil—too-high temperatures kill the scent), skimming off floating dirt and stirring occasionally to release wax trapped in the berries, then set aside to cool until a hard cake of olive-green wax forms on the surface. Remove the wax and melt it in a clean pot, strain it through cheesecloth into a tall container such as a coffee tin, and add enough paraffin (from 3 to 5 pounds) to bring the wax level up to the height desired for the candle. Melt the mixture together, then keep it warm over a low flame while you do the dipping. Using a three-braided wick (available at hobby stores), dip quickly, then lift the wick out to let the layer of wax harden; continue dipping the wick until the candle is the thickness that you want.

flower heavily for many, many years. However, if our young couple is thinking about buying a bigger house within a few years, or anticipate the husband's transfer to another city, they might be better advised to choose shrubs like deutzia or Froebel spirea that blossom quickly after planting, even though those plants may have shorter life spans.

If you keep such considerations in mind, you will find that choosing properly is not difficult and that you can save yourself many later regrets. There are so many varieties of flowering shrubs that you will discover numbers of them suited both to your immediate plans and to any site in your garden. The chart on pages 146 to 151, as well as the entries in the encyclopedia section, will help you greatly in making your choices.

SHOPPING FOR SHRUBS

Once you have made your selection it is best to order your shrubs by their Latin names, rather than their common English names, to make sure you get precisely what you want. Common names vary from one part of the country to another and often apply to a number of shrubs of a species, some of which may grow 20 feet tall while others may be only waist high. Specifying the exact variety you desire guarantees getting the flower color and plant size you want.

Now, if you are buying plants in person rather than by mail, you must make the final selection of the individual shrubs you will take home. How can you make sure you get vigorous and healthy ones? How big should they be?

Unless you are shopping at a nursery that specializes in mature shrubs, do not be tempted to buy big, old shrubs in the hope that they will enhance the look of your garden immediately. In the first place they are much more expensive than younger plants; in the second place, unless they have been specially treated in the years before their sale and then been very carefully dug up and moved, they are bound to suffer so much shock in the process of transplanting that they may never regain their original grace, which was what attracted you in the first place.

Buy young plants, about half the size they will reach at maturity; if, for example, the encyclopedia specifies that a plant grows 6 to 10 feet tall, buy one that is no more than 3 to 5 feet tall. If the plant is of a kind that spreads rather than soars, its most important dimension at maturity will be its diameter rather than its height, but the same rule of thumb applies—if the eventual spread will be 6 feet, buy the plant when it spreads no more than 3 feet.

JUDGING PLANTS FOR VIGOR

As you are walking around the nursery, look for the signs that distinguish strong and healthy plants from weaker stock. The best shrubs have a number of canes—stems that branch out from the central stem close to the ground. Look for dense, bushy plants with many stems coming off the main branches, and with leaves that are free of blemishes. The more buds there are on the branches and stems, the better.

Equally plain are the signs of plants you should shy away from: bark that is shriveled, or stems with many dead twigs, or brown leaves indicate that the plant is diseased or has been injured. Nor should you buy a plant that displays yellow-green leaves; it is probably undernourished, growing in the wrong soil or suffering from damage to its roots.

A number of symptoms can tell you whether a plant is being attacked by pests. Look at leaves for discolored spots that indicate fungus disease, or holes that show the presence of insects. Examine the leaf nodes (the joints where leaves are attached to stems or canes) for stuff that resembles soft white cotton—the "cotton" is a colony of mealy bugs. To check for spider or other mites, hold a piece of white paper beneath the leaves and shake the plant; if tiny dots start dancing on the paper, the plant should be passed over. Examine the stems for the presence of cankers, malformations that resemble dark knots; they are also a compelling reason for rejecting a plant, for they cut off the flow of sap, eventually spreading and killing the plant unless the afflicted stems are cut away.

HOW SHRUBS ARE SOLD   You will face another choice—one specified in jargon that may be mystifying at first—when you must pick the form in which to take your new plants home. Their form affects their price and the ease with which they take hold in the garden.

In the most common—and least expensive—form, flowering shrubs are dormant and their roots are bare of soil. These are known as bare-rooted plants. The lack of soil around the roots exposes the plants to danger while they are waiting to be planted. The roots must not be permitted to dry out, even momentarily. Good nurseries and mail-order houses pack the roots in dampened material such as fibrous sphagnum moss and wrap them in plastic, moss and all, to conserve moisture. But some sales lots offer shrubs whose roots have been allowed to lie exposed to air and sun. No matter how appealing the price of such shrubs may seem to you, spurn them. They are worthless.

Many shrubs can also be purchased with their roots inside the ball of soil in which they have been growing all along. This ball may be wrapped in burlap—in nurserymen's jargon, balled and burlaped, or B&B—or inside a container, a plastic pot or a large tin can. Certain shrubs, in fact, must be sold balled and burlaped or in containers after they reach a height of 3 feet or so because they will not survive digging and transplanting in bare-rooted form;

these include azaleas, which have a profusion of shallow roots, tamarix, which has unusually sparse, stringy roots, and other shrubs noted in the encyclopedia. Still other shrubs, such as barberries, which could be sold as bare-rooted plants when dormant, are more commonly sold balled and burlaped or in containers because that way they can be moved from the nursery to your yard with little danger at any time, even when they are in full bloom. Balled-and-burlaped and container-grown shrubs cost more than the bare-rooted kind, because of the labor that is involved in the nursery in preparing them for sale.

Some container-grown plants are satisfactory and others are not. The good ones have been grown in the containers in which you purchase them. The poor buys were grown in fields and then dug up and stuffed into cans for easier handling and sales display. The trouble with such plants is that they lost perhaps half their roots to the spade when they were dug up. This loss could have been compensated for if they had been cut back at the top, so that the remaining roots would have less growth to support. But many plant dealers, knowing that the taller plants are, the more they can charge for them, refrain from cutting back. Once such shrubs are planted in your garden, they either die back from the top, or produce weak growth and tiny leaves. You could rejuvenate them by cutting them back severely enough to bring roots and top growth into balance (*drawings, page 49*), but you would do better in the first place—and save yourself time and effort—by purchasing container-grown plants that were properly raised.

You can distinguish between container-grown plants and field-grown plants stuffed into containers. If roots stick out above the soil and over the rim of the can, the shrub was probably field grown. If there is no such obvious sign, ask the nurseryman to lift the shrub and its soil partway out of the container; a few inches will suffice. If you see many roots, resembling a tangle of spaghetti, tightly packed on the outside of the ball of soil, the plant was probably started in the can and it is satisfactory. But if roots are sparse or invisible around the soil ball, or if the soil ball itself is loose and crumbly, the shrub probably has not been long in the container and is one that you should reject as a poor specimen.

Many gardeners believe that spring is the only season in which plants may be set out. It is the best time for shrubs that need all summer to grow so they can be well established in the garden before facing the rigors of winter (those plants are identified in the encyclopedia section). But tougher shrubs can be planted at other times. If they are bought balled and burlaped or container grown, most can be set out whenever the soil can be worked. And for shrubs

THE MANY USES OF SHRUBS

Over the centuries shrubs have served as more than garden ornaments and, in fact, many derive their names from their practical uses. The lilac's botantical name, Syringa, comes from the Greek word for Pan's pipes—the shrub's pithy shoots were made into wind instruments by early musicians. Euonymus, or spindle tree, was not only employed in spindles to hold yarn for spinning, but was also burned to make fine sketching charcoal. In Shakespeare's England, housewives used green branches of Cytisus, or broom, to sweep out their houses. And for years gardeners have celebrated the fragrance of Clethra by calling it summer sweet—and sometimes using it as soap, rubbing the blossoms together with water to make a perfumed lather.

WHEN TO PLANT

in any form—balled and burlaped, container grown or bare-rooted —fall planting may be preferable. The soil, frequently muddy in spring, usually contains less moisture in fall and thus is easier to work. Also, a shrub that is hardy enough to stand fall planting will be able to start new growth in the spring considerably earlier than a spring-set plant could.

The fall planting season for balled-and-burlaped or container-grown shrubs begins in late summer; for bare-rooted plants it begins as soon as the shrubs' leaves begin to fall. In either case the planting season continues until the ground freezes in the North, although it is best to plant as early as possible after the season's growth has matured to give the roots a chance to get established before cold weather. From Zone 7 south, where the soil seldom or never freezes, the planting season extends through the winter; bare-rooted shrubs can be planted until springtime temperatures become mild enough to start the shrubs' growth (balled-and-burlaped or container-grown shrubs, of course, can be planted still later in the year).

HOW TO SPACE SHRUBS Give your shrubs room to grow by setting them rather far apart, unless you want to make a hedge, which requires a special technique described farther on in this chapter. How far apart depends on your taste, on the presence of other plants and on the shrubs, but as a general rule place them no closer together than they will spread when full grown (encyclopedia). A honeysuckle that grows 8 to 10 feet tall with an equal spread should be spaced 8 to 10 feet away from a similar plant; within three to five years the tips of their branches will touch. It is usually better to allow too much rather than too little room for such elegant specimens as azaleas, enkianthuses and stewartias, which are prone to lose their shape and grace when crowded by other plants.

Flowering shrubs planted close to a house should be set far enough away so that when mature they will not touch the walls. Sometimes it almost takes an act of faith to plant a young shrub 5 to 6 feet from a building, but if it is of a species that grows 5 to 6 feet tall and spreads out an equal distance, it will need at least that much room—not only to avoid a cluttered look around the house, but to protect the health and shape of the shrub. Space between house and plant permits air circulation that lessens the chance of mildew and other diseases, and in a sunny location it also prevents the plant from being baked dry by heat reflected from the house walls. Avoid planting any shrub under an overhanging roof where rainfall never reaches to provide necessary moisture, and never plant directly under the drip line of a roof where plants are likely to be damaged by falling icicles or clumps of snow.

To be sure you keep to the proper spacing, set a stake in each spot where a shrub is to grow. Then dig a separate hole for each —because of the relatively great separation, digging separate holes is easier than cultivating the entire area, as you would for a flower bed. As you dig, make separate piles of the topsoil and the subsoil. There is usually a distinct demarcation between them—the topsoil is darker because of the presence of decayed organic material—and they need to be separated because later, as each plant is set into its hole, the layers will be reversed; the rich topsoil will be used to fill in around and nourish the roots, while the subsoil will be used at the top of the ground. To give the roots growing room, dig holes at least 6 inches wider on all sides than the roots of the plants that will go into them. Holes should also be deep enough to allow plants to grow at the same level that they did in the nursery. For example, a bare-rooted shrub 3 to 5 feet in height generally requires a hole 2 feet across and about 1½ to 2 feet deep.

There is more to the proper planting of shrubs, of course, than just digging holes in the ground. Flowering shrubs do not need coddling, but they will look handsomer and flower more abundantly if they are given soil of the proper acidity and texture.

ADDING ORGANIC MATTER

Soil texture affects the roots' supply of air and moisture. Some types of shrubs can grow in swamps and others on dry banks, but nearly all of them do best in a well-drained, moderately porous soil. The best way to provide this condition is by adding organic material such as peat moss, leaf mold, compost or decayed sawdust. These materials serve several functions. They open up nonporous clay soils to improve drainage and admit the air necessary for good root growth. Yet they are also needed in very porous earth, for they retain moisture in light, sandy soils that otherwise leak precious rain water like sieves. Peat moss, perhaps the best and most widely available of these organic materials, is sold in many grades; for conditioning soil for shrubs, I prefer the chunky kind made up of pieces of fibrous moss ½ inch or more in diameter. Wet the peat moss repeatedly before using; otherwise it will remain impermeable by water for a long time, then actually draw moisture from the surrounding soil to the detriment of the roots.

The only chance you ever get to work the proper amount of organic material deep enough into the soil to do your plants any good is before planting. Shrub plantings are unlike vegetable gardens or annual flower beds, which can be turned over and enriched at the start of each new growing season. Once shrubs are in the ground, it is difficult or impossible to add organic materials to the soil without injuring the roots. Proper soil conditioning at planting-time can therefore make a great difference for years. To prepare the soil excavated from each planting hole, use about 1 part of peat moss or other organic material to 2 parts of soil, and mix it well into the pile of subsoil as well as the pile of topsoil. It is not essential at this point to add fertilizer but I generally use some. A light dusting of bone meal or dried cow manure, thoroughly mixed with the peat moss and soil, will give a good start to shrubs that do not require an acid soil. For acid-loving shrubs, such as azaleas and brooms, use a fertilizer such as cottonseed meal, which leaves an acid residue as it decays; apply it at the rate of 2 cupfuls for a 3- to 4-foot shrub and mix it thoroughly with the soil.

CHANGING SOIL ACIDITY The acidity of the soil may need adjustment as much as its texture. A great many flowering shrubs do well in soil that is very mildly acid, registering between 6.0 and 7.0 on the chemists' pH scale, just on the acid side of the 7.0 neutral point. But some of the most desirable shrubs, among them azaleas, serviceberries, summer sweets, brooms, enkianthuses, bayberries and blueberries, require soil that is definitely acid, with a pH reading of 4.5 to 5.5. Such soils are common in the East, the Great Lakes region and the Pacific Northwest, but alkalinity prevails on the prairies and most of the nonmountainous regions west of the Mississippi. However, geographical limits are imprecise, for within the broad areas of acidity, pockets of alkalinity exist, and vice versa. So, for success with flowering shrubs—and any other plants, for that matter—it is wise to test the pH of your garden's soil, either with an inexpensive kit available at garden centers or by sending soil samples to a state or county agricultural agency or private laboratory.

Excess alkalinity is the problem that must be corrected for

(continued on page 48)

Luring birds to the garden

The sight and sound of birds the year round can add immeasurably to the enjoyment of a garden—and planning a garden that will satisfy both you and the birds you want to attract requires little effort. Birds are fond of grounds like those of the Massachusetts garden shown at right, whose flowering shrubs were chosen primarily to provide the birds with a varied diet of fruit and nectar, along with insects that are also attracted by the shrubs. A birdbath, nestled close to the protection of the shrubs at right, and a birdhouse provide water, shelter and safety from predators. In this bird haven large cotoneasters and Amur honeysuckles (to the right of the bath) were planted for their red berries, which are eaten by robins, cedar waxwings, cardinals and winter finches. To appeal to ruby-throated hummingbirds, three nectar-rich flowering shrubs were set out: a roseshell azalea in the right foreground above the ferns, a Sargent crab apple behind the birdhouse to the left and a weigela to the right. Similar shrubs can be selected to serve the same purposes where you live (chart, overleaf).

Hermit thrush on nannyberry

Cardinal on winterberry

Pine grosbeak on Sargent crab apple

A selection of flowering shrubs to attract birds

REGION	SHRUB	FRUIT OR FLOWER	SEASON	BIRDS MOST OFTEN ATTRACTED
NORTHEAST Connecticut Delaware Illinois Indiana Iowa Kentucky Maine Maryland Massachusetts Michigan Minnesota Missouri New Hampshire New Jersey New York Ohio Ontario Pennsylvania Quebec Rhode Island Vermont Virginia West Virginia Wisconsin	**AMERICAN ELDER**	Blue-black berries	Late summer to midfall	BLUEBIRDS, CATBIRDS, FLICKERS, MOCKINGBIRDS, ROSE-BREASTED GROSBEAKS, WOODPECKERS
	AMUR HONEYSUCKLE	Red berries	Fall to midwinter	CARDINALS, CEDAR WAXWINGS, ROBINS, THRASHERS, THRUSHES, TOWHEES, WINTER FINCHES
	ARROWWOOD	Blue-black berries	Fall	BLUEBIRDS, CATBIRDS, FLICKERS, ROBINS, THRUSHES
	BAYBERRY	Gray berries	Fall to early spring	BLUEBIRDS, CAROLINA WRENS, DOWNY WOODPECKERS, HERMIT THRUSHES, MYRTLE WARBLERS, TREE SWALLOWS
	BLACK HAW	Blue-black berries	Fall	CEDAR WAXWINGS, PILEATED WOODPECKERS, SWAINSON'S THRUSHES, YELLOW-BILLED CUCKOOS
	HIGH-BUSH BLUEBERRY	Blue-black berries	Midsummer to midfall	BLUEBIRDS, CHICKADEES, HERMIT THRUSHES, ORCHARD ORIOLES, ROBINS, TOWHEES
	NANNYBERRY	Black berries	Fall	CATBIRDS, CEDAR WAXWINGS, FLICKERS, HERMIT THRUSHES, ROBINS, ROSE-BREASTED GROSBEAKS
	PINXTER-BLOOM AZALEA	Pink or white flowers	Spring	RUBY-THROATED HUMMINGBIRDS
	SARGENT CRAB APPLE	White flowers	Spring	RUBY-THROATED HUMMINGBIRDS
		Dark red fruit	Fall	CEDAR WAXWINGS, EVENING AND PINE GROSBEAKS, PURPLE FINCHES, ROBINS
	SIBERIAN DOGWOOD	Blue-white berries	Fall	CARDINALS, CHATS, FINCHES, FLYCATCHERS, MOCKINGBIRDS, TREE SWALLOWS
	TATARIAN HONEYSUCKLE	Pink or red flowers	Late spring	RUBY-THROATED HUMMINGBIRDS,
		Red or yellow berries	Summer	BROWN THRASHERS, CATBIRDS, CEDAR WAXWINGS, PURPLE FINCHES, ROBINS
	WINTERBERRY	Red berries	Late summer to midwinter	BLUEBIRDS, BROWN THRASHERS, CARDINALS, CEDAR WAXWINGS
SOUTH AND SOUTHEAST Alabama Arkansas Florida Georgia Louisiana Mississippi North Carolina South Carolina Tennessee	**AMERICAN ELDER**	Blue-black berries	Late summer to midfall	BROWN THRASHERS, CARDINALS, CAROLINA CHICKADEES, CHATS, FLICKERS, INDIGO BUNTINGS, MOCKINGBIRDS, PHOEBES
	ARROWWOOD	Blue-black berries	Fall	BROWN THRASHERS, CATBIRDS, PHOEBES, ROBINS, WHITE-EYED VIREOS
	BAYBERRY	Gray berries	Fall to early spring	DOWNY WOODPECKERS, HERMIT THRUSHES, MYRTLE WARBLERS, TREE SWALLOWS
	BLACK HAW	Blue-black berries	Fall	CAROLINA CHICKADEES, DOWNY AND RED-BELLIED WOODPECKERS, HERMIT THRUSHES, MOCKINGBIRDS
	HIGH-BUSH BLUEBERRY	Blue-black berries	Midsummer to midfall	CATBIRDS, CHATS, ORIOLES, PHOEBES, TANAGERS
	HYBRID WEIGELA	Pink, red or white flowers	Spring	RUBY-THROATED HUMMINGBIRDS
	MANY-FLOWERED COTONEASTER	Red berries	Fall	BLUEBIRDS, CEDAR WAXWINGS, MOCKINGBIRDS, ROBINS
	SAPPHIREBERRY	Blue berries	Fall	BLUEBIRDS, CARDINALS, CATBIRDS, MOCKINGBIRDS, SUMMER TANAGERS
	SIBERIAN DOGWOOD	Blue-white berries	Fall	BLUEBIRDS, CATBIRDS, CEDAR WAXWINGS, MOCKINGBIRDS, WOOD THRUSHES
	SMOOTH SUMAC	Red berries	Fall to early spring	BLUEBIRDS, CAROLINA CHICKADEES, CATBIRDS, DOWNY WOODPECKERS, MOCKINGBIRDS

(continued on next page)

A selection of flowering shrubs to attract birds (CONTINUED)

REGION	SHRUB	FRUIT OR FLOWER	SEASON	BIRDS MOST OFTEN ATTRACTED
NORTH AND SOUTH CENTRAL **Kansas Manitoba Nebraska North Dakota Oklahoma South Dakota Texas**	BEAUTY BUSH	Pink flowers	Early summer	RUBY-THROATED AND RUFOUS HUMMINGBIRDS
	CORALBERRY	Purple-red berries	Fall to midwinter	HERMIT THRUSHES, PURPLE FINCHES, ROBINS, WAXWINGS, WOODPECKERS
	FRAGRANT SUMAC	Dark red berries	Summer	BLUEBIRDS, RED-HEADED WOODPECKERS, ROBINS, THRASHERS, YELLOW-SHAFTED FLICKERS
	NANNYBERRY	Black berries	Fall	CARDINALS, CATBIRDS, CEDAR WAXWINGS, FLICKERS, HERMIT THRUSHES, ROBINS
	ORANGE-EYED BUTTERFLY BUSH	Blue, pink, purple or white flowers	Midsummer to frost	RUBY-THROATED HUMMINGBIRDS
	SIBERIAN DOGWOOD	Blue-white berries	Fall	BLUEBIRDS, CARDINALS, CHATS, EVENING GROSBEAKS, THRUSHES, TREE SWALLOWS, WAXWINGS
	SIBERIAN PEA TREE	Yellow flowers	Spring	RUBY-THROATED AND RUFOUS HUMMINGBIRDS
	WINTERBERRY	Red berries	Late summer to midwinter	BLUEBIRDS, BROWN THRASHERS, CARDINALS, CEDAR WAXWINGS, PURPLE FINCHES, ROBINS
WEST AND SOUTHWEST **Alberta Arizona Colorado Idaho Montana Nevada New Mexico Saskatchewan Utah Wyoming**	AMERICAN ELDER	Blue-black berries	Late summer to midfall	LEWIS'S WOODPECKERS, MAGPIES, MOUNTAIN BLUEBIRDS, SPARROWS, THRUSHES, WARBLING VIREOS
	BLACK HAW	Blue-black berries	Fall	HERMIT THRUSHES, ROBINS, TOWNSEND'S SOLITAIRES, VEERIES, WAXWINGS
	NANNYBERRY	Black berries	Fall	BLUEBIRDS, BOHEMIAN AND CEDAR WAXWINGS, CATBIRDS, FLICKERS, HERMIT THRUSHES
	RED OSIER DOGWOOD	White berries	Summer	BULLOCK'S ORIOLES, CARDINALS, HERMIT THRUSHES, MOCKINGBIRDS, SWAINSON'S THRUSHES
	RUNNING SERVICEBERRY	Purple-black berries	Summer	GREEN-TAILED TOWHEES, LEWIS'S WOODPECKERS, MAGPIES, SWAINSON'S THRUSHES, TOWNSEND'S SOLITAIRES
	SIBERIAN PEA TREE	Yellow flowers	Spring	BROAD-TAILED HUMMINGBIRDS
	SNOWBERRY	White berries	Midsummer to midwinter	EVENING AND PINE GROSBEAKS, MAGPIES, ROBINS, RUFOUS-SIDED TOWHEES
	STAGHORN SUMAC	Red berries	Fall to early spring	EVENING GROSBEAKS, HERMIT THRUSHES, MAGPIES, ROBINS, TOWNSEND'S SOLITAIRES
	TATARIAN HONEYSUCKLE	Pink or red flowers	Late spring	BROAD-TAILED HUMMINGBIRDS,
		Red or yellow berries	Summer	BOHEMIAN AND CEDAR WAXWINGS, HERMIT AND SWAINSON'S THRUSHES
FAR WEST **British Columbia California Oregon Washington**	BEAUTY BUSH	Pink flowers	Early summer	ANNA'S, BLACK-CHINNED, CALLIOPE AND RUFOUS HUMMINGBIRDS
	BLUE ELDER	Blue-black berries	Late summer	BLACK-HEADED GROSBEAKS, CALIFORNIA THRASHERS, PHAINOPEPLAS, STELLER'S JAYS, SWAINSON'S THRUSHES
	JAPANESE ROSE	Orange-red fruit	Fall	EVENING GROSBEAKS, ROBINS, THRUSHES, TOWHEES, TOWNSEND'S SOLITAIRES
	MAGELLAN FUCHSIA	Red and violet flowers	Early summer to frost	ANNA'S, BLACK-CHINNED, CALLIOPE AND RUFOUS HUMMINGBIRDS
	SNOWBERRY	White berries	Midsummer to midwinter	BLACK-HEADED, EVENING AND PINE GROSBEAKS, ROBINS, SPOTTED TOWHEES, VARIED THRUSHES, WREN TITS

Cedar waxwing on many-flowered cotoneaster

the great majority of flowering shrubs; the remedy is an application of finely ground sulfur or iron sulfate. Sulfur remains effective for years, but acts more slowly than iron sulfate and should be applied a month or two before planting to allow it to be assimilated into the soil. To lower the pH ½ to 1 unit, apply sulfur at the rate of ½ pound per 100 square feet. Three pounds of iron sulfate per 100 square feet will also lower the pH ½ to 1 unit. Since it acts quickly, it does not have to be applied far in advance of planting, and it contains iron, which promotes the production of dark green leaves and richly colored flowers. But iron sulfate drains away quickly and must be replaced every two or three years by sprinkling the powder on the ground under and around the shrub and watering it into the soil.

If your soil is too acid for the shrubs you want to grow, you can correct it by adding finely ground dolomite limestone to the soil of the planting hole; it is preferable to work the limestone into the soil throughout the entire area in which the shrubs are to grow and spread more on the surface between the holes as well. For most garden soils, about 5 pounds of limestone to every 100 square feet will raise the pH about 1 unit; if you have a heavy, poorly drained soil or if you have added a great deal of peat moss, which is naturally acid, increase the amount of limestone by about one third. The effect of the limestone will not be felt for several months, so it is best to apply it well in advance of planting—in the fall for spring planting and in the spring for fall planting.

PREPARING THE SHRUBS All holes should be dug and soil prepared before your shrubs arrive, particularly if they are bare-rooted, because bare-rooted shrubs ought to go into the ground as soon as possible to keep their roots from drying out. If you can plant them the day they come, do so, keeping them in their wrappings until the last minute. If you have to delay planting for two or three days, leave the shrubs in their wrappings and store them out of the sun in a spot where the temperature will be cool but not freezing. If you must postpone planting longer than a few days, you can keep your shrubs healthy by a temporary technique called heeling in. Dig a trench about 6 inches deep in a shaded, out-of-the-way part of the yard. Unwrap the shrubs and lay them almost flat and close together with their roots in the trench. Cover the roots with moist soil, and the rest of the shrubs with more moist soil or with leaves, hay, damp burlap or half a dozen sheets of wet newspaper. If the plants are emerging from dormancy and the weather is dry, bare-rooted shrubs can be heeled in for as long as a week without injury. If they are still dormant and the weather is wet, they can be heeled in for as long as two weeks with safety.

Container-grown plants can be left in their containers until you are ready to plant them, as long as you give them some water during dry spells. Balled-and-burlaped plants can also be left above-ground indefinitely, provided that the soil ball is kept constantly moist and protected with damp sawdust, peat moss or any other kind of organic mulch heaped up around the sides of the ball.

When you are ready to plant a shrub, the first thing you should do is set it in its hole to see if the hole is too deep or too shallow (drawings, below). Depth is important because roots require air as well as moisture; they suffer when extra soil over them reduces their air supply. In fact, if a choice had to be made, it would be better to plant shrubs too shallow than too deep.

A shrub grows best, however, only if planted at the depth at

PROPER PLANTING

HOW TO PLANT A BARE-ROOTED SHRUB

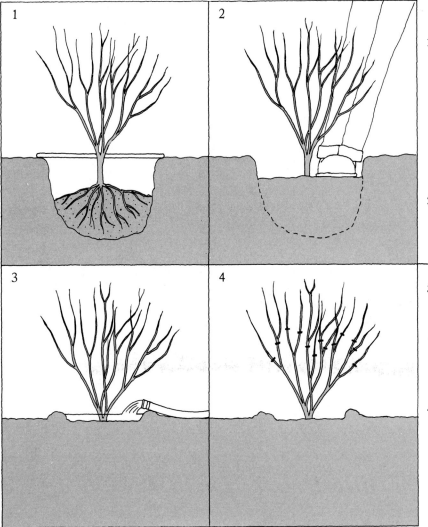

1. *A board laid across the planting hole helps set a bare-rooted shrub at the depth at which it originally grew. Dig the hole 6 inches wider all around than the roots, placing topsoil and subsoil in separate piles. Set the shrub in the hole atop a mixture of 2 parts topsoil and 1 part peat moss so that the shrub's soil line is level with the board; spread the roots.*

2. *Fill the hole three fourths full with the topsoil mix and tamp down the soil with your foot. Fill the remaining space with water.*

3. *When the water has drained away, fill the hole completely with soil and water again. When filling the hole, use up the topsoil mixture first, then use subsoil mixed with peat moss. A 2-inch dike of soil around the hole holds the water so that it soaks in.*

4. *Cut one third to one half off the stems (lines) to compensate for roots lost when the plant was dug up at the nursery. Do not cut the shrub back to an even height, but take proportional lengths from each stem so that you follow the shrub's natural shape.*

THE CHANGEABLE HYDRANGEA

The odd tendency of the hydrangea to change color like a chameleon has long been known. In 1796 an English botanical magazine described a plant, owned by the Countess of Upper Ossory, that produced pink flowers one year and blue the next. By 1875 gardeners knew that watering with an alum solution or adding iron filings or rusty nails to the soil would turn otherwise pink flowers blue, although a gardening writer of the day properly advised against such "trickery"—the best blue (or pink) hues are obtained by selecting plants notable for the color that is desired and then cultivating them in the soil they prefer. Today plant physiologists have determined that certain hydrangeas—notably the big-leaved, or French, types —need aluminum to produce rich blue blooms, and that the soil in which they grow must be quite acid to make the aluminum it contains available to the plants. The nails or iron filings were effective because as they rusted they formed iron oxide, which turned into ferrous sulfate and finally into sulfuric acid. But the speed of this chemical change was unpredictable, and standardized agricultural chemicals are now used to control the colors (page 116).

which it grew in the nursery. You can determine that depth by looking at the bark near the base of the plant, where there is an easily visible line of demarcation; bark that formed below ground level is usually lighter in color than bark that has always been aboveground. This demarcation line ought to be level with the surface of the ground after the shrub is planted, but when you first place the shrub in the hole, the line should be a bit below ground level. You make up the difference by filling in under the shrub with the mixture of topsoil and peat moss. This soil must be well compacted or the plant will settle later, so step into the hole and firm the loose soil with your foot. Try the shrub in the hole again, filling or taking away soil until you have just the right amount. Then set the shrub in the hole, checking to make sure that the side of the plant with the best branches is facing in the direction from which the plant will be most frequently seen.

When planting a bare-rooted shrub, spread the roots so that they reach out toward the sides of the hole. Then toss in a shovelful of the topsoil and peat-moss mixture, and with your hands work it under, over and around the roots. When the roots have been thoroughly covered, and the hole is about three quarters filled, firm the soil again with your foot; exert pressure around the outer fringes of the roots, but be careful that you do not step on the plant's crown (the point from which the main stems emerge) or press down so hard that you are likely to injure the roots.

At this point a bare-rooted shrub can stand erect without support. Give the plant a big enough drink to saturate the soil, using a garden hose at gentle pressure; the water will make a puddle and filter in under the roots, carrying down dirt to settle the soil and fill in any air pockets. When all the water has drained away, fill in the rest of the hole, using the balance of the topsoil and peat-moss mixture first, then finishing with the subsoil mixture. After the hole has been filled to the level of the surrounding ground, make a 2-inch-high dike of soil around the hole and allow the garden hose to run gently into this "saucer" until the soil is thoroughly soaked. This last soaking can be delayed if a number of shrubs are to be planted at the same time; in such cases, give each plant only its initial watering and go on to the next shrub. When you have planted them all, go back and finish filling the holes, making the dikes, and providing the second watering.

The planting procedure for balled-and-burlaped and container-grown shrubs is virtually the same as for bare-rooted plants, only simpler. A container-grown plant must be taken out of its container; do this so as to disturb the cylinder of soil around the roots as little as possible. Then set the cylinder in the hole so that the top of the cylinder is level with the ground. Fill in with a mixture of top-

branch that rubs on another, since it may cut through the bark, opening a site for infection or insect infestation. This is a good time to look carefully at the major stems, especially the older ones, for any signs of an infection of scale, which manifests itself as a crust of tiny bumps along the stems. Scale can easily multiply for some time without being noticed because of the summer-long canopy of foliage. Remove badly infected canes and spray the entire plant to eradicate the infestation (symptoms of and remedies for shrub ailments are described in the pest and disease chart, pages 152-153). Maintenance pruning of this kind is not an arduous job and requires little time if it is done annually. All too often routine pruning is left undone for years until the homeowner is desperate; then he attacks the plants as though he were at war with them.

Most pruning is remedial—eliminating dead or undersized branches, cutting back overgrowth. But some is preventive, intended to keep a shrub well shaped, vigorous and productive of flowers. Most shrubs are pruned to make them produce more stems and thus more flowers, but it is important that this treatment be carried out at the right time so that it will not interfere with the flower production it is supposed to induce.

PRUNING FOR MORE FLOWERS

All flowering shrubs can be divided into two categories as far as flower production is concerned. The categories are determined not by the time the flowers bloom, but by the time the buds form. Some shrubs, such as forsythias, flowering quinces, lilacs and big-leaved hydrangeas, blossom from buds formed on stems that grew during the previous summer; the current season's growth produces no flowers until the following year. These shrubs should be pruned soon after they have flowered on the previous year's growth and before buds start to form on the current year's growth. A lady complained to me some years ago, when I was a nurseryman, that she never got any flowers on the big-leaved hydrangea I had sold her. It turned out that she was doing her pruning in early spring. She was cutting off the buds before they could bloom, and she was getting great masses of foliage but no blossoms. When she learned what she had been doing wrong and undertook her pruning in summer, after the blossoms had faded and before buds had formed, she was rewarded with masses of flowers.

Other shrubs, such as roses of Sharon, peegee hydrangeas and crape myrtles, blossom from buds formed on the current season's growth. These shrubs should be pruned early in spring before the new growth starts, that is, just as the buds that will produce new stems begin to swell; trimming then will induce each stem to put out several strong flower-bearing shoots. You need not be timid about early-spring pruning. In fact you can prune back the shrubs so that only two or three buds are left on each stem, without sacrificing all the blossoms; such hard pruning reduces the number of blossoms on each plant, but results in enormous flowers.

REJUVENATING OLD SHRUBS Eternal youthfulness is no more possible for plants than it is for man, but with proper pruning flowering shrubs can come close to it. Shrubs regenerate themselves by sending up new stems from beneath or close to the ground level; to keep them regenerating year after year, remove some of the oldest stems, cutting them down to within 2 to 4 inches of the ground. This kind of pruning will force the development of new buds that break through the bark at the base of the plant and produce new stems; if you remove some old stems every year, the plant will always have stems of various ages coming along to take the place of the old ones. This technique of removing old stems entirely is the only kind of pruning that should be employed for such plants as deutzias, weigelas, and mock oranges, whose symmetry is easily disturbed by the cutting away of the top parts of the stems.

Occasionally extensive rejuvenation is needed. If a planting of shrubs becomes heavily overgrown, drastic measures are called for. Rather than dig up and replace the shrubs with younger ones, an expensive and time-consuming job, try cutting every stem all

PRUNING AFTER FLOWERS FADE

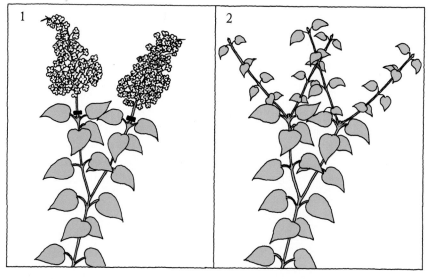

Shrubs that blossom on previous season's growth should be pruned after the flowers fade. Cut the stems below a blossom and above a bud (lines). A third of the oldest main stems may be cut close to the ground.

The energy that would have gone into producing seeds in each faded flower now goes into producing one or more flower stems. In similar fashion, the energy diverted from old main stems goes to form new ones.

the way back to the ground in early spring. This operation will not kill the shrub, but will force great numbers of very fast-growing canes to arise from the stumps. These fresh stems may not flower for two or three years, but when they do they will have great numbers of blossoms. Subsequent normal pruning will keep them from again becoming too tall. If such complete rejuvenation is called for, do not do a half-hearted job. Cut the plants down with a pruning saw, leaving only stubs that are from 2 to 4 inches high.

Such complete cutting may have to be an annual routine for some plants in Northern areas. There the roots of a number of shrubs will survive the winter, but their stems will be killed by the cold each year. This dieback affects such shrubs as bluebeards, orange-eyed butterfly bushes and chaste trees, and their winter-injured or dead stems should be cut to within 2 to 4 inches of the ground each spring to make room for the new stems that will arise in their place. In the South, where butterfly bushes and chaste trees become 15 feet tall and are not injured by cold temperatures, the entire plant may be cut back similarly to keep it smaller and to make it flower more heavily.

A number of other plants should be cut to the ground every few years unless they are being used as tall screens. Among such shrubs are red- and yellow-stemmed dogwoods, which are valued

PRUNING FOR COMPLETE REJUVENATION

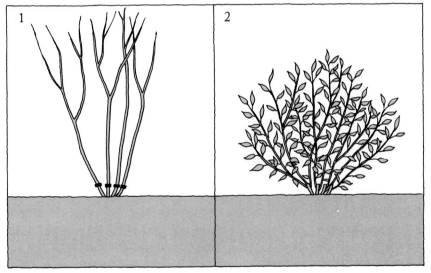

If a shrub becomes either heavily overgrown or extremely lanky, with few branches at the bottom, prune drastically in early spring, cutting every stem back to within 2 to 4 inches of the ground (lines).

This severe pruning will force great numbers of fast-growing stems to rise from the stumps. The new stems may not blossom until their second year or later. They can then be pruned normally (pages 54 and 56).

for the bright colors that their stems display in winter. Since it is the young stems that are the brightest in color, keep your plants young by taking out the older, darker stems each spring.

PLANTING A HEDGE

The planting and pruning of shrubs differ in some ways when shrubs are grouped into hedges instead of being set alone. For one thing, formal hedges (but not informal ones) require shearing periodically, sometimes as often as four times during a single growing season. And the planting procedure for both formal and informal hedges is a special one.

Because one characteristic of a good hedge is dense growth, plants for hedges are deliberately set closer together than they would be elsewhere. Spacing at plantingtime may vary from 1 to 3 feet, depending upon the kind of plant and its ultimate size (spacing for shrubs recommended as hedge plants is given in the encyclopedia). Ordinarily, hedge plants are set in a single row, but a staggered double row of plants *(drawings, page 59)* will produce quicker results and guarantee a dense hedge. Such double hedges take up more room because the rows should be 8 to 10 inches apart, but they have an added advantage—a wire fence, an unsightly barrier by itself, can be hidden between the rows to keep dogs in or out of the yard or children from falling into a pool.

Plants for hedges are usually set into a trench rather than individual holes, because the trench allows you to adjust the spacing between shrubs before you begin the actual planting; if you should discover that you are running short of shrubs for the length of hedge you want, you can move them slightly farther apart. Also, trenching assures that the soil into which the roots will spread has been loosened and properly prepared.

Locate the trench far enough from your property line so that the mature plants will not grow over into your neighbor's yard, and allow enough room so that they will not overhang a sidewalk. A formal hedge requires ground space roughly equal to its height to give you room to work around it when you trim it; a hedge 4 feet tall, for example, may spread 2 feet across but you should allow another foot on each side so you can get at it with your shears. An untrimmed hedge requires considerably more space; a multiflora rose (*Rosa multiflora*), for example, may grow 15 feet tall and spread 20 feet across. Such a rose hedge can become a thorny problem indeed when it starts to wrap around your neighbor's porch or garage, and that is one of the reasons I do not recommend it for the average homeowner. A better choice would be the Mentor barberry, which grows only 6 or 7 feet high and 4 feet wide.

The trench should be dug 18 to 24 inches wide and 12 to 18 inches deep for a single row of shrubs, depending on the size of the

BARBERRY'S REPRIEVE

The attractive barberry, widely used in hedges, was long under suspicion as the cause of black stem rust, a fungus that destroys wheat, barley and rye, and as early as 1726 a law in Connecticut required the destruction of barberries found near grain fields. More than a century later, scientific evidence clinched the case: in 1865 the German botanist Heinrich Anton DeBary worked out the life cycle of the fungus and showed that although it lives on wheat in summer and winter, it grows on barberry in spring. DeBary's discovery might have been the death knell for the valued shrub; but later studies proved that not all species and varieties act as hosts to the fungus. Today there are over 60 kinds of rust-resistant barberries, and these types can be grown safely in any part of the country; three of the best are described on page 96.

plants, and up to about 30 inches wide for a double row of plants. After preparing the soil with organic matter and adding sulfur or limestone as necessary to adjust the pH, stretch a string on stakes above the trench as a guideline to make sure you line up the plants correctly. Set the plants at the depth at which they grew in the nursery and firm the soil in place around them with your foot. Leave a shallow trough along each edge of the trench to collect and hold water; then give the plants a thorough soaking.

If the hedge is to be a dense, formal one, the initial pruning will take a certain amount of nerve, for I propose that the 2- or 3-foot-high plants you have just set in the ground be cut back to a height of 4 inches from the ground. This is where many an amateur gardener balks, and understandably. A newlywed friend of mine who had just put in a new hedge was hesitantly pruning it not long ago when I chanced by and advised him to cut it back to a far lower level. He objected, saying, "I'll kill the plants." Reluctantly he took my advice and cut back with a vengeance. Within a few months his cut-back plants were as tall as they had been to begin with, for all deciduous shrubs sprout new stems immediately below a cut surface. More important, they sprout two to six new stems for every old one and thus become far bushier and denser than they were be-

PRUNING HEDGES

PLANTING A DOUBLE-ROW HEDGE

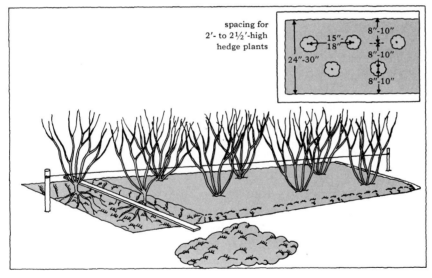

For a dense hedge in minimum time, plant two staggered rows of shrubs (inset) in a trench; tie string between stakes as a guide. Set plants in the trench as you would set bare-rooted shrubs in individual holes *(page 49). Cover the roots as you go, to keep them from drying out. After covering and watering all plants, finish filling, leaving a narrow trough around the trench for water. Water again with a soaking hose.*

fore. So don't do a halfway job the first time you prune a formal hedge; if you compromise, as my young friend was about to before I intervened, and make your cut 12 inches from the ground instead of the recommended 4 inches, the thick new growth will start there, and the bottom will remain forever barren.

The initial drastic pruning is all the trimming the plants in a formal hedge should get during their first season; they should be allowed to grow without any shearing. The following spring begin shaping the hedge. The top should be somewhat narrower than the base, because sloping sides allow sunshine to reach the leaves on all the branches, including the lower ones. If you trim in what seems to be an easier, more natural way—wide at top, narrow at bottom— the lower branches will be constantly shaded and will die, leaving the lower part of the hedge bare. As long as the top is narrower than the bottom, it can be either rounded or precisely flat. However, a rounded top and sloping sides are preferable for hedges growing in northern areas to prevent the accumulation of heavy loads of snow—a burden of snow can add so much weight to branches that they break or are forced apart, making the hedge wider at the top than it is at the bottom.

After the first year, a formal hedge should be sheared lightly every time new stems become about 6 inches long. Such regular trimming will induce each clipped stem to send out several side twigs, adding to the hedge's thickness. Do not clip after midsummer in colder regions, because new growth must have time to mature before winter arrives.

If the hedge is to be an unclipped, informal one, do not cut the shrubs back to the ground after planting. Instead, remove about one third to one half of their top growth; do not shear all the stems to an even height but maintain the shrub's natural shape by removing a proportionate part of the top of each stem, making each cut about ¼ inch above an outward-facing bud. New growth will quickly fill in the spaces to make a dense and beautiful hedge.

EARLY BLOOMS FROM SHRUBS

Among the rewards of many deciduous shrubs—and a by-product of pruning them—are the cut flowers they provide for bouquets to be enjoyed in the house, not only during their normal blooming period but even before it. By using a technique called forcing, a number of shrubs can be encouraged to blossom indoors in midwinter and early spring; among them are forsythia, Japanese barberry, winter honeysuckle, pussy willow, flowering quince, several spireas, winter hazel and witch hazel.

There is generally a correlation between the time the shrubs normally blossom in the garden and the time that they can be picked for use indoors: the closer to the normal outdoor blooming season a shrub is cut, the quicker most blossoms will open. For example, witch hazel blooms so early that its stems can be cut any time from November or December on and buds will open quickly indoors. Any plant whose buds are completely dormant will respond poorly, if at all, to indoor warmth, but if the swelling of buds is evident, the branches can be cut even in midwinter.

The best time to cut branches for forcing is when outdoor temperatures are above freezing, so that the transition from outdoor cold to indoor warmth is less abrupt. The life within the branches is then easily awakened by filling their cells with moisture, and the easiest way to accomplish this is to lay the branches in a bathtub partly filled with tepid water and leave them there overnight. If they are too long for the tub, stand them up in a vase or pail and give them a prolonged shower.

WHEN TO CUT BRANCHES

After their bath, the branches continue to need plenty of water. Most plants seem to absorb water more easily if their stems are slit up 3 to 4 inches from the bottom or their bark is peeled back the same length. Water in vases should be changed every day or two unless you have added a cut-flower food, as is often done to lengthen the flowers' indoor life.

Branches being forced into bloom need not only water in a

FORCING BRANCHES TO BLOOM INDOORS

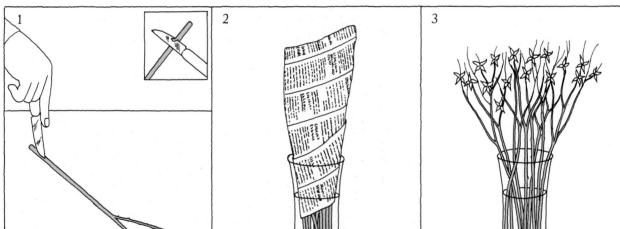

To bring cut branches into blossom in the house before they flower outdoors, slit each stem 3 to 4 inches from the base or shave off 3 inches of bark (inset). Lay the stems in a tub of tepid water overnight.

Keep the branches moist by placing them upright in a vase of tepid water and wrapping them in damp newspaper or clear plastic. Leave them wrapped for a few days, until their buds show some color.

The budding branches come into bloom after you remove the wrapping and place them in a cool, brightly lighted room. Do not place the vase in direct sunlight, which could dry out the buds.

vase but a high level of humidity in the air around them. Outdoors in spring, the humidity rarely falls below 60 per cent, but indoors in a heated house the humidity is usually about 10 to 25 per cent; dormant stems subjected to such desert-dry air dehydrate and die, or at best blossom weakly. To keep the branches properly moist until they blossom, put them in deep, tepid water in a vase and place the vase in the coolest place in the house—the cooler the air, the higher the relative humidity. A cool porch, garage or basement is ideal provided the temperature there does not drop to freezing at night. Another way to maintain humidity is to wrap the stems in damp newspaper or in clear plastic and leave them in the wrapping for a few days until the buds begin to show color. This wrapping technique helps if you cannot store the branches at low temperature, but it is useful even if you can, especially early in the year when forcing is more difficult.

After the first few days indoors, bright light helps to speed blooming—if you can find a brightly lit place that is also cool. Do not, however, put the branches in full sunshine, which has a drying effect on dormant buds. When the blossoms open, their colors usually are less brilliant than they are in the garden, but this is a small price to pay to be able to enjoy flowers indoors in midwinter. The length of time that flowers will last indoors depends upon the species and the temperature at which they are kept. The cooler the room, the longer the flowers will last.

CUT FLOWERS IN SEASON   All the shrubs that can be forced to bloom in winter—and many others—also make lovely bouquets when cut during their normal blooming period outdoors. The best time of day to cut stems is late in the afternoon after the plants have had a full day's sunshine in which to build up energy. Choose stems whose first flowers are just beginning to open; such stems will usually hold their flowers longest because many of the blooms will not yet have been pollinated. Any flower that has already been visited by a bee and fertilized will have completed its function as a flower and will then proceed to drop its petals and make seeds. Unpollinated flowers that open indoors, after cutting, generally last much longer than do those that open while still on the bushes.

When cutting flowers during the outdoor blooming period, remove all leaves that will be below the water level and put the stems in warm water immediately (I carry a vase or a bucket of warm water outdoors with me). Then place them in a cool, shady, draftless place. This technique fills their cells thoroughly with water and forestalls wilting. Some shrub blossoms, such as those of frangipani and hydrangeas, last longer if the ends of the stems are seared very briefly over a flame before they are put in water; the searing prevents the stems from oozing a coagulating substance that closes off the water ducts.

Cutting stems for flower arrangements is a form of pruning, and can be used consciously to shape plants or to lower their height. It is usually a healthful rather than a detrimental operation, since the plant does not have to devote energy to producing seeds, but can make more flower buds for another year.

Even if you do not pick a shrub's flowers, it is generally advisable to remove the faded blooms before seeds form, except on shrubs whose flowers are followed by attractive fruit. By preventing the formation of seeds, you make more of the plant's energy available for flower production. The procedure is usually easy; for lilacs, for example, take a pair of small hand shears to the garden, along with a basket in which to throw the old seed heads. Cut each one off at its place of origin in the "V" between the remaining twigs at the ends of the branches. You will find that the seed pods of azaleas can be snapped out easily by hand, but the faded plumes of false spirea have to be cut off with hand shears.

On many shrubs the berries and fall foliage are as attractive as the flowers, and they are often cut for display indoors. Although the ripening of fruit is usually connected with the harvest season, the berries of certain shrubs, such as February daphne and winter honeysuckle, become ripe in early summer. The fruits of cornelian cherry, blueberry and cherry elaeagnus are ripe by midsummer and color has begun to appear in most other fruits by late summer. The length of time the fruit remains on plants depends on the species and on how much the birds relish it; some shrubs are laden with handsome fruit one day and virtually stripped of fruit the next. But some berries cling until March or later, apparently because birds find them unpalatable or will not eat them until the supply of more palatable berries is exhausted. Such shrubs as Japanese barberry, many sumacs, European cranberry bush, linden viburnum, bayberry, and Amur and ibolium privet hold their fruit most of the winter and these lend color to indoor arrangements. To cut stems with berries or leaves for bouquets, take them from a plant when the fruit or foliage has reached its peak.

Certain berried shrubs such as sumac, as well as flowering branches of peegee hydrangea and other shrubs, can be dried for use in arrangements that will last indoors right through the winter. Simply hang stems of these plants upside down somewhere in a dry cellar, workshop or storage room; leave them there for a couple of weeks until they dry before taking them down and arranging them in a vase. Indoors as well as out, this will enable you to enjoy your shrubs all the more, year after year.

BERRIES AND LEAVES

A pretty way to solve a problem

Few plants can match the versatility of flowering shrubs. Whether you need a utilitarian hedge to hide a row of garbage cans or a flower-bright composition for a garden picture *(right),* there is a variety of shrubs to fill the bill. Whatever the prospective use, however, a shrub should be analyzed on four main counts before it is chosen and planted. The relative importance of these criteria will vary with the purpose and situation, but all must be considered:

Form. The shape in which a plant grows is almost always a key factor in its use. The arching, fountainlike sprays of most spireas and forsythias, for example, are well suited to loose, informal hedges where ground space is no problem, but would soon be in the way along a narrow garden path, where a more compact shrub like the dwarf European cranberry bush or the truehedge columnberry would be a better choice.

Texture. The size, arrangement and character of the twigs and leaves are every bit as important as the flowers, particularly in shrubs whose blooming period is short but whose foliage or bare branches will be visible all year long. Dense twigs and foliage make effective privacy screens and windbreaks; loose, feathery ones create quite a different pattern and allow welcome views and breezes through.

Color. In addition to the colors of the blossoms, consider the colors of the berries, the leaves—which range from a dark green in some shrubs to almost silver hues in others—and even the shading of the bark *(pages 18-33).* Judge them not only in relation to your own tastes but also to surrounding plantings and the colors of your house; then pick just a few to use repeatedly, for rhythm and harmony.

Size. This is the one criterion most people forget—they plant shrubs that outgrow their surroundings. Choose plants that grow to, and stay at, the mature height you want.

For the gardener who takes the time to think about these characteristics in the plants he is considering, shrubs can do almost any landscaping job for which they are intended, in both practical and pretty ways.

Bursts of orange, yellow, white and pink azalea blossoms transform a wooded backyard into a colorful focal point.

Choosing plants for a boundary line

Most houses without some landscaping elements placed out toward the front and sides are likely to appear naked and two-dimensional, particularly when viewed from the street *(above)*. One successful solution is to plant a row of shrubs along the boundary line, which not only creates a feeling of space between house and street, but also provides the homeowner with a sense of enclosure and establishes a frame for other landscaping. When planning a boundary marker, the important thing to remember is to select the type of shrub best suited to the site and its surroundings. The loose row of tall, informally arching forsythias shown at right is in keeping with the semirural site; it might, however, be out of scale and character on a narrower suburban lot, where a similar effect could be achieved with smaller plants such as dwarf garland spirea or dwarf winged euonymus.

Spring-blooming forsythias brighten a roadside, screening off the

ouse from traffic while providing a pleasant approach. In summer the leaves will form a green background for roses on the fence.

Blending plants and architecture

Plantings close to a house are not only highly visible elements in any landscape design, but ones that must be chosen with care so they do not clash with or overwhelm the architecture. The traditional solution to this problem—a garnishing of evergreens, including a couple of sentinels posted by the door *(below)*—is generally dull and often awkward. Far more attractive than evergreens alone around the front door, many gardeners have found, are summer displays of flowering shrubs like the hydrangeas at right —potted in movable tubs, if desired, so they can be replaced with other seasonal displays. To brighten the scheme further, low-growing flowering shrubs like the cranberry cotoneaster, golden St.-Johnswort or bush cinquefoil—all of which have fine foliage—can be combined with evergreens in year-round plantings under windows and in front of foundations.

The graceful arch of this Spanish-style doorway is echoed b

rounded shrubs, big-leaved hydrangeas. Attractive from spring to fall, they are easy to grow and blossom for two months in summer.

Decorating
a garden path

Planting along a path, whether it is a straight strip of concrete or a pleasant, grassy curve like the one shown here, might seem a simple enough task. Yet a surprising number of otherwise knowledgeable gardeners put in plants, like the tall, sprawling spirea sketched below, that soon spill over the walk, getting in the way unless pruned back to an unnatural shape. An obviously better choice is a plant that matches the scale of the path as well as the character of the surroundings—and that remains within bounds. Straight paths, for example, can be enhanced by low, neat borders of compact box barberry, dwarf cut-leaved stephanandra or dwarf purple osier. Curving paths lend themselves more to the informality of plants like kerria or Mollis Hybrid azaleas (right). To add to the pleasure of walking through the garden, fragrant plants like February daphne or Korean spice viburnum can be chosen to provide a welcome bonus of perfume.

Deep pink and white Mollis Hybrid azaleas, which tolerate the

light shade of their location, brighten a grassy garden walk, providing strollers with an attractive splash of color in a sea of green.

A massive hedge of purple and white lilacs forms an attractive garden screen, permitting a view of distant treetops while effectively

concealing whatever lies immediately behind its dense foliage.

Screening an eyesore

What do you do when your garden vista is flawed by a large and highly visible eyesore, like the neighbor's garage illustrated above? Often the only solution is to mass plants that are tall enough and thick enough to form a screen, yet are attractive enough to justify their prominence. The most effective shrubs are those whose branches and stems form a thick growth even when bare of foliage, like Amur privet, winged euonymus or the lilac shown at left. Tall screen plantings are also useful in breaking the full force of wind, blocking the lights of passing cars and even modifying some of the noise of a busy street. Among the most effective year-round screens for such uses is a planting of closely spaced evergreens such as hemlocks or spruces, fronted by shorter shrubs whose bright blossoms will stand out strikingly against the dark green background when they bloom.

Beautifying a terrace

In most backyards, a terrace or patio fills the role of an outdoor living room, a place to relax and enjoy the garden view. The best kinds of terrace plantings lend a slight sense of enclosure without walling the terrace off from the rest of the garden. In the example pictured here, a retaining wall was built around three valued shade trees to preserve them from a drop in ground level when the terrace was built; the result, while beginning to enclose the outdoor room on one side, still left something to be desired (*sketch, below*). The solution was to transform the earth-filled double wall into a bed for bright hydrangeas (*right*), which complete the design and are not too high or ornate to interfere with the view. Similar effects could have been achieved on more conventional terraces by planting shrubs in ground-level beds edging the terrace or by setting them in large tubs.

An arc of color around one side of a sitting area (left) is created

by plantings of big-leaved hydrangeas along a wall. The flowers blend harmoniously with the reddish stone and red bougainvilleas.

Using a spot screen

More than one suburban gardener has been confronted by a problem like the one illustrated in the sketch above: a neighboring house so close that it looms above any low plantings or fences on the property line, becoming an undesirable center of attention. A tall hedge, used in an attempt to screen the house completely *(pages 72-73),* would be out of scale in a small yard, making it seem boxed in and even smaller. A better—and cheaper —solution is a spot screen, a single tall shrub like the tall border privet pictured at right. Planted in a line between the neighboring house and the spot from which it will be most frequently seen, such as a terrace or a picture window, it partially obscures the house and replaces it as a new center of interest. Among other tall (10 to 15 feet) shrubs ideal for such use are Siberian pea trees, as well as smoke trees and nannyberries.

A single border privet in full flower makes a striking spot screen.

Even when not completely hiding the house next door, as in this view, it successfully diverts the focus of attention toward itself.

Highlighting a garden feature

A pleasing way to create a center of attraction in a garden is to landscape an interesting feature—a large rock, a piece of statuary, a bench or a decorative pool. Water in the garden presents a particularly exciting opportunity—it adds life and motion to the scene and can double the effect of plants placed around it by reflecting their colors, lights and shadows. Yet the opportunity is often missed, as in the example sketched above: the evergreens are too few, too tall and too stiff; they rise abruptly from the water's edge, and their dark, one-colored forms are only dully mirrored by the pond's surface. A much more natural, and harmonious, arrangement is pictured at right: an informal grouping of shrubs of various kinds that steps down from high plants in back to low ones with handsome flowers in front, where they can best be seen and reflected in the water.

The yellow blossoms of bush cinquefoil and the pink flower

clusters of Bumalda spirea stand out in a planting of shrubs around a pond, whose still surface picks up and reflects the blooms.

Six ways to multiply your plants 3

At one corner of my house—not far from the Persian lilac I raised from a bare-rooted 14-cent shrub—stands a huge purple lilac that an uncle gave me more than 20 years ago, when it was nothing but a single branch 2 feet high with a chunk of root attached. I still treasure his gift, but it did not cost my uncle even 14 cents. He had simply dug out one of the young plants that had sprung up from the base of a venerable shrub in his own yard, severed it from its parent and brought it over for me to put in my backyard. Within a few years it grew into the bush that for two weeks every spring makes a mass of deep purple in the garden and wafts sweet scent up the street in front.

Lilacs are among the easiest of the flowering shrubs to multiply, but hardly any shrubs pose great difficulty in this regard. A number of different techniques work, and generally you can choose the simplest one—though what is simplest may depend not only on the plant but also on the season of year, on your working habits and on how many new plants you need. Once you know how and when to use the methods, you will find propagating shrubs to be rewarding, for there are several reasons for growing your own shrubs instead of buying them.

Often you have a chance to duplicate a prized variety—from your garden or a friend's—that may not be easy to obtain from a nursery. And you can be certain of its suitability for your home conditions; if the parent plant grows well in your yard, so should its offspring. Economy is also a consideration. Not that most shrubs are very costly to buy. But in many cases you may want large numbers of plants. Enough of them to make a 50-foot-long hedge add up if they have to be purchased; if they are propagated from an existing plant, they cost nothing except a little effort on your part. But the best reason of all for propagating plants from your own stock is simply the pleasure it affords; few gardening activities that I know of can bring more satisfaction than growing plants that you have helped to create yourself.

Clusters of brilliantly colored Exbury azaleas border a lake on the Rothschild estate at Exbury, England. It was here that Lionel de Rothschild, an ardent plant breeder, developed these hybrids.

MULTIPLYING BY DIVISION

Division, which is the simplest method of multiplying shrubs such as common lilacs and oak-leaved hydrangeas that send out underground shoots called suckers, is best done in early spring before the leaves of the plants have opened. Choose a healthy sucker that has sprouted a foot or 2 above the ground. With a spade, cut a deep circle 6 to 8 inches in diameter around the sucker; this will sever the sucker from the main stem of the shrub. Then dig up the sucker, carefully going deep enough to bring it up with all of its own root system. Replant the sucker elsewhere at its original depth and water it well.

The lilac that my uncle multiplied was propagated by the general method called—in language he probably would have scorned as highfalutin—vegetative reproduction. His gift was reproduced from a piece of the older shrub's own vegetation, a living, growing segment of the plant. In his case the vegetation was a stem with a piece of root, but the same result can often be achieved by treating a segment of branch or root alone. Such a piece of vegetation contains in its cells exactly the same genetic material as the rest of the shrub, and the new plant will thus be exactly like the old one—not so much an offspring as a twin.

Vegetative reproduction is one of two basic ways in which plants can be propagated. The other is to grow them from seed, which might seem easier. But the seeds of most shrubs do not sprout readily; in fact, most must undergo many months of cool, moist conditions, and some may lie dormant for two years or more before they germinate. When they do sprout, seedlings may not resemble their parents. Bees may have introduced new genetic factors in the course of transporting pollen from one plant to another, and undesirable characteristics may turn up in the seedling; and if the parent plant is a hybrid—the result of professional interbreeding —seedlings may favor a grandparent rather than the parent. These problems do not entirely rule out the use of seeds. Some plants grow easily no other way. And the variability of seed propagation in itself is valuable. Seeds of azaleas, particularly, may produce beautiful specimens the likes of which have never been seen before. But generally you will be better off multiplying your shrubs by vegetative reproduction, which guarantees that your new plants will exactly duplicate the old ones.

The technique my uncle used—one of the simplest and most widely practiced—is called division *(drawing, left)*. It works well not only with lilac but with oak-leaved hydrangea, fragrant sumac, Siberian dogwood, kerria and other plants that send out suckers —underground branches—from which one or more stems emerge and shoot straight up. The best time to practice the division technique is early spring, before the leaves have appeared.

Flowering shrubs that do not send out suckers cannot be divided, but many of them can be propagated from pieces of their stems. Depending on their maturity, such cuttings are described as softwood, semihardwood or hardwood. A softwood cutting is taken in late spring or early summer from new growth: a stem still young and green but with new leaves established. If it snaps when bent, the way a fresh stalk of asparagus will, it is just mature enough. A semihardwood cutting is taken in mid- to late summer and will be slightly tougher so that it will bend almost in half before it breaks; when it does break, a stringy fringe of bark and some wood adhere at the breaking point. A hardwood cutting, taken in fall or winter, consists of tough, mature wood that is leafless because the plant from which it is severed has become dormant.

Which kind of cutting you use depends partly on your own convenience, and partly on the habits of plants you plan to start. Most shrubs root most easily and quickly from softwood cuttings, but if you are going to be away from home in late spring or early summer and unable to tend your cuttings, or if you simply do not get around to the job in spring, then semihardwood cuttings, taken in summer, serve perfectly well. If you've been too busy all summer, hardwood cuttings can be taken still later in the year and, while they take a considerably longer time to root, they require less care and are less perishable than either softwood or semihardwood cuttings because they are more mature.

The time to take softwood cuttings in Zones 5 and 6 is between June 1 and July 15; in Southern areas the period comes a few weeks earlier and in Northern sections a couple of weeks later. Semihardwood cuttings can be taken in Zones 5 and 6 between July 15 and the end of August, with about the same differential for Southern and Northern zones. Both types of cuttings are handled the same way, as shown in the drawings on page 84. Cut pieces of the current year's growth, 5 to 7 inches long, choosing the ends of stems that are neither weak nor excessively vigorous. Weak growth, indicated by stunted stems, will produce weak plants. Excessively vigorous growth, indicated by extremely long stems, widely spaced nodes (the places where leaves or buds appear) and few, if any, side branches, may fail to root.

MAKING STEM CUTTINGS

Some stems, such as those of forsythia and stephanandra, will root no matter where you cut them. If you have ever brought stems of pussy willow or forsythia indoors for forcing, for example, you may have noticed that some of the stems started to form roots while in their vase of water; these can be planted outdoors in your garden and will grow into full-sized shrubs. Many gardeners simply cut branches of forsythia right off the bush and stick them in the ground; many root without further attention, and if some do not, nothing is lost—you still get more shrubs than you can probably use, and any extras you cannot use yourself may be offered to friends. But most cuttings root most easily if the stem is cut about ½ inch below a node, and if they are given special treatment.

Once cut, softwood and semihardwood stems wilt quickly, so get all the materials you need ready before you start. Work with

PROPAGATING FROM SOFTWOOD CUTTINGS

1. *To grow shrubs from cuttings of softwood, the young growth of late spring or early summer, remove 5 to 7 inches of healthy stem tips. Use a sharp knife and make a cut ½ inch below a leaf joint. Sprinkle the stems with water and wrap them in damp burlap to keep them moistened.*

2. *When you are ready to root the cuttings, trim the leaves on large-leaved plants to reduce their size by one third to one half. Remove any flowers, buds and leaves on the lower third of the stems.*

3. *Dip about half an inch of each stem base in rooting hormone.*

4. *Set the cuttings about 2 inches deep and 3 inches apart in a half-and-half mix of coarse sand and peat moss. Water, then cover with a plastic bag supported with sticks and tuck the ends under. Set in light shade outdoors. If no new leaves appear by fall, remove the plastic and place the cuttings in a cold frame; if new leaves appear, signaling root growth, pot each stem in potting soil, then move to a cold frame. Transplant them to the garden in spring.*

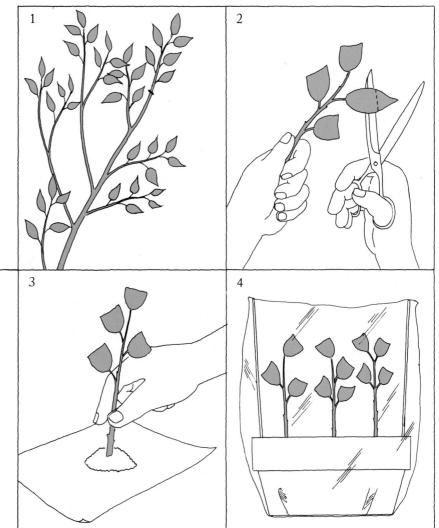

the cuttings in the early morning when the stems are full of water and stay in the shade to protect them from the drying effects of strong sun. They will need moisture immediately but do not put them in water because it will dilute their sap and inhibit their ability to form roots. Instead, sprinkle the stems with water, cover them with dampened burlap or cheesecloth and put them in a cool place until you can set them in rooting medium.

Among the suitable rooting media are coarse sand, peat moss or a mixture of equal parts of the two. Equally good are vermiculite, perlite and finely ground sphagnum moss. All of these materials retain the moisture the cuttings need, yet allow vital air to penetrate to the buried sections that will sprout roots. Any container that has good drainage—a flowerpot or a gardener's flat —will serve if it is deep enough to contain the 3 to 4 inches of rooting medium that most cuttings need.

When you are ready to plant your cuttings, remove any flowers or flower buds, which would drain energy needed for root formation. Also take off leaves on the lower third of the cutting, which will be below the level of the rooting medium. Plants with medium-sized or large leaves—hydrangeas and orange-eyed butterfly bushes, for example—lose moisture fast because of their leaf area, and should have the leaves reduced in size—part of each leaf is cut off to maintain a balance between the moisture the stems can draw up and the moisture lost from the leaves. On such plants, snip off one third to one half of each of the remaining leaves (drawings, left). On small-leaved plants like most cotoneasters, barberries and Thunberg spirea, the moisture balance is adequate and cutting back of leaves is not necessary.

After removing and trimming leaves, if required, dip the bottom ½ to 1 inch of each cutting into synthetic rooting hormone, a powder available at garden centers—and a blessing to modern-day gardeners. Growing many plants from cuttings was difficult a generation ago; the rooting hormone now makes the task relatively easy. The powder contains naphthaleneacetic acid, a natural substance present in all plants to a greater or lesser degree. It helps to induce the formation of root cells by a process that is not yet fully understood. Nonetheless, the rooting powder works. For best results, buy the concentrated grade that is recommended for shrub cuttings; the lower grades that are available may not be sufficiently strong to induce rooting. After dipping the end of the cutting in the hormone, tap the cutting lightly to remove excess powder, then insert the cutting about 2 inches deep in the rooting medium and firm the surface with your fingers.

Once the cuttings have been set in place, the rooting medium should be thoroughly moistened, but not soaked; it is a good idea to

THE DOWSER'S WITCH HAZEL

A forked branch from a witch hazel shrub is a traditional tool of dowsers, who claim to locate water-producing well sites with its aid. Subsurface water attracts the witch hazel branch, the dowsers say, causing it to dip toward the ground where a plentiful source is to be found. To try your hand at dowsing, cut a Y-shaped witch hazel branch about 2 feet long and grip the ends in both hands, palms up, pointing the branch skyward at a 45° angle. Walk around a likely-looking area, and if you feel the branch ends twist in your hands as if the butt were being pulled down, you may have dowsed a well. Success in dowsing seems to depend more on the dowser's pragmatic knowledge of geology than on any attraction between water and wood (a theory for which there is not a shred of scientific evidence), but an estimated 25,000 practitioners of this mystical art are still active in the United States today.

use an atomizerlike misting device. Then enclose the cuttings and their container in clear plastic film to maintain a relatively high humidity around them. To enclose a few cuttings set in flowerpots, use plastic food bags propped with sticks inserted in the rooting medium to keep the bags from sagging down on the cuttings. If you are rooting a dozen or more cuttings in a flat, cover them with a tent of clear plastic sheeting held up on a framework of bent wire (old coat hangers will do). In either case, the bottom of the plastic film should be tucked under the container. Set this miniature greenhouse in a lightly shaded place outdoors and sprinkle the rooting medium whenever it shows signs of drying out.

The time it takes cuttings to form roots may vary from two to three weeks in the case of shrubs like forsythia, broom, euonymus, pussy willow and orange-eyed butterfly bush to six months or more in the case of shrubs like flowering quince, enkianthus, azalea, lilac, viburnum and cotoneaster. If your cuttings root relatively quickly—the signal is new leaf growth—remove them gently from the rooting medium, plant them in individual pots in packaged potting soil, available at garden centers, and place them in a cold frame for the fall and winter; the following spring plant them in the garden. (A cold frame is easily built out of boards for sides and a sloping sash of glass or plastic for a roof.) If the cuttings root slowly, take off the plastic covers in fall but leave the cuttings in the rooting medium and place the containers in a cold frame until early the next spring; then, before they sprout new leaves, remove them gently from the rooting medium and set them into beds or rows in the garden where they can continue their growth.

MAKING HARDWOOD CUTTINGS The technique of propagating new plants from hardwood cuttings differs considerably from that used for softwood and semihardwood cuttings. Stems of the current year's growth are cut in late fall or early winter after they have matured completely and the leaves have fallen off. Stunted stems or overvigorous stems whose buds are widely spaced should be avoided. The best tool for making hardwood cuttings is a pair of sharp hand pruning shears; the wood is usually too tough to cut easily with a knife. Take cuttings up to 2 feet long from the plant's stems and divide them into pieces about 5 to 8 inches long *(drawings, right)*.

Hardwood cuttings should not be stuck upright into a rooting medium. Instead, store them over the winter by laying them on their sides in a box in damp sawdust or a slightly moistened mixture of equal parts of peat moss and coarse sand. Ideal storage temperatures are 50° to 55° for three to four weeks, then 35° to 40° for the rest of the winter. In areas where the ground does not freeze, the box can be left outdoors in a cool, moist but well-drained shaded place out of the wind to remain until the following spring. In colder regions the box can be stored in an unheated garage or the coolest part of a cellar; except in parts of Zones 3 and 4 where winters are exceptionally severe, the box can also be buried outdoors in a well-drained location in the yard and covered with a pile of leaves about a foot high to protect it from freezing solid.

When you retrieve the cuttings in spring, you may be dismayed to find that many, perhaps most, have not developed any roots. However, close examination of the lower end of each cutting will disclose a ridge of whitish new tissue, called callus tissue. From this callus roots usually emerge, although some species send out roots all along the stems.

Hardwood cuttings are planted outdoors as early in the spring as you can work the soil. Put them for the time being in rows in a

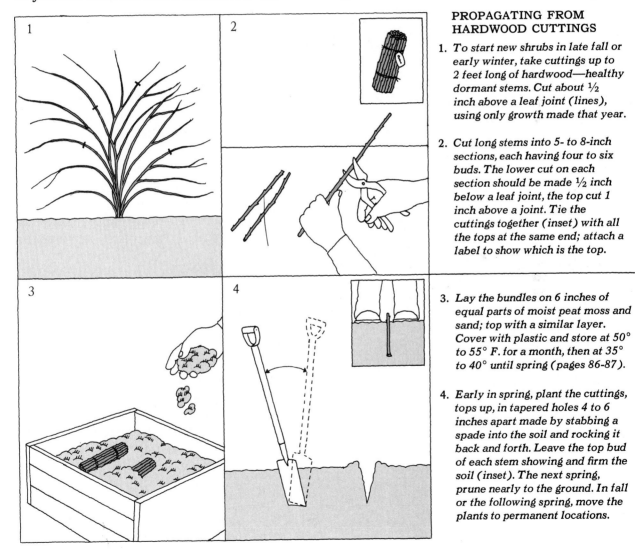

PROPAGATING FROM HARDWOOD CUTTINGS

1. *To start new shrubs in late fall or early winter, take cuttings up to 2 feet long of hardwood—healthy dormant stems. Cut about ½ inch above a leaf joint (lines), using only growth made that year.*

2. *Cut long stems into 5- to 8-inch sections, each having four to six buds. The lower cut on each section should be made ½ inch below a leaf joint, the top cut 1 inch above a joint. Tie the cuttings together (inset) with all the tops at the same end; attach a label to show which is the top.*

3. *Lay the bundles on 6 inches of equal parts of moist peat moss and sand; top with a similar layer. Cover with plastic and store at 50° to 55° F. for a month, then at 35° to 40° until spring (pages 86-87).*

4. *Early in spring, plant the cuttings, tops up, in tapered holes 4 to 6 inches apart made by stabbing a spade into the soil and rocking it back and forth. Leave the top bud of each stem showing and firm the soil (inset). The next spring, prune nearly to the ground. In fall or the following spring, move the plants to permanent locations.*

nursery bed, a small out-of-the-way spot in the garden where they can grow up with plenty of light and moisture, since the new plants that will form will be too small to enhance your main garden immediately and could be overwhelmed by larger plants there. Set the cuttings so that only the top bud of each cutting shows above the soil. Do not let them become dry between the time you take them from their box and the time you plant them; if any delay in planting should become necessary, cover them with damp burlap to keep them moist.

Later in spring, with the arrival of mild weather, the cuttings begin sending up new stems, and during their first summer they become miniature shrubs. The following spring, cut the plants back nearly to the ground—this drastic treatment will force them to send up more stems and become bushier during their second growing season. At the end of the second summer they will be large enough to assume their permanent positions in the garden and should be moved there that fall or the following spring.

MAKING ROOT CUTTINGS

Certain shrubs such as bottle-brush buckeye, serviceberry, staghorn sumac, rose acacia and sweet shrub can be grown from small sections of their roots, which should be cut off in fall or spring when the plants are dormant and leafless. This method *(drawings, right)* is in some ways simpler than taking stem cuttings, since there is no need to develop the new plants in several stages in pots or cold frames. The root segments, cut into small pieces, can be planted directly into a nursery bed. Within a few months a young plant will appear from each section. It can grow where it is for one or two years before it is moved to its permanent location in the main garden.

PLANTS FROM GROWING STEMS

If you want only one or two new plants, there is a propagation method that requires even less effort than rooting cuttings; it takes advantage of a natural phenomenon you may have observed: When the long flexible branches of certain plants such as forsythia, cotoneaster or flowering quince bend over far enough to touch the ground, they sometimes send down roots at that spot and make new plants. To force this rooting action to take place, simply bury a branch in a hole as shown in the drawings on page 90 and let the mother plant continue to supply nourishment until the new plants are established enough to be separated and replanted on their own. No special care is needed. The best time to practice the technique, called simple layering or ground layering, is in early spring.

AZALEAS FROM SEEDS

One of the several methods of vegetative reproduction is the best choice for multiplying most flowering shrubs, but there is one plant, the azalea, that is worth the trouble of growing from seeds. New plants are expensive to buy, compared to such shrubs as forsythia and spirea, and they are difficult to root from cuttings. There is good reason for the high price of azaleas—a plant requires four to six years of careful attention before it reaches 3 feet in height, whereas a forsythia or a spirea usually is that tall at the end of its second growing season. But any gardener who wants numbers of azaleas can have dozens or even hundreds of them for less than the cost of a single blossoming-sized plant simply by investing his time and a small amount of money in seeds. From seeds to flowers may require four years, but you can count on a tremendous pride of accomplishment at each stage in your plants' growth.

All kinds of azaleas can be grown from seeds; in fact, the elegant named varieties all began as seedlings. The seedlings' blossom sizes and colors may vary somewhat from one to another—and

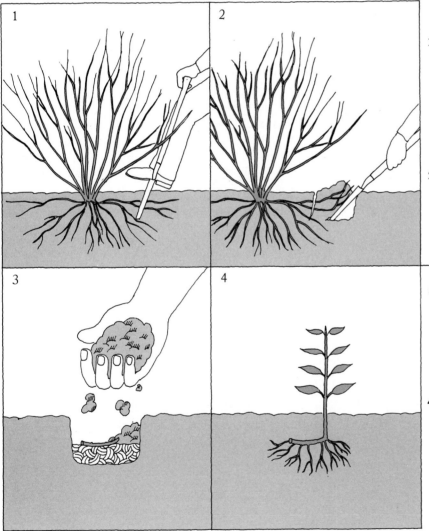

PROPAGATING FROM ROOT CUTTINGS

1. *Use a sharp spade to get root cuttings for new shrubs. Drive it into the ground about one third of the way in from the outermost spread of branches, cutting off a section of the spreading roots. Root cuttings should be taken in early spring or late fall when the plant is dormant and leafless.*

2. *About 18 inches out from the first cut, pry up the earth with the spade to expose the root ends. Pull the root sections out and cut them into pieces 2 to 3 inches long with hand pruning shears.*

3. *Each cutting goes into a nursery-bed hole, about 3 inches deep and 4 inches wide, atop a 1-inch layer of damp peat moss, and is then covered with enough soil to fill the hole. Firm the soil into place by pressing down with your foot.*

4. *The root cutting will send out new roots along its length and in a few months a young plant will appear, growing from the end of the cutting that was nearest the mother plant. The baby shrub may be moved the following year from the nursery row to its permanent place in the garden.*

from the parent plants. If the seeds are those of a modern hybrid such as Exbury or Mollis, the results are more unpredictable. But this variability is what makes seed propagation so fascinating. And there is always the chance that one of your seedlings will produce flowers superior to varieties now being grown.

Azalea seeds are extremely tiny, almost dustlike. You may buy them from seedsmen or gather them yourself from particularly fine plants in your own or a friend's garden. If you decide to gather your own, pick the seed pods in the fall after they have begun to turn brown but before they have split open to discharge seeds. A single pod may contain hundreds of seeds. Put the pods of different species or varieties in separate envelopes, marked with the name of the plant—if you know it—and the color of the blossoms from which the pods came. Store the envelopes in a cool, dry place until you are ready to plant the seeds.

A good time to start azalea seeds is in midwinter, indoors; the young plants then have a long season in which to grow before the arrival of the following winter, a critical time for seedlings. Provide separate containers for different varieties of seeds because some grow faster than others. A 4- or 6-inch plastic flowerpot of the pan type—half as tall as it is wide—provides a suitable container. Fill the pots to within ½ inch of the top with fine-grade peat moss and

PROPAGATING SHRUBS BY GROUND LAYERING

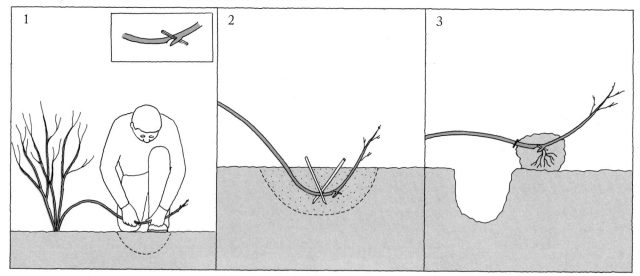

To start new plants from flexible shrubs in spring, bend a stem to touch the ground a foot from the tip; dig a dish-shaped hole 6 inches deep. At the bend cut partway through and wedge with a matchstick (inset).

Dust the cut with rooting powder and bury it 3 inches deep, anchored with crossed sticks, in soil mixed with equal parts of damp peat moss and coarse sand; water thoroughly. About 6 inches of stem should show.

By the following spring the buried stem will have produced roots. Cut it from the parent stem just below the soil ball (line), set the ball to its original depth in a prepared hole in its new location, and water well.

moisten and firm it well. Then add a ¼-inch layer of finely ground, or milled, sphagnum moss. Ordinarily, this moss is moist when purchased; if it has dried out, wet it with very hot water—it is nearly impermeable by cold water—and be sure that the moss is thoroughly and evenly moistened before you sow the seeds. Then take a pinch of seeds between your thumb and forefinger and drop them sparingly across the surface. Do not cover the seeds. After sowing, treat the surface of the moss to prevent the fungus-caused rot called damping off. This can be best accomplished by sprinkling with a solution containing a fungicide such as folpet, thiram or captan, using 1 tablespoon to a gallon of water.

Next, slip the flowerpots into clear plastic food bags and place them on a brightly lighted, but not sunny, window sill where the temperature is between 55° and 75° F. Unless the surface moss becomes obviously dry, no further watering is needed until the young plants peep about ¼ inch above the surface. At that time the plastic should be loosened for a day or two, then removed entirely. Water the plants by placing the pots in saucers and filling the saucers until the surface of the moss becomes moist; repeat waterings whenever the moss begins to dry out. Once a month, simultaneously water and feed the plants with a solution made by dissolving ⅓ teaspoon of ammonium sulfate in a gallon of water.

The seedlings will develop their first true leaves—which closely resemble those of mature azaleas and come after the initial pair of seedling leaves—about two to three months after planting. Then transplant them into moist peat moss, setting them one to a pot in small flowerpots, or 2 inches apart in flats. Place the pots or flats in a shaded cold frame to remain until the following spring, when they will be slightly more than a year old. Then set them 8 to 12 inches apart in an outdoor nursery bed in a soil mixture composed of one half peat moss or leaf mold and one half coarse sand. A shading of lath, such as snow fencing, is advisable during the hot summer months, but it should be removed in late summer to allow the fall sunshine to ripen and toughen the young plants before the arrival of cold weather.

When the young plants have become about 12 inches tall, usually about two to three years after planting, they are large enough to go into their permanent garden spots. They need moist acid soil (pH 4.5 to 5.5) and should be mulched with pine needles, decayed sawdust or other organic material to control weeds and to maintain a cool, moist condition around the roots. By the spring of the third or fourth year, your carefully raised plants should reward you with their first flowers. And as with any plants you have propagated yourself, regardless of the method, that is the moment that makes it all worthwhile.

THE MYSTERIOUS FRANKLINIA

The fragrant franklinia, one of the few shrubs that bloom in fall, is notable on another count—all the specimens now growing in gardens are descended from a handful of shrubs found two centuries ago by a father-son team who were among America's first plant hunters. John Bartram and his son William happened on the white-flowered shrubs growing wild along the Alatamaha River in southern Georgia in the fall of 1765. They brought them back to their Philadelphia garden for propagation and named the species Franklinia alatamaha after the river and John's friend Benjamin Franklin. In 1783 William Bartram went back and collected a few more specimens but these apparently were among the last of the rare breed growing in nature. Plant historians theorize that the shrub was on the verge of extinction; in any case, none have been found in the wild since 1790.

An illustrated encyclopedia of flowering shrubs 4

Two questions to ask before choosing a flowering shrub are: what role do you want it to play in your landscape, and how much space do you have for it? Characteristics such as shape and size at maturity, as well as suitability for various landscaping uses, are described and illustrated in the following encyclopedia chapter, which includes 77 genera of flowering shrubs. The entries also list the soil and light requirements of each plant, the climate zones for which it is recommended and the seasons in which it flowers, bears fruit and turns color; the zones are keyed by number to the map on page 154, and an accompanying table lists the months approximately corresponding to spring, summer and fall in each zone.

Unless otherwise noted, plants can be purchased in three forms: bare-rooted, with their roots bare of soil; balled and burlaped, with roots in their original soil ball, which is wrapped in burlap; and in containers, usually plastic pots or large tin cans. The latter two forms can be set into the garden any time that the ground can be worked, but bare-rooted plants must be planted when dormant. Shrubs planted in groups should be set apart a distance equal to their spread at maturity; for plants used in hedges, specific spacing instructions are given. Most species reach maturity within five years. Fast growers may add 3 or more feet a year if not pruned, moderate growers about 2 feet a year, slow growers about a foot. Most plants require light pruning in spring to remove dead or damaged wood; the time to prune for shape and more or larger flowers varies and is given in each entry.

The plants are listed alphabetically by their internationally recognized Latin botanical names; for example, in *Berberis thunbergii atropurpurea,* the red-leaved Japanese barberry, *Berberis* indicates the genus, *thunbergii* the species and *atropurpurea* the particular variety. Common names, which often vary from region to region, are cross-referenced to the Latin genus names. For quick reference, a chart of the characteristics and uses of the recommended species and varieties appears on pages 146-151.

Shrub flowers to suit every fancy appear in a painting by Allianora Rosse, including the tight red petals of the strawberry bush, the white cup of franklinia (center) and the pink stars of daphne (lower left).

KOREAN ABELIALEAF
Abeliophyllum distichum

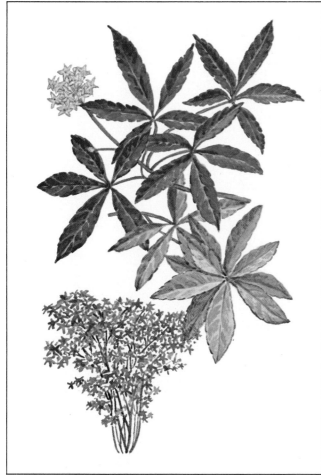

FIVE-LEAVED ARALIA
Acanthopanax sieboldianus

A

ABELIALEAF, KOREAN See *Abeliophyllum*

ABELIOPHYLLUM
A. distichum (Korean abelialeaf, white forsythia)

Often called white forsythia, although true forsythia is another genus *(page 112),* Korean abelialeaf bears masses of flowers in early spring at the same time as true forsythias. The ½-inch slightly fragrant blossoms appear in thick clusters on the leafless twigs of densely packed and arching branches. At first they are pale pink, but they quickly fade to white with orange centers. Oval 1- to 2-inch blue-green leaves are borne on the shrub during the summer. It carries deep purple buds through the winter, and the stems may be cut in midwinter and easily made to bloom indoors. Korean abelialeaf usually grows 3 to 4 feet tall, but sometimes reaches 5 feet. Since the flowers usually bloom when it is still chilly outside, it is best planted in a spot that allows it to be seen and enjoyed from indoors.

HOW TO GROW. Korean abelialeaf grows in Zones 5-8 in almost any well-drained soil in full sun or light shade. It should be given a protected location in northern limits of Zone 5 so that its exposed flower buds will not be damaged by cold during the winter. Flowers form on the previous season's growth, not on new growth, so do not prune until after the flowers fade. New plants can be started from softwood cuttings of young growth taken in late spring or early summer, from semihardwood cuttings of more mature growth taken in mid- or late summer, or from hardwood cuttings of dormant leafless growth taken in late fall or early winter.

ACACIA, ROSE See *Robinia*

ACANTHOPANAX
A. sieboldianus, also called *Aralia pentaphylla* (five-leaved aralia, angelica shrub)

Five-leaved aralia is a tough pest-resistant shrub that tolerates shade or dry soil as well as the soot and grime of the city. It has inconspicuous flowers and fruit but attractive foliage. The shiny dark green leaves, each composed of five to seven 2-inch leaflets, hold their color until late autumn, when they turn yellow before falling. Plants usually grow to a height of 4 to 6 feet. They are well suited for informal hedges because the stiff upright branches, which have sharp spines at the bases of the leaves, make effective barriers.

HOW TO GROW. Five-leaved aralia grows in Zones 4-9 in almost any soil in full sun or shade. Plants used as hedges should be set 18 to 24 inches apart. If the plant becomes too tall or gawky, prune in early spring, cutting the stems off at ground level; many fresh new shoots will then quickly crop up. New plants can be started from softwood cuttings of young growth in late spring or early summer, from semihardwood cuttings of more mature growth in mid- or late summer, or from hardwood cuttings of dormant leafless growth in late fall or winter. New plants can also be propagated from root cuttings.

AESCULUS
A. parviflora (bottle-brush buckeye, dwarf horse chestnut)

No lawn shrub is more stunning in mid- and late summer than the bottle-brush buckeye, whose deep green mounds of foliage are adorned with hundreds of 8- to 16-inch flower spikes that do indeed resemble the bristly bottle brushes for which they are named. Each spike consists of dozens of ½-inch white flowers with pink-tipped pollen-bearing stamens that may be twice as long as the flower petals. The flowers are followed by 1-inch fruit that look like horse chestnuts but have smooth rather than prickly husks. The mounds of foliage grow 3 to 10 feet tall, often with greater spread; the palm-shaped leaves have five to seven fingerlike leaflets, each 3 to 8 inches long, and turn yellow in autumn. Bottle-brush buckeyes, natives of the southeastern section of the United States, spread slowly by underground roots and eventually require a wide space in which to grow; for this reason they are seldom used in borders, but are very effective as clumps set against dark green evergreen plants.

HOW TO GROW. Bottle-brush buckeyes grow in Zones 4-10 in full sun or light shade in almost any soil, but do best in full sun in moist soil that has been liberally enriched with peat moss or leaf mold. Plant in early spring. Pruning is seldom required. New plants can be started from root cuttings or by forcing a branch to grow roots by the method known as ground layering.

ALDER, BLACK See *Ilex*
ALDER, WITCH See *Fothergilla*
ALLSPICE, CAROLINA See *Calycanthus*
ALMOND, FLOWERING See *Prunus*
ALTHEA, SHRUB See *Hibiscus*

AMELANCHIER
A. stolonifera (running serviceberry)

Running serviceberry is particularly useful to owners of homes on the seacoast because of its ability to stabilize shifting banks of sand. In the spring, just as the leaves unfold, this 2- to 4-foot upright shrub bears 1½- to 3-inch clusters of white flowers less than an inch across. The 1- to 2-inch leaves are almost white underneath in spring, but turn handsome shades of red and yellow in the fall. The sweet-tasting purplish black berries, which ripen in midsummer, are relished by birds. The running serviceberry looks best in a semiwild setting.

HOW TO GROW. Running serviceberry grows in Zones 4-8 and does best in full sunshine and in dry well-drained soil. Pruning is almost never required. The plant spreads naturally by means of its roots, and new plants are most easily started from divisions of these offshoots. Plants can also be propagated from root cuttings.

ANGELICA SHRUB See *Acanthopanax*
ARALIA, FIVE-LEAVED See *Acanthopanax*
ARALIA PENTAPHYLLA See *Acanthopanax*

ARONIA
A. arbutifolia (red chokeberry), *A. melanocarpa* (black chokeberry), *A. prunifolia* (purple chokeberry)

The richly colored chokeberries lend bright touches to shrub borders from late spring through fall. In late spring they bear 2-inch clusters of ½-inch white or pink flowers. The flowers are followed by bright masses of tiny berries that have an astringent taste—hence the name chokeberry. Even the birds do not like them. In the fall the 2- to 3-inch oval leaves turn a brilliant red.

Red chokeberry grows 6 to 9 feet tall and bears clusters of berries, less than ½ inch in diameter, that turn red in early fall and remain on the shrub until early winter. It has smooth oval leaves with either white-green or gray-green tints. Brilliant chokeberry, *A. arbutifolia brilliantissima*, grows to a similar size, but has more and brighter red fruit and leaves than the regular species. Black chokeberry, which grows only 1½ to 3 feet tall, has black berries that ripen in late summer and drop off soon thereafter. The leaves are smooth, shiny and pale green.

BOTTLE-BRUSH BUCKEYE
Aesculus parviflora

RUNNING SERVICEBERRY
Amelanchier stolonifera

For climate zones and months of flowering, see page 154.

Purple chokeberry bears shiny purple berries that ripen in autumn but fall off after the first frost. It grows 10 to 12 feet tall and makes a fine shrub where a tall screen planting is desirable.

HOW TO GROW. Chokeberries grow in Zones 4-10 in almost any soil—red chokeberry even tolerates wet soil, and the black chokeberry adapts well to dry soil. All chokeberries bear more abundant fruit and have brighter autumn colors if they are grown in full sunshine, but very light shade is also suitable. The shrubs rarely need pruning. New plants can be started in any of several ways: by digging up and replanting underground offshoots known as suckers, from softwood cuttings of young growth taken in spring or by forcing a branch to grow roots by the method known as ground layering.

ARROWWOOD See *Viburnum*
AZALEA See *Rhododendron*

B

BARBADOS PRIDE See *Caesalpinia*
BARBERRY See *Berberis*
BAYBERRY See *Myrica*
BEAUTY BUSH See *Kolkwitzia*
BEAUTY-BERRY See *Callicarpa*
BENZOIN See *Lindera*

BERBERIS

B. koreana (Korean barberry), *B. mentorensis* (Mentor barberry), *B. thunbergii* (Japanese barberry)

So many hedges have been made of barberries that it is easy to forget that individual shrubs, allowed to grow naturally without pruning, are attractive enough to be planted alone. Their small yellow flowers, some tinged with red, open in late spring at the same time that the new 1-inch-long green leaves unfold. In the fall, the leaves turn red or orange and the flowers are followed by red berries, which may cling to the plants until the next season's flowers open. The berries of the Japanese species are a source of food in late winter for birds. The arching branches, dense foliage and low height of barberries make them suitable for planting near a house or in the front of a shrub border; their spiny branches make them effective barrier plants. In certain areas of the country where wheat is a major crop, laws prohibit the growing of some kinds of barberries because the plants act as hosts for a wheat-destroying fungus called black stem rust; the shrubs listed here do not harbor this fungus, and they can be planted wherever climate and soil are suitable.

Korean barberry grows 4 to 6 feet tall and bears both its tiny flowers and round red berries in hanging clusters. Mentor barberry is a 5- to 7-foot hybrid that has dull red berries and is semievergreen: it holds its spiny leaves throughout the year in Zones 7-10 but drops them late in the fall in colder areas. Japanese barberry, in its normal green-foliaged form, has been planted by the millions for more than a century. It grows 4 to 7 feet tall and has bright red oval berries that hang like little pendants from its branches. In addition to the normal green-foliaged form, there are several fine varieties of this species of special interest. The red-leaved Japanese barberry, *B. thunbergii atropurpurea,* has deep purplish red foliage that turns greenish late in the summer, especially if it is grown in shady places. Another type of the red-leaved variety, Redbird, is more highly colored and retains its brightness throughout the season. Crimson Pygmy is a compact dwarf variety that grows less than 2 feet tall and has bright red foliage. Truehedge columnberry, *B. thunbergii erecta,* has leaves,

BRILLIANT CHOKEBERRY
Aronia arbutifolia brilliantissima

JAPANESE BARBERRY
Berberis thunbergii

flowers and berries that are similar to those of the species, but its branches are upright rather than arching, making the truehedge columnberry one of the finest shrubs for either formal or informal hedges. The box barberry, *B. thunbergii minor,* has small green leaves and grows slowly into a dense, bushy plant 2½ to 3½ feet tall.

HOW TO GROW. Japanese barberries grow in Zones 4-10; Korean and Mentor barberries grow in Zones 5-10. All do well in almost any soil in full sun but will tolerate light shade. Barberries that are grown as sheared hedges may need to be trimmed to shape two or three times during a season, but plants grown singly rarely need pruning. For hedge planting, set them 1 to 2 feet apart. If plants become straggly, they can be cut to within 2 inches of the ground in early spring; they will soon send up an abundance of new growth. All of the barberries described above can be propagated from softwood cuttings of young growth taken in late spring or early summer, from semihardwood cuttings of more mature growth taken in mid- or late summer, or from hardwood cuttings of dormant leafless growth taken in fall or winter.

BLADDER SENNA See *Colutea*
BLUEBEARD See *Caryopteris*
BLUEBERRY See *Vaccinium*
BRIDAL WREATH See *Spiraea*
BROOM See *Cytisus*
BUCKEYE, BOTTLE-BRUSH See *Aesculus*
BUCKTHORN, ALDER See *Rhamnus*
BUCKTHORN, SEA See *Hippophae*

BUDDLEIA, also called BUDDLEJA
B. alternifolia (fountain butterfly bush), *B. davidii* (orange-eyed butterfly bush, summer lilac)

Butterfly bushes are late starters—they do not begin growth until the end of spring, after most other plants have put out new leaves. But their tiny fragrant flowers, borne on long arching branches, are worth waiting for. The fountain butterfly bush becomes 8 to 10 feet tall, with a spread of as much as 15 feet if it is given enough room. It bears ¾-inch clusters of lilac-purple flowers in late spring and early summer. Its 1- to 4-inch willowlike leaves, light green above and silvery beneath, cling until late in the fall. The orange-eyed butterfly bush grows 3 to 8 feet tall in a single summer, and in frost-free climates can become 15 to 20 feet tall with an equal spread. Its spectacular varieties bear flower spikes up to 18 inches long that are densely packed with blossoms from midsummer until frost. The flowers of the original species are bluish purple with orange centers, but the varieties such as those shown come in many colors. Among the best selections are: Fascinating, pink; Flaming Violet, violet; Purple Prince, purple; Fortune, lilac; Empire Blue, blue; and White Profusion, white. They make excellent cut flowers and will last longer if the stem ends are placed in warm water (about 100° F.) as soon as they are cut. Orange-eyed butterfly bushes have very attractive silvery gray fuzzy leaves, which vary from 4 to 8 inches in length. Since the tops of orange-eyed butterfly bushes either die or are badly injured in winter in cold parts of the country, the plants are often set at the back of perennial borders along with plants that normally die down to the ground each year.

HOW TO GROW. Butterfly bushes grow in Zones 5-10 in full sun and well-drained soil that has been liberally enriched with peat moss, leaf mold or compost. In Zones 5-7 plant in spring to give them a full growing season to establish themselves; in Zones 8-10 butterfly bushes can be set into the ground at any time. Pruningtime varies by spe-

FOUNTAIN BUTTERFLY BUSH
Buddleia alternifolia

ORANGE-EYED BUTTERFLY BUSH
TOP TO BOTTOM: *Buddleia davidii* 'Fascinating,' *B. davidii* 'Flaming Violet,' *B. davidii* 'Purple Prince,' *B. davidii* 'Fortune'

For climate zones and months of flowering, see page 154.

BARBADOS PRIDE
Caesalpinia pulcherrima

PURPLE BEAUTY-BERRY
Callicarpa dichotoma

cies. The flowers of the fountain butterfly bush form on the previous season's growth, not on new growth, so do not prune until after the blossoms have faded; then cut the plants back to about two thirds of their original height to force the development of long new stems. The flowers of the orange-eyed butterfly bush form on the current season's growth; prune in early spring before new growth starts so that the current season's stems can produce flowers. The plants can be cut to the ground to encourage the growth of large flower spikes, even in mild climates where no winter damage has occurred. New plants of both species can be started from softwood cuttings of young growth in late spring or early summer or from semihardwood cuttings of more mature growth in mid- or late summer. The fountain butterfly bush can also be propagated from hardwood cuttings of dormant leafless growth in late fall or winter. In Zones 5-7 protect young plants started from cuttings in a cold frame over winter (*page 86*). Transplant them to the garden in spring as soon as the ground can be worked; they will grow quickly when warm weather arrives.

BURNING BUSH See *Euonymus*
BUTTERFLY BUSH See *Buddleia*

C

CAESALPINIA
C. pulcherrima, also called *Poinciana pulcherrima* (Barbados pride, Barbados flower fence, dwarf poinciana)

Barbados pride is a fast-growing shrub, popular in the gardens of Florida and Southern California. Brilliant 2-inch orange-red flowers, arranged in upright clusters 6 to 8 inches across, bloom throughout the summer. The flowers are distinguished by many red pollen-bearing stamens, which extend 2 inches or more from the centers of the blossoms. The light green leaves of Barbados pride are composed of many ½-inch leaflets, giving the plant a light and airy appearance. Most shrubs reach a height of 5 to 6 feet, but old plants may grow to 10 feet with an equal spread. Barbados pride is excellent for shrub borders because of the long season of bloom.

HOW TO GROW. Barbados pride grows in Zones 9 and 10, but frost in Zone 9 may occasionally nip it back. It does best in full sun, but will stand light shade. Plant in a well-drained, slightly acid soil supplemented with leaf mold or peat moss. Prune plants back at any time to encourage fresh branching. To ensure a long season of bloom, remove faded flowers. New plants can be propagated from seeds sown in the spring to begin flowering in late summer.

CALLICARPA
C. dichotoma, also called *C. gracilis, C. koreana, C. purpurea* (purple beauty-berry); *C. giraldiana,* also called *C. bodinieri giraldii* (Girald beauty-berry); *C. japonica* (Japanese beauty-berry). (All also called jewel berry)

As their common name indicates, beauty-berries are grown for their colorful fruit rather than for flowers or foliage. The inconspicuous white or pink blossoms are hidden beneath 2- to 4-inch leaves in midsummer, but are followed in the fall by tiny berries that are borne in clusters along the stems. The berries last two or three weeks after the leaves fall. Beauty-berries may grow 6 to 10 feet tall in mild climates but the stems are apt to die to the ground during cold winters. Even in warm regions the stems are normally pruned each year; as a result, the maximum height of these shrubs is usually about 3 feet. Since these shrubs bear berries on the current season's growth, a full crop of fruit can be expected each year. Beauty-berries are most effective when they are planted in groups at the front of a shrub border. An advantage of having several plants close together is that there is better cross-pollination of flowers, resulting in larger crops of berries.

The purple beauty-berry has deep lilac berries set on purplish stems and leaves that turn purplish late in the fall. The Japanese beauty-berry has purple berries, and its leaves become a golden color in the autumn. The Girald beauty-berry has shining bluish berries; its foliage turns pinkish purple in the fall.

HOW TO GROW. Beauty-berries grow in Zones 5-8 in almost any well-drained soil. Though they tolerate light shade, they do much better in full sun. For the greatest crops of berries, cut the stems to within 4 to 6 inches of the ground early each spring. New plants can be started from softwood cuttings of young growth in late spring or early summer, from semihardwood cuttings of more mature growth in mid- or late summer, and from hardwood cuttings of dormant leafless growth in fall or winter. Plants can also be started by forcing a branch to grow roots by the method known as ground layering.

CALYCANTHUS
C. floridus (sweet shrub, Carolina allspice)

The sweet shrub, native to the Southeastern states, has been cherished by gardeners since colonial days. At one time the cinnamon-flavored bark was used as a seasoning, but its principal charm today lies in its distinctive flowers; each blossom, about 2 inches across, is composed not of true petals but of many ribbonlike outer petals called sepals. The flowers, which bloom in late spring, have the fragrance of strawberries when they first open, gradually taking on the scent of ripe apples as they become full blown. Even the dark green leathery leaves are aromatic when crushed or rubbed. The leaves also contribute color —on their undersides they have a brownish fuzz, which is also apparent on new twigs, and they turn a clear yellow in the fall. Sweet shrubs usually grow 5 to 6 feet tall and spread to a width equal to their height. Sweet shrubs have special appeal when planted close to a house because of their pleasant fragrance. A similar shrub, *C. fertilis* or *C. laevigatus* (pale sweet shrub), is often mistaken for *C. floridus*, but its blossoms have only a faint fragrance. *C. fertilis* can be easily identified because the bottoms of its leaves lack the brownish fuzz of the true sweet shrub.

HOW TO GROW. Sweet shrubs grow in Zones 4-10 in moist soil enriched with peat moss or leaf mold. They tolerate full sun but do best in light shade where they have protection from the wind. Prune in early spring before new growth starts so that the current season's stems can produce flowers. New plants can be started from softwood cuttings of young growth in late spring or early summer, from semihardwood cuttings of more mature growth in mid- or late summer, or from hardwood cuttings of dormant leafless growth in fall or winter. Plants can also be propagated by digging up and replanting the underground offshoots known as suckers or by forcing a branch to grow roots by the method known as ground layering.

CARAGANA
C. arborescens (Siberian pea tree)

Originally from the bleak and windy regions of northern Asia, the Siberian pea tree is now widely grown in the high plains of western United States and Canada. It is resistant to winter cold, and withstands wind, heat and dryness equally well. With its dense growth of stiff branches, the Siberian pea tree is well suited for hedges and serves as an excellent windbreak. The shrub usually has several stems and grows upright to a height of 15 to 20 feet with a 6- to 8-

SWEET SHRUB
Calycanthus floridus

SIBERIAN PEA TREE
Caragana arborescens

For climate zones and months of flowering, see page 154.

BLUEBEARD
Caryopteris clandonensis 'Heavenly Blue'

CHINESE REDBUD
Cercis chinensis

foot spread. In late spring, small clusters of fragrant ¾-inch yellow pea-shaped flowers line the branches, to be followed in summer by small and slender pods. The bright green 1½- to 3-inch leaves are divided into 8 to 12 leaflets so that they resemble feathers. The young twigs are yellow-green. Weeping Siberian pea tree, *C. arborescens pendula,* assumes an unusual shape when it is grafted to an upright stem of the regular species; the stiff branches grow downward and give the shrub the shape of an umbrella. Lorberg's pea tree, *C. arborescens lorbergii,* has threadlike leaflets that give it a misty appearance. Its flowers are larger than but not as abundant as those of the ordinary species.

HOW TO GROW. Siberian pea trees grow in Zones 2-9 in almost any well-drained soil, but do best in sandy soil and in full sun. Prune the previous season's growth back about one third immediately after the shrub has flowered. To produce dense growth, cut the plants all the way down to the ground in early spring; you will then have to wait until the next spring for flowers. For a hedge, plant 2- to 3-foot Siberian pea trees about 1½ to 2 feet apart. New plants can be started from softwood cuttings of young growth taken in late spring or early summer, from semihardwood cuttings of more mature growth taken in mid- or late summer, or from hardwood cuttings of dormant leafless growth taken in late fall or winter. New plants can also be propagated from root cuttings.

CARYOPTERIS
C. clandonensis (bluebeard, caryopteris)

Autumn-flowering shrubs are rare, especially those that have blue flowers; it is for these reasons that bluebeards are of special interest to gardeners. From late summer until frost, varieties of this hybrid bluebeard, such as Blue Mist, with light blue flowers, and Dark Knight and Heavenly Blue, with dark blue flowers, bear clusters of small misty-looking blossoms along wiry stems lined with slender 2- to 3-inch leaves. Bluebeards grow to a height of about 2 to 4 feet and, because of their low stature, are most impressive when used in groups of at least three to five plants near a house, at the forefront of shrub borders or in perennial borders.

HOW TO GROW. Bluebeard grows in Zones 5-9 and does best in full sunshine and light well-drained soil. Since the tops are apt to be damaged by winter cold in almost any part of the country, the plants should be cut back to within 2 to 4 inches of the ground in early spring before new growth begins. This pruning forces the growth of fresh new stems with fine foliage and many lovely flowers. In Zones 5 and 6 spring planting is recommended; also mound mulch over the crowns, or tops of the root structure, late in fall and remove it in spring. New plants can be started from softwood cuttings of young growth in late spring or early summer or from semihardwood cuttings of more mature growth in mid- or late summer.

CERCIS
C. chinensis (Chinese redbud, Chinese Judas tree)

The Chinese redbud is a small tree in its Asian home, but in North America it is a bushy shrub usually only 4 to 8 feet tall. Before the leaves unfold in spring, its twigs, its branches and even its main stems are studded with clusters of rosy purple ¾-inch pea-shaped flowers. As the flowers fade, 5-inch heart-shaped leaves appear, hiding the flat 5-inch seed pods that follow the blossoms. Late in autumn the leaves turn golden yellow before falling. Since the Chinese redbud does not grow very tall, it is often placed toward the front of a shrub border or near a house. Its stems may be cut in midwinter and forced into bloom indoors.

HOW TO GROW. Chinese redbud grows in Zones 6-9 in well-drained soil. It does best in a spot protected from the wind where there is light shade during the hot part of the day. Do not buy bare-rooted plants, which are difficult to establish, but get container-grown plants or the balled-and-burlaped ones, sold with their roots in their original soil ball wrapped in burlap. Set them into the garden in spring. Newly set plants are often slow in sending out leaves the first spring. Pruning is seldom needed. Propagate new plants from seeds sown in the spring. Soak the seeds overnight in tepid water before sowing. Young plants begin to blossom when they are four or five years old.

CHAENOMELES
C. japonica (Japanese quince); *C. speciosa*, also called *C. lagenaria, Cydonia japonica, Pyrus japonica* (flowering quince); *C.* hybrids (hybrid flowering quince)

Quinces bear 1- to 2-inch flowers in white and shades of red and pink. Some have a single ring of petals, others many overlapping petals. The 1½- to 3-inch leaves are bronzy in early spring before they turn dark green. In fall quinces produce greenish yellow fruit about 2 inches in diameter, which is used for jelly. Low-growing types (3 feet or less) look good beneath windows or in shrub borders. Taller types (5 to 6 feet) are valuable as hedges, isolated specimens and borders and for espaliering on walls or fences. Branches cut in midwinter bloom indoors.

The true Japanese quince grows about 3 feet tall and has orange-red flowers. Its variety, alpine Japanese quince, *C. japonica alpina,* grows 15 inches tall and bears bright orange flowers. Flowering quince usually grows 5 to 6 feet tall and is available in many named varieties. Good ones are: Nivalis and Snow, white; Phylis Moore and Gaujardii, deep pink; Apple Blossom and Marmorata, pink and white; and Cardinalis, red. Hybrid flowering quinces are available in both tall- and low-growing types. Excellent tall ones are: Enchantress, pink; Clarke's Giant Red, bright red; and Toyo Nishiki, an intriguing variety that has pink, pink-and-white, white and red flowers all on the same plant. Low-growing hybrids are: Cameo, pink; Jet Trail, white; Rowallane, bright red; and Texas Scarlet, fiery scarlet.

HOW TO GROW. Japanese and flowering quinces grow in Zones 4-10, hybrid quinces in Zones 6-10. All do best in full sun and will grow in almost any soil. Since they begin growth so early in the spring, it is advisable to plant them in the fall if they are bought bare-rooted. Do not prune until flowers have faded on the current season's growth. For hedges, set them 2½ to 4 feet apart. New plants of named varieties can be started in any of several ways. They can be propagated from softwood cuttings of new growth in late spring or early summer, from semihardwood cuttings of more mature growth in mid- or late summer, or from hardwood cuttings of dormant leafless growth in fall or winter. Quinces can also be propagated by taking root cuttings, by digging up and replanting underground offshoots known as suckers, and by forcing a branch to grow roots by the method known as ground layering.

CHASTE TREE See *Vitex*
CHERRY See *Prunus*
CHERRY, CORNELIAN See *Cornus*
CHOKEBERRY See *Aronia*
CINQUEFOIL See *Potentilla*

CLETHRA
C. alnifolia (summer sweet, sweet pepper bush)
The medium-sized very colorful shrubs called summer

HYBRID FLOWERING QUINCE
Chaenomeles hybrid

PINK SUMMER SWEET
Clethra alnifolia rosea

For climate zones and months of flowering, see page 154.

101

BLADDER SENNA
Colutea arborescens

SWEET FERN
Comptonia peregrina

sweets provide an abundance of tiny delightfully scented blossoms in dense 3- to 5-inch spikes in late summer. The flowering season lasts for four to six weeks. Most of the types of summer sweet bear white blossoms, but there is also a very fine variety with pale pink flowers that is named *C. alnifolia rosea,* pink summer sweet. The plants usually grow to be 4 to 6 feet tall and are thickly covered with 1½- to 4-inch deep green leaves that turn to a clear yellow in autumn. Summer sweets grow wild in the eastern part of North America. They can be used successfully in the salty, windy conditions of seashore areas as well as inland, and they grow naturally in locations where the soil is too wet for many other plants to survive.

HOW TO GROW. Summer sweets grow in Zones 3-10 in full sun or light shade; however, they will do best if they are set into a moist acid soil that is generously supplemented with organic material such as peat moss or leaf mold. Pruning is not usually necessary to control the size or stimulate the growth of these shrubs, but some gardeners dislike the appearance of the seed pods that form after the flowers fade and clip the pods off to maintain neatness. If the plants become taller than desired, you can prune them in early spring so that the current season's growth can produce flowers. New plants can be started by any of several methods of propagation: from softwood cuttings of young growth in late spring or early summer, from semihardwood cuttings of more mature growth in mid- or late summer, or by cutting away and replanting a rooted off-shoot of the plant.

CLOVER, BUSH See *Lespedeza*

COLUTEA

C. arborescens (bladder senna)

The bladder senna is a fast-growing shrub from the Mediterranean region that is of particular value to gardeners because it can grow in poor sandy soil where few other blooming plants do well and because it produces its blossoms over an unusually long period, beginning in the late spring and continuing well into early fall. The yellow flowers are of a kind seldom seen. They are borne in clusters of three to eight that spring from the leaf joints of the stems and produce inflated bronze seed pods about 2 inches long. Each of the leaves is composed of 9 to 13 leaflets with an overall length of 2 to 4 inches. The plants generally grow to be 4 to 6 feet tall but they may reach 10 feet under favorable conditions. Because of this fast growth, these shrubs are especially useful for screen plantings.

HOW TO GROW. Bladder sennas grow in Zones 5-9 and do best in full sun in very well-drained soil. Set plants into the garden in early spring. Because the plants are apt to be gangly, prune the stems back one third to one half in early spring to encourage branching; this trimming should be done before new growth starts so that the current season's stems can bear flowers. New plants can be started from softwood cuttings of young growth in late spring or early summer, from semihardwood cuttings of more mature growth in mid- or late summer, or from hardwood cuttings of dormant leafless growth in late fall or winter.

COMPTONIA

C. peregrina, also called *C. asplenifolia* (sweet fern)

The sweet fern, a plant grown for its handsome foliage rather than for its inconspicuous flowers, is a graceful 1½- to 4-foot-tall shrub that is to be found growing wild over much of the northern part of the continent from Alaska and Labrador to Virginia. It is well known to nature lovers who have hiked through the open fields where this plant thrives.

The slender, aromatic dark green leaves are 3 to 5 inches long and have edges set with rounded lobes. These plants are particularly useful when they are placed in a semi-wild setting, and they make a dependable ground cover for sunny, sandy banks.

HOW TO GROW. Sweet fern grows in Zones 2-7 in full sun and moist, acid, well-drained soil that has been liberally supplemented with peat moss. This species has a thin, stringy root system and is difficult to establish in the garden unless, before planting, all stems are cut to ground level. This seemingly drastic treatment ensures survival since new stems quickly grow from beneath the soil. Although few nurseries stock this plant, most can get it for you if you ask. It is difficult to propagate.

CORAL TREE See *Erythrina*
CORALBERRY See *Symphoricarpos*

CORNUS
C. alba (Tatarian dogwood); *C. mas* (cornelian cherry); *C. sericea,* also called *C. stolonifera* (red osier dogwood)

Those who think that all dogwoods have large white or pink flowers are missing some of the most interesting members of the genus. The species described here offer conspicuous clusters of small blossoms, showy fruit, bright autumn foliage and, in many instances, vividly colored bark that provides unusual patterns of color in winter. These species are handsome bushy shrubs of broadly rounded shape, usually about 5 to 10 feet tall, not trees as the more familiar dogwood species are.

The Tatarian dogwood, from Asia, and the native red osier dogwood are similar in all respects except that the red osier dogwood spreads by sending out underground stems, or stolons, to form large clumps. Both species have bright red branches that bear 2-inch clusters of tiny white flowers in late spring. In late summer tiny white or bluish white berries appear and the 2- to 5-inch-long leaves later turn red. One of the best varieties of the Tatarian dogwood is *C. alba sibirica,* the Siberian dogwood. Unpruned, Siberian dogwoods can become 7 to 9 feet tall, but most gardeners prune the plants regularly in order to produce new stems, which are brighter in color than old ones. The stems of a similar variety called Westonbirt are a particularly vivid red. Two other excellent Tatarian dogwood varieties are *C. alba argenteo-marginata,* the silver-edged dogwood, whose white-edged leaves make it an interesting accent plant in shrub borders, and *C. alba spaethii,* the yellow-edged dogwood, with leaves edged in yellow. Two recommended varieties of the red osier dogwood are *C. sericea kelseyi,* Kelsey dogwood, whose bright red stems rarely exceed 2 feet in height, and *C. sericea flaviramea,* the yellow-twigged dogwood, whose new stems are bright yellow instead of red. The cornelian cherry is entirely different from the Tatarian and red osier dogwood species. In the earliest days of spring its branches are laden with a golden mist of tiny flowers. The branches may be cut in mid-winter and brought indoors to blossom earlier than the normal blooming season. Flowers are followed in late summer by ¾-inch cherrylike fruit, which is excellent for preserves. Finally, in autumn, the 2-inch leaves turn deep, dramatic shades of red. Two excellent varieties are *C. mas aureo-elegantissima,* variegated cornelian cherry, whose leaves are unusually large for cornelian cherries—about 4½ inches long—and are marked with creamy yellow and red; and *C. mas flava,* the yellow-fruited cornelian cherry, which, as its name implies, has yellow rather than red fruit.

HOW TO GROW. Tatarian dogwood grows in Zones 5-10, red osier dogwood in Zones 2-9 and cornelian cherry in

SIBERIAN DOGWOOD
Cornus alba sibirica

CORNELIAN CHERRY
Cornus mas

For climate zones and months of flowering, see page 154.

SPIKE WINTER HAZEL
Corylopsis spicata

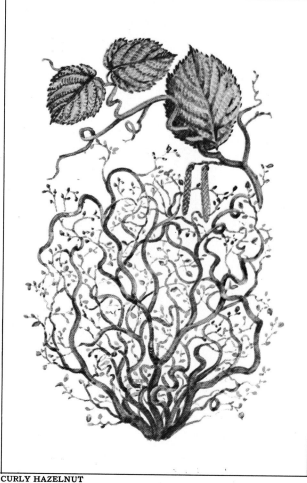

CURLY HAZELNUT
Corylus avellana contorta

Zones 4-8. All three types tolerate light shade but are best planted in sun, which brings out the full color of their stems. They grow in almost any soil, and all—especially Tatarian and red osier dogwoods—do well in wet places, such as near a pond. Prune Tatarian and red osier dogwoods in early spring before new growth starts, cutting old stems to the ground to force an abundance of brightly colored new growth. Cornelian cherry rarely needs pruning unless it is being trained into tree form; whatever pruning is required should not be done until after the flowers have faded, since the flowers form on the previous season's growth, not on new growth. New plants of all three types of dogwoods can be started from softwood cuttings of young growth in late spring or early summer, from semihardwood cuttings of more mature growth in mid- or late summer, or from hardwood cuttings of dormant leafless growth in late fall or winter. Tatarian and red osier dogwoods can also be propagated from underground branches, or suckers, or by forcing a branch to grow roots by the method known as ground layering.

CORYLOPSIS

C. glabrescens (fragrant winter hazel), *C. pauciflora* (buttercup winter hazel), *C. spicata* (spike winter hazel)

Three species of winter hazels are of interest because of their fragrant bell-shaped yellow flowers, borne in pendulous clusters in early spring before the leaves unfold. During the summer their oval 2- to 4-inch leaves are dark green with deep parallel veins; in the fall they turn clear gold. The plants are usually as broad as they are tall.

The fragrant winter hazel grows 8 to 15 feet tall and has ½-inch flowers in 1- to 1½-inch pendant spikes. The buttercup winter hazel grows 4 to 5 feet tall and has two or three flowers in ⅝-inch clusters set sparsely along its branches. The spike winter hazel, the most colorful of the three species, grows up to 4 feet tall and 4 to 5 feet across and bears an abundance of ½-inch flowers in drooping clusters about 1 to 1½ inches long.

HOW TO GROW. The fragrant winter hazel grows in Zones 5-9; the buttercup and spike winter hazels grow in Zones 6-9. All winter hazels will grow in full sun or light shade and do best in a moist acid soil well supplemented with peat moss or leaf mold. They blossom so early in the spring that they are susceptible to late frosts; for that reason, they should be given a sheltered position in the garden. Pruning is almost never required but, if necessary, it should be done immediately after the flowers fade. New plants may be started from softwood cuttings of young growth in spring, from semihardwood cuttings of more mature growth in summer, or by forcing a branch to grow roots by the method known as ground layering.

CORYLUS

C. avellana (hazelnut, filbert), *C. maxima purpurea* (purple-leaved hazelnut)

Hazelnuts are easy-to-maintain shrubs that are most often grown not for their hard-shelled edible nuts—squirrels are apt to harvest the nuts before the homeowner gets a chance—but for their colorful foliage, unusual forms and delicate, pendulous, scaly flower clusters called catkins. The male catkins, which develop in fall and hang on the plants during winter, expand in early spring to a length of 2½ inches and become bright yellow with pollen. The inconspicuous female flowers are followed by ¾-inch seed husks that hold the ½-inch roundish or egg-shaped nuts within them; they ripen in early fall. Among the recommended varieties of the *C. avellana* species are two unusual ones. Golden-leaved hazelnut, *C. avellana aurea,* which grows

8 to 15 feet tall, has 4-inch leaves that are bright yellow in spring and become greenish during the summer. *C. avellana contorta,* known as curly hazelnut or Harry Lauder's Walking Stick, grows 8 feet tall and has fantastically twisted branches. It is so unusual looking that it is best used alone as a garden accent. The purple-leaved hazelnut usually grows 12 to 15 feet tall. It has 5-inch leaves that, as the name implies, are dark purple; they hold their color throughout the summer and fall.

HOW TO GROW. Hazelnuts grow in Zones 4-9 in almost any soil in full sun or light shade. Pruning is rarely required except to remove suckers, fast-growing stems that rise from the bases of old plants. These can be cut away at any time. New plants can be started by digging up and replanting the suckers or by forcing a branch to grow roots by the method known as ground layering.

COTINUS

C. coggygria, also called *Rhus cotinus* (smoke tree); *C. obovatus,* also called *C. americanus* (American smoke tree)

A more appropriate name could not have been chosen for smoke trees, whose 8-inch-long clusters of minute fluffy blossoms rise above the plants from mid- to late summer on slender wirelike stems, creating an illusion of smoke. The stems become hairy as the flowers fade, continuing the illusion until early fall. Three excellent varieties of the *C. coggygria* species are: Royal Purple, with bronze-hued "smoke"; Notcutt, with reddish purple smoke; and Velvet Cloak, with fawn-colored smoke. All three varieties bear dramatic purple foliage, which holds its color most of the summer before taking on shades of yellow and orange in fall. These varieties usually grow 10 to 12 feet tall with an equal spread, but very old plants may become as much as 25 feet tall if left unpruned. The American smoke tree is grown primarily for its outstanding autumn foliage, which provides brilliant shades of orange and scarlet. It has 5-inch clusters of pale purple smoke. The plants grow to a height of 20 feet or more. Female smoke trees have more impressive smoke and all named varieties sold by nurserymen are of this sex.

HOW TO GROW. Smoke trees grow in Zones 5-10 in full sun in almost any well-drained soil. Plant in spring. Prune in early spring before new growth starts so that the current season's stems can produce flowers. New plants can be started from softwood cuttings of young growth in late spring or early summer, from semihardwood cuttings of more mature growth in mid- or late summer, or from hardwood cuttings of dormant leafless growth in fall or winter.

COTONEASTER

C. adpressa praecox (early cotoneaster), *C. apiculata* (cranberry cotoneaster), *C. dielsiana* (Diel's cotoneaster), *C. divaricata* (spreading cotoneaster), *C. multiflora* (many-flowered cotoneaster), *C. racemiflora soongorica* (Sungari cotoneaster)

Cotoneasters are grown more for their berries and bright red-to-orange fall foliage than for their early summer clusters of small pink or white flowers. The berries, ½ inch or less in diameter, generally turn red in early fall and cling to the plants until late winter. Most species have gleaming dark green leaves less than 1 inch long on gracefully arching branches. Early cotoneaster is a low-spreading variety whose branches rarely become more than 1½ feet tall. The cranberry cotoneaster—its berries do indeed look like cranberries but are tasteless—usually grows 2 to 3 feet tall with a spread of 3 to 4 feet. Diel's cotoneaster grows 5 to 6 feet tall, with widely arching branches that spread to make a mound 6 to 8 feet across. The popular spreading coto-

SMOKE TREE
Cotinus coggygria 'Notcutt'

CRANBERRY COTONEASTER
Cotoneaster apiculata

For climate zones and months of flowering, see page 154.

SPREADING COTONEASTER
Cotoneaster divaricata

SUNGARI COTONEASTER
Cotoneaster racemiflora soongorica

neaster grows upright 4 to 5 feet before spreading and is very heavily laden with berries in fall. A white-flowered species with many berries is the many-flowered cotoneaster; 5 to 6 feet tall, it bears its blossoms in clusters along long arching stems. The 6- to 8-foot Sungari cotoneaster, also white-flowered, has gray-green leaves up to 1½ inches long, which is large for a cotoneaster, and bears multitudes of red berries. The drooping branches of cotoneasters are especially attractive on top of a wall or a bank. Because the plants can stand dry soil, wind and salt spray, they are ideal for seaside gardens.

HOW TO GROW. Early and cranberry cotoneasters grow in Zones 4-10; Diel's, spreading and many-flowered cotoneasters in Zones 5-10; Sungari cotoneasters in Zones 3-10. All grow in almost any well-drained soil but do best in full sun. Cotoneasters have sparse, stringy root systems and should not be moved bare-rooted. It is best to purchase shrubs that have been grown in containers; they may be planted at any time. If you buy shrubs balled and burlaped —with their roots in the original soil ball wrapped in burlap —plant in early spring. Allow plenty of room for the plants to develop fully—the arching branches lose much of their beauty if they have to be clipped off. Keep pruning to a minimum. New plants can be started from softwood cuttings of young growth in late spring or early summer, from semihardwood cuttings of more mature growth in mid- or late summer, or from hardwood cuttings of dormant leafless growth in fall or winter.

CRANBERRY BUSH See *Viburnum*
CURRANT, INDIAN See *Symphoricarpos*
CYDONIA See *Chaenomeles*

CYTISUS
C. hybrids (hybrid broom), *C. kewensis* (Kew broom), *C. nigricans* (spike broom), *C. praecox* (Warminster broom), *C. purpureus* (purple broom), *C. scoparius* (Scotch broom)

Brooms are fast-growing shrubs noted for their abundant 1-inch or smaller pea-shaped, often fragrant blossoms; the flowers are mostly yellow but also come in red, pink and purple, as well as combinations. The long arching stems of many brooms are green year round. Some are nearly leafless, others have small simple or three-leaflet leaves. Brooms include low, spreading types ideal for large rock gardens or sunny embankments, as well as plants several feet tall appropriate for borders, and others of intermediate size suitable near a house. All are excellent for seaside or windy locations.

Most hybrid brooms are closely related to the Scotch broom. Tall-growing varieties, usually 5 to 7 feet in height, are: Burkwoodii, garnet red and yellow; Hollandia, pinkish purple; St. Mary's, white; and San Francisco, deep red. Dwarf varieties, under 2 feet in height, are: Lilac Time, deep reddish purple; and Peter Pan, deep red. All of these varieties blossom in spring.

Kew broom, a remarkable hybrid not related to Scotch broom, grows only 6 inches tall but creeps along the ground, forming a carpet that may reach a diameter of 6 feet. In spring its green twigs are covered with masses of pale yellow flowers, and the less-than-½-inch leaflets are softly hairy and very narrow.

Spike broom grows about 3 feet tall and bears bright yellow flowers in spikes at the ends of its branches in mid- to late summer. Warminster broom, 5 to 6 feet tall, has masses of lemon-yellow blossoms on green twigs in spring; its variety, *C. praecox albus,* grows about 4 to 5 feet tall and has white blossoms. Purple broom, 1 to 1½ feet tall, has purple flowers in spring.

Scotch broom usually becomes 4 to 6 feet tall. It can spread widely and become a nuisance, but if you plant it where it will not overrun your garden, it is an interesting shrub with bright yellow blossoms in spring.

HOW TO GROW. Hybrid and Kew brooms grow in Zones 6-10; spike, Warminster, purple and Scotch brooms in Zones 5-10. All need full sun and well-drained soil. Bare-rooted plants are exceedingly difficult to establish in the garden, especially when they are large, so nurseries generally sell small container-grown plants. Set these out in early spring to give them a full season to become established before winter. They grow very rapidly and usually begin to blossom during their second season.

Proper pruning is crucial to brooms. Spring-blooming varieties—that is, all listed here except spike brooms—bear blossoms on the previous season's growth, not on current growth, so do not prune until after the flowers have faded. Then cut back stems that have blossomed by two thirds. Do not cut branches more than one year old, for they usually will not sprout again. For this reason, tired old plants cannot be rejuvenated by being cut to the ground, and should simply be pulled out and replaced. The summer-flowering spike broom should be pruned in the spring before new growth starts so that the current season's stems can produce flowers. Cut back to strong low buds of the previous season's growth, removing as much as desired of the one-year-old stems.

To multiply existing plants, take softwood cuttings of young growth in spring or force a branch to grow roots by the method known as ground layering. However, if you do not require duplicates of existing stock and are willing to experiment, interesting plants of unpredictable flower colors can easily be grown from seeds. They should be sown in spring after soaking overnight in tepid water; plants begin to blossom when two or three years old.

D

DAPHNE

D. genkwa (lilac daphne), *D. mezereum* (February daphne, mezereon)

Daphnes are cherished by gardeners for their early spring blossoms that, on some species, are extremely fragrant. It must be noted, however, that all parts of the plants —particularly their tiny attractive berries—are poisonous. Daphnes are useful at the front of a border or set near a home. These two deciduous species grow about 3 feet tall. Daphnes are relatively slow growing and require about five years to reach their mature height. The lilac daphne is particularly well named because its ½-inch slightly fragrant flowers are not only lilac in color but are also borne in clusters along the upper ends of the leafless branches in early spring much like those of lilacs. The flowers are followed in early summer by small white berries that are mostly hidden by the 2-inch oval leaves. The February daphne opens its intensely fragant ½-inch bright rosy purple flowers in February in mild areas but not until early April in colder climates. The flowers are stemless and appear along the upper portions of the branches. They are followed in early summer by bright red berries partly hidden by the 2- to 3-inch wedge-shaped gray-green leaves. The white February daphne, *D. mezereum album,* has white blossoms and yellow berries.

HOW TO GROW. Lilac daphne grows in Zones 6-9, February daphne in Zones 4-9. (Some gardeners who live north of the lilac daphne's recommended growing areas cultivate it successfully, for it will often live through their winters without trouble; if it does not and dies to the ground, it can usually be revived by pruning back to ground level as

KEW BROOM
Cytisus kewensis

WARMINSTER BROOM
Cytisus praecox

For climate zones and months of flowering, see page 154.

FEBRUARY DAPHNE
Daphne mezereum

LEMOINE DEUTZIA
Deutzia lemoinei

soon as the damage is apparent.) Both species do best in full sun or light shade in well-drained soil that has been supplemented with peat moss or leaf mold; the soil should be mulched to keep it as cool as possible during summer months. Daphnes are difficult to grow from bare-rooted plants. It is advisable to buy container-grown or balled-and-burlaped plants—plants with their roots in their original soil ball wrapped in burlap. Set them out in the spring so that they will have an entire season in which to become established before winter. Pruning is rarely required. New plants can be started in a number of ways: from softwood cuttings of young growth in late spring or early summer, from semihardwood cuttings of more mature growth in mid- or late summer, from hardwood cuttings of dormant leafless growth in fall or winter, from root cuttings, or by forcing a branch to grow roots by the method known as ground layering.

DESMODIUM See *Lespedeza*

DEUTZIA
D. gracilis (slender deutzia); *D. lemoinei* (Lemoine deutzia); *D. rosea* (rose-panicled deutzia); *D. scabra,* also called *D. crenata* (fuzzy deutzia)

All deutzias have in common pest resistance and an unfailing ability to cover themselves so completely with flowers each spring or early summer that their leaves are nearly hidden. Most varieties have white flowers, but many are pink when they open and fade with age. The blossoms, ½ to 1 inch across, are borne in short spikes or clusters and come in singles, with one ring of petals, or doubles, with numerous overlapping petals; the flowers are followed by small brown seed pods. Deutzia leaves are 2 to 4 inches long; they do not become brightly colored in fall.

The most widely grown species, slender deutzia, grows 2 to 4 feet tall and makes a fine low informal hedge. Its delicate arching or upright stems are laden with white flowers before other late-spring-blooming deutzias. Its variety, pink slender deutzia, *D. gracilis rosea,* has pale pink flowers. The branches of slender deutzia, as well as those of Lemoine deutzia, can be cut in midwinter for forcing into bloom indoors. The 5- to 7-foot Lemoine deutzia bears large quantities of snow-white blossoms in late spring. Of the many varieties of the rose-panicled deutzia, a hybrid that blooms in late spring, two excellent ones are the 4- to 6-foot pinkchoice deutzia, *D. rosea eximia,* which has large clusters of single pink flowers, and the 3- to 4-foot Pink Pompon, with thick clusters of double pink blossoms. Two varieties of the fuzzy deutzia are of special interest: the snowflake deutzia, *D. scabra candidissima,* has pure white double flowers, and Pride of Rochester (which has no Latin varietal name) has double white flowers whose outer petals are brushed with pink. Both grow 6 to 8 feet tall and blossom in early summer.

HOW TO GROW. Slender and Lemoine deutzias grow in Zones 4-9, rose-panicled and fuzzy deutzias in Zones 5-9. All grow in almost any soil in full sun or light shade. Plant them in the spring to give them an entire season to become established before winter. In cold areas the tips of the stems of many deutzias are killed during the winter and should be removed in early spring. For other pruning, wait until flowers have faded since flowers form on the previous season's growth, not on new growth. For hedges, set slender deutzias 2 to 2½ feet apart. New plants can be started from softwood cuttings of young growth in late spring or early summer, from semihardwood cuttings of more mature growth in mid- or late summer, or from hardwood cuttings of dormant leafless growth in fall or winter.

DIERVILLA See *Weigela*
DOGWOOD See *Cornus*

E

ELAEAGNUS

E. angustifolia (Russian olive, oleaster); *E. argentea,* also
called *E. commutata* (silverberry, wolf willow); *E. multiflora,* also called *E. longipes* (cherry elaeagnus, gumi);
E. umbellata (autumn elaeagnus)

Elaeagnus species have a well-founded reputation as dependable easy-to-care-for shrubs that produce sweetly fragrant flowers and small mealy fruit relished by birds. Most
of them have silvery foliage that, when seen at the far end
of a garden, creates the illusion of a long, distant vista. All
are tough plants, as broad as they are tall, suitable for borders, windbreaks and seaside plantings.

The Russian olive has slender 1½- to 3½-inch silvery gray leaves and ordinarily becomes a many-branched
12- to 15-foot shrub, although if lower branches are removed to leave one main stem, it may grow into a small
tree 20 feet tall. It can even be grown as a formal hedge because it will tolerate close shearing. It is a mainstay in
windbreak plantings on the high plains of western Canada
and the United States. Old plants have crooked pictur-
esque trunks with loose brown bark. The tiny yellow fragrant flowers bloom in early summer and are followed by
½-inch yellow but silvery-scaled sweet berries in late summer and early fall. The silverberry, native from Alaska
south to Utah and from the Pacific eastward to Quebec,
grows 8 to 12 feet tall and has 1½- to 2½-inch leaves
that are silvery on both sides. It has inconspicuous but
very fragrant yellow flowers in late spring, followed by ⅜-
inch silvery berries that last from midsummer to early fall.
The cherry elaeagnus, a smog-resistant shrub that grows
well in city gardens, grows up to 9 feet tall and has ¾-
inch fragrant pale yellow flowers in late spring. The flowers are followed by ½- to ¾-inch red cherrylike fruits in
early summer that are exceptionally attractive to birds.
The leaves of the cherry elaeagnus are 1½ to 2½ inches long and are green above and silvery beneath. The autumn elaeagnus has tiny yellowish white fragrant flowers
in late spring and unusual berries—they are a scaly, silvery brown in summer and do not ripen to scarlet until
midautumn. This species grows 12 to 15 feet tall and has 2-
to 4-inch leaves that are dark green above and silvery beneath; the tips of new growth are notably silvery also.

HOW TO GROW. Russian olive grows in Zones 2-9, silverberry in Zones 1-7, cherry elaeagnus in Zones 4-10 and
autumn elaeagnus in Zones 3-8. All thrive in almost any
well-drained soil in full sun. Pruning is seldom required.
For hedges, plant Russian olives 3 to 5 feet apart. New
plants can be started from softwood cuttings of young
growth in late spring or early summer, from semihardwood
cuttings of more mature growth in mid- or late summer, or
from hardwood cuttings of dormant leafless growth in fall
and winter. They can also be grown by forcing a branch to
grow roots by the method known as ground layering.

ELDER See *Sambucus*
ELDERBERRY See *Sambucus*

ENKIANTHUS

E. campanulatus (redvein enkianthus); *E. perulatus,* also
called *E. japonicus* (white enkianthus)

Enkianthuses offer two seasons of elegant beauty: once
when their 2- to 3-inch clusters of tiny bell-shaped flowers
open in the spring and again in the fall when their 1- to
3½-inch leaves turn orange and scarlet. Enkianthus flow-

FUZZY DEUTZIA
Deutzia scabra 'Pride of Rochester'

CHERRY ELAEAGNUS
Elaeagnus multiflora

For climate zones and months of flowering, see page 154.

ers open just in advance of their leaves and cling until well after the leaves have fully expanded. The shrubs are frequently companion plants for rhododendrons and azaleas because they require similar growing conditions.

Redvein enkianthus grows about 6 to 8 feet tall in cold regions and up to 20 feet tall in mild areas. Its creamy flowers are conspicuously netted with red. Its variety *E. campanulatus albiflorus,* white redvein enkianthus, has lovely pure white blossoms without the red veins. White enkianthus, which has white flowers, grows about 6 feet tall and blossoms about a week before the redvein enkianthus.

HOW TO GROW. Redvein enkianthus grows in Zones 4-9 and white enkianthus in Zones 5-9. Both are equally at home in full sun or light shade, provided they have a moist acid soil enriched with peat moss or leaf mold. Pruning is almost never required. New plants can be started from softwood cuttings of young growth in late spring or early summer, from semihardwood cuttings of more mature growth in mid- or late summer, or from hardwood cuttings of dormant leafless growth in fall or winter. They can also be propagated by forcing a branch to grow roots by the method known as ground layering.

ERYTHRINA
E. bidwillii (Bidwill's coral tree)

Coral trees are spectacular shrubs for mild-climate gardens, bearing great clusters of 2- to 3-inch-long red flowers intermittently throughout the year but mostly during hot weather. Bidwill's coral tree, a hybrid species with flower spikes up to 2 feet long, puts on its biggest display in midsummer, although flowers may also appear at other times of the year. The shrub generally grows 8 to 10 feet tall with an equal spread, but old plants unscathed by frost may reach twice that height. All coral trees have thorny branches with large three-leaflet leaves. They are primarily used as dramatic free-standing ornaments.

HOW TO GROW. Coral trees grow in Zones 9 and 10 in almost any soil and do best in full sun. To keep plants neat and to encourage continued blossoming, cut off each flower spike after the blossoms fade. If heavy pruning is required, do it in early spring before new growth starts so that the current season's stems can produce flowers; wear gloves to protect your hands from the thorns. Propagate Bidwill's coral tree from softwood cuttings of young growth in late spring or early summer.

EUONYMUS
E. alatus (winged euonymus, burning bush); *E. americanus* (strawberry bush); *E. europaeus* (European spindle tree); *E. hamiltonianus yedoensis,* also called *E. yedoensis* (Yeddo euonymus)

Deciduous euonymuses offer little color until fall, when they bear fascinating pink, red or, more rarely, white fruit capsules set among some of the most brilliant red autumn foliage known to gardeners. The fruit capsules split open as they ripen and reveal bright orange centers. The inconspicuous flowers, pale and tiny, appear late in the spring. Most species are rather tall growing and are useful at the back of a shrub border, but shorter ones are ideal for low informal hedges.

The 8- to 9-foot-tall winged euonymus has several unusual characteristics. Prominent corky ridges called wings line its stems. And in fall, its green summer foliage turns from pink to scarlet if the plant is in the sunshine, but remains a rosy pink if it is in the shade. The scarlet seed capsules, orange-centered, are seldom noticed because of the brilliance of the 1½- to 2½-inch leaves, which turn color at the same time the fruit appears. The dwarf va-

REDVEIN ENKIANTHUS
Enkianthus campanulatus

BIDWILL'S CORAL TREE
Erythrina bidwillii

110

riety of winged euonymus, *E. alatus compactus,* grows to a height of 4 to 5 feet and has smaller wings, but is very densely branched so that it makes an excellent plant for a hedge. Strawberry bush grows 6 to 7 feet tall and has strange warty fruits, pink to red in color, that are slightly reminiscent of strawberries. They open to reveal orange seed coverings within the capsules. The 1½- to 3-inch leaves turn dark red in the fall. The ordinary European spindle tree, a 20-foot-tall plant whose hard wood was formerly used to make butchers' skewers and spindles for spinning thread, is generally too big for house gardens, but several smaller varieties are more shrublike and very useful. Among these varieties are: white European spindle tree, *E. europaeus albus,* which grows 8 to 10 feet tall and has white fruit; Aldenham spindle tree, *E. europaeus aldenhamensis,* which can reach a height of 10 to 12 feet and is noted for the abundance of its pink fruit; intermediate spindle tree, *E. europaeus intermedius,* which is very practical for many gardeners because it grows only 4 to 5 feet tall and has many red fruit capsules; and Red Cascade, a 10-foot variety with many large clusters of deep rosy red fruit. All varieties of the European spindle tree have dark green 1½- to 3-inch leaves that turn dark red in the fall. Yeddo euonymus grows 10 to 15 feet tall and its leaves, up to 5 inches long, turn bright red in the autumn. The pink fruit usually hangs from the branches long after the leaves have fallen.

HOW TO GROW. Winged euonymus and European spindle tree grow in Zones 3-9, strawberry bush in Zones 6-9 and Yeddo euonymus in Zones 4-9. All are very easy to grow, and do well in full sun or light shade in almost any soil or situation. Pruning is rarely required. For hedges, plant dwarf winged euonymuses about 2 feet apart; plant intermediate spindle trees about 3 feet apart. Start new plants from softwood cuttings of young growth taken in late spring or early summer, from semihardwood cuttings of more mature growth taken in mid- or late summer, or from hardwood cuttings of dormant leafless growth taken in late fall or early winter. Plants can also be propagated by forcing a branch to grow roots by the method known as ground layering.

EXOCHORDA
E. giraldii wilsonii (Wilson pearlbush); *E. macrantha* 'The Bride' (The Bride pearlbush); *E. racemosa,* also called *E. grandiflora* (common pearlbush)

Pearlbushes get their common name from their stringlike clusters of pearl-shaped flower buds. In midspring, just as the 1½- to 2-inch leaves unfold, the buds open into white blossoms about 1¼ to 2 inches across. The flowers usually last only about a week to 12 days, but they are so lovely that this plant is well worth growing. Wilson pearlbush grows 12 to 15 feet tall and produces an abundance of flowers up to 2 inches across. The Bride pearlbush grows only 3 to 4 feet tall and is particularly useful in small gardens; its flowers are 2 inches across. The common pearlbush grows 10 to 12 feet tall and has flowers about an inch or more across.

HOW TO GROW. Pearlbushes grow in Zones 5-9 in almost any soil, provided the site is sunny. They are not easy to establish in the garden if planted bare-rooted and should ordinarily be bought as container-grown plants or balled and burlaped, with their roots in their original soil ball wrapped in burlap. Plant in early spring so the shrubs have a season to grow before winter comes. To counteract their natural tendency toward gangliness, the tips of young stems should be pinched off from time to time; the pinching rechannels growing energy outward through many shoots and side

DWARF WINGED EUONYMUS
Euonymus alatus compactus

PEARLBUSH
Exochorda macrantha 'The Bride'

For climate zones and months of flowering, see page 154.

111

BORDER FORSYTHIA
Forsythia intermedia 'Beatrix Farrand'

LARGE FOTHERGILLA
Fothergilla major

shoots. It is also a good idea to remove weak branches because only the strong ones produce a wealth of flowers. Such pruning should be done immediately after the flowers fade. Plants can be propagated from softwood cuttings of young growth taken in late spring or early summer or by forcing a branch to grow roots by the method known as ground layering.

F

FERN, SWEET See *Comptonia*
FILBERT See *Corylus*
FLOWER FENCE, BARBADOS See *Caesalpinia*

FORSYTHIA

F. 'Arnold Dwarf' (Arnold Dwarf forsythia), *F.* 'Arnold Giant' (Arnold Giant forsythia), *F. intermedia* (border forsythia), *F. ovata* (Korean forsythia), *F. suspensa* (weeping forsythia), *F. viridissima* (green-stemmed forsythia). (All also called golden bell)

There are no more colorful or easily recognized harbingers of spring than the golden forsythias, which open the season in Southern gardens in February, and by March and April have gilded the countryside as far north as New England and the Pacific Northwest. Their branches, picked in midwinter, are among the easiest to force into bloom indoors. All forsythia flowers are yellow, but the shades range from pale primrose to deep brass; the leaves are mostly 2 to 3 inches long, although some of the dwarf varieties have proportionally smaller leaves. Forsythias vary in size from shrubs that grow only 1 foot tall to others that reach 8 to 10 feet. Give forsythias enough room to grow without the necessity of hacking off their tops to keep the plants in bounds, for their real beauty lies in the graceful manner in which their branches grow. Forsythias make excellent informal shrub borders and hedges, screen plantings and individual specimens. The taller types can be espaliered —trained to grow flat against a wall—and the shorter ones make fine ground covers. They are tolerant of the poor growing conditions in cities.

The Arnold Dwarf forsythia is valued less for its pale yellow flowers, which appear only rarely, than for the deep green insect-free foliage that makes lustrous mounds of green throughout the summer. Although plants may become 4 feet tall, they are usually under 2 feet in height; they spread by the rooting of branch tips, making an excellent ground cover. The Arnold Giant forsythia has deep yellow flowers about 2 inches across. It reaches a height of 8 feet and has stiff, upright branches.

All of the hybrid varieties of the 6- to 8-foot-tall border forsythia bear large quantities of 2-inch blossoms on upright stems. Excellent varieties are Beatrix Farrand, Karl Sax, Lynwood Gold and Spectabilis, all with deep yellow flowers, and Spring Glory, with pale yellow blossoms. The Korean forsythia grows 6 to 8 feet tall; although its flowers are not as large or as plentiful as those of other recommended hybrids, this species has the advantage of growing well in Northern zones. Two varieties of the weeping forsythia are of special interest: Fortune's weeping forsythia, *F. suspensa fortunei,* which grows 7 to 8 feet tall and has long arching canes, and Siebold's weeping forsythia, *F. suspensa sieboldii,* which seldom grows more than 5 feet tall but has such limber canes that they trail across the ground 10 feet or more, rooting as they go; this latter variety is excellent atop a wall, where the overhanging branches can move with each passing breeze. The dwarf variety of green-stemmed forsythia known as Broxensis rarely exceeds 1 foot in height but spreads to twice that distance and bears great numbers of pale yellow flowers.

Its 1- to 1½-inch leaves turn a lovely purple red in fall.

HOW TO GROW. All forsythias grow in Zones 5-9 and Korean forsythia will also grow in Zone 4. They thrive in full sun or light shade in almost any soil. In cold areas, exposed buds may be killed by a severe winter; yet even after such damage to the upper parts of the branches, the lower sections may bloom if they were protected by a blanket of snow. Each year prune about one fourth to one third of the main stems that are more than four years old by cutting them back to within 4 inches of the ground. Flowers form on the previous season's growth, not on new growth, so pruning should be done immediately after the flowers have faded. For hedges, plant forsythias 4 to 6 feet apart. New plants can be started from softwood cuttings of young growth in late spring or early summer, from semihardwood cuttings of more mature growth in mid- or late summer, or from hardwood cuttings of dormant leafless growth in late fall or early winter. New plants can also be propagated by forcing a branch to grow roots by the method known as ground layering.

FORSYTHIA, WHITE See *Abeliophyllum*

FOTHERGILLA
F. gardenii, also called *F. carolina* (dwarf fothergilla); *F. major* (large fothergilla); *F. monticola* (Alabama fothergilla). (All also called witch alder)

The little-known fothergillas, indigenous to the Southeastern United States, are somewhat neglected in competition with imported shrubs. Yet they are outstandingly beautiful in two seasons of the year: in spring, when they display fragrant flower heads 1 to 2 inches across composed of tiny white flowers, and in fall, when their 1- to 4-inch-long leaves turn brilliant shades of yellow, orange and scarlet. The flowers have no petals; shaped like lathered shaving brushes, they are made up of long pollen-bearing stamens and are particularly effective against an evergreen background. Dwarf fothergilla rarely grows more than 3 feet tall. Its 1½-inch flower clusters open before its 2½-inch leaves unfurl. The 2-inch-tall flower heads of the large and Alabama fothergillas open at the same time that the leaves unfold. The large fothergilla usually grows 9 feet tall and the Alabama fothergilla 6 feet tall; both have broad 2- to 4-inch-long leaves.

HOW TO GROW. Fothergillas grow in Zones 5-9 and do best in light shade and a moist acid soil that has been enriched with peat moss or leaf mold. New plants can be started by forcing a branch to grow roots by the method known as ground layering, but the process may take two years. New plants can also be started from softwood cuttings of young growth in late spring or early summer or from root cuttings taken in spring or fall.

FRANGIPANI See *Plumeria*

FRANKLINIA
F. alatamaha, also called *Gordonia alatamaha* (franklinia)

Franklinia, a native of Georgia, was named in honor of Benjamin Franklin when it was first discovered in the 18th Century, but it has not been found growing wild since 1790. The shrub is unusual because it provides so much conspicuous, contrasting color at one time. The 3-inch cup-shaped fragrant white blossoms—each filled with golden pollen-bearing stamens—bloom in fall, at the same time that the plant's 5-inch, bright green and shiny leaves turn to brilliant shades of red or orange. In the South it is not uncommon for franklinias to grow to become 30 feet tall, but in the northern part of their growing area the shrubs rare-

FRANKLINIA
Franklinia alatamaha

For climate zones and months of flowering, see page 154.

MAGELLAN FUCHSIA
Fuchsia magellanica

CHINESE WITCH HAZEL
Hamamelis mollis

ly exceed 10 feet in height. This shrub should not be buried among others in a border; it is a choice, relatively rare plant that deserves a special location where it can stand on its own and get the attention it merits.

HOW TO GROW. Franklinias grow in Zones 6-9 in full sun or light shade, but they have brighter autumn foliage and more blossoms when they are grown in sunny places. They need a moist, well-drained acid soil liberally enriched with organic matter such as leaf mold or peat moss. New plants can be grown from softwood cuttings of young growth in late spring or summer or by forcing a branch to put out roots by the method known as ground layering.

FUCHSIA
F. magellanica (Magellan fuchsia)

Fuchsias are outdoor shrubs mainly on the West Coast. Magellan fuchsia, however, grows elsewhere if treated as a dieback shrub—one that dies to the ground over winter but sprouts after pruning each spring. It then grows to about 3 feet and bears many 1½-inch red and violet flowers in early summer. Flower production continues until frost where summers are cool and air is moist. The 2-inch oval leaves are bright green. Magellan fuchsia is a one-of-a-kind plant for most gardens and is usually placed where it can be appreciated.

HOW TO GROW. Magellan fuchsia grows in Zones 6-8 as well as in coastal parts of Zones 9 and 10 in the West. It needs a moist but well-drained soil and will grow in sun or light shade. A good soil mixture contains equal parts of leaf mold, sandy loam and well-rotted cow manure. In Zone 6 it is advisable to mound soil around the base of the plants in fall so that the lowest parts of the stems are protected from winter cold. The aboveground stems die and must be cut off in the spring, but new growth will blossom the same season. New plants can be started from softwood cuttings of young growth taken in late spring or early summer or from semihardwood cuttings of more mature growth taken in mid- or late summer.

G

GOLDEN BELL See *Forsythia*
GORDONIA See *Franklinia*
GUMI See *Elaeagnus*

H

HAMAMELIS
H. 'Arnold Promise' (Arnold Promise witch hazel), *H. mollis* (Chinese witch hazel), *H. vernalis* (vernal witch hazel), *H. virginiana* (common witch hazel)

Witch hazel gets its name from the fact that the forked twigs are sometimes used as divining rods in water witching, but the shrub wins popularity among gardeners for its unusual flowers and wide choice of blooming seasons. Some species are among the last to bloom in fall, others the first to unfold in spring, and some send out a very sweet fragrance over a long period as their yellow blossoms open and close in response to warm and cool days. The ½- to 1½-inch flowers are odd in appearance, formed of four leaflike petals, or sepals, and four slender petals that are shaped like twisted ribbons. They usually appear when the plants are leafless. Witch hazels are excellent shrubs for the edge of a woodland where the golden or red hues of their leaves in autumn add a second season of interest. They are also tolerant of the grime and polluted air of cities. The lotion witch hazel is distilled from the twigs of the common witch hazel.

Arnold Promise is a hybrid that grows 15 to 18 feet tall and has 1½-inch yellow flowers in late winter or early spring. Its 4- to 5-inch leaves turn red and yellow in fall. Chinese witch hazel usually grows 10 to 15 feet tall. It has unusually fragrant 1-inch yellow flowers in early spring, and 3- to 6-inch round leaves that are downy beneath and turn yellow in the fall. The variety *brevipetala* has orange-yellow flowers with petals shorter than those of the regular species. Vernal witch hazel, native to the South Central states, grows 6 to 10 feet tall and has ½-inch yellow flowers in late winter or early spring. Its leaves turn yellow in fall. Common witch hazel usually grows 6 to 10 feet tall. It has ¾-inch yellow flowers late in autumn, often at the same time its yellow leaves begin to fall.

HOW TO GROW. Arnold Promise, vernal and common witch hazels grow in Zones 4-9, Chinese witch hazel in Zones 5-9. All types will grow in full sun or light shade but do best in moist soil liberally supplemented with peat moss or leaf mold. Plant witch hazels in fall. Pruning is rarely needed, but if necessary should be done immediately after the flowers fade. New plants can be started from softwood cuttings of young growth taken in late spring.

HAW, BLACK See *Viburnum*
HAZELNUT See *Corylus*

HIBISCUS

H. syriacus (rose of Sharon, shrub althea)

The rose of Sharon, a native of India and China, has been cherished in Europe for 400 years and in this country for nearly 200. It is particularly useful in gardens because it blooms in late summer and early fall, long after most other shrubs have finished blossoming. Depending on the variety, the 2½- to 4-inch flowers may be single, each with one row of petals; semidouble, with several rows; or double, with numerous overlapping petals; colors range from white through shades of pink, red and blue to purple and combinations of these hues. The 2- to 3-inch leaves are soft gray-green and may be of a simple oval shape with lobed edges or may be divided into three lobes. Roses of Sharon usually grow 6 to 12 feet tall, with branches that are stiffly upright when young but spread broadly when older if the plants are left unpruned. They are fine shrubs for borders, as individual accents standing alone or for planting near a house. They are sometimes trained as small single-trunked trees. Roses of Sharon are tough and will tolerate city and seashore conditions. Some of the better varieties are: Anemonaeflorus, double blossoms, deep pink with a red center; Ardens, semidouble, light purple; Blue Bird, single, light blue; Coelestis, single, light violet; Hamabo, single, white with red center; Woodbridge, single, deep rose with red center; and W. R. Smith, single, pure white.

HOW TO GROW. Roses of Sharon grow in Zones 5-9 and do best in full sun, but will tolerate light shade. They thrive in a moist but well-drained soil supplemented with peat moss, leaf mold or compost. Roses of Sharon are difficult to establish when large; it is best to set out plants no larger than 5 feet tall in early spring. In Zones 5 and 6 plants may suffer some frost damage the first two or three years after planting, and dead tips of branches may have to be pruned in spring. Roses of Sharon are very late in sending out leaves in spring and inexperienced gardeners are apt to conclude they have died. They grow rapidly once they begin, however, and bear flowers on current season's growth. Some gardeners choose not to prune roses of Sharon, allowing them to produce large crops of medium-sized flowers on natural-looking plants. Others cut back each stem of the previous season's growth to two buds in early spring, a technique that produces fewer but much bigger flowers. New plants can be started from softwood cut-

ROSE OF SHARON
Hibiscus syriacus 'Blue Bird'

For climate zones and months of flowering, see page 154.

tings of young growth in late spring or early summer, from semihardwood cuttings of more mature growth in mid- or late summer, or from hardwood cuttings of dormant leafless growth in late fall or early winter.

HIPPOPHAE
H. rhamnoides (sea buckthorn)

Gardeners who live by the seashore are loud in their praise of sea buckthorn, a rambling, thorny shrub that spreads by means of underground stems, or suckers, which hold sand dunes in place. In late spring the plants bear inconspicuous flowers on bare branches, but in fall female plants bear enormous quantities of ⅓-inch bright orange berries along their stems. Both male plants, which usually grow upright, and female plants, which tend to spread, are necessary for fruit production. The fruit, disliked by birds, remains on the shrub through winter until the early spring. The leaves of the sea buckthorn are silvery green, slender and about 2 inches long. It usually grows 8 to 12 feet tall and looks best in a semiwild setting.

HOW TO GROW. Sea buckthorns grow in Zones 3-7 in any well-drained soil in full sun; they spread faster in poor soil than in a fertile soil. To ensure good berry production, plant one male to every six females. New plants can be started from underground stems, or suckers, from root cuttings or by forcing a branch to grow roots by the method known as ground layering. The offspring of such vegetative reproduction will be the same sex as the parent plant.

HOLLY See *Ilex*
HONEYSUCKLE See *Lonicera*
HORSE CHESTNUT See *Aesculus*
HORTENSIA See *Hydrangea*

HYDRANGEA
H. arborescens grandiflora (hills-of-snow hydrangea); *H. macrophylla*, also called *H. hortensis, H. opuloides* (big-leaved or French hydrangea, hortensia); *H. paniculata grandiflora* (peegee hydrangea); *H. quercifolia* (oak-leaved hydrangea)

Hydrangeas are notable for their enormous clusters of summer-blooming white, pink or blue flowers. The most attractive blossoms are sterile—that is, unable to produce seeds; they are flat, four-petaled and 1 inch or so across. Some plants bear clusters containing only sterile flowers, but most have clusters that include fertile ones, tiny star-like blossoms usually at the centers of the clusters.

Hills-of-snow hydrangea is appropriately named, for it grows 3 to 4 feet tall and bears 6- to 8-inch rounded clusters of pure white sterile flowers from mid- to late summer. One type, Annabelle, has flower clusters 10 inches across. All types have soft green oval leaves about 3 to 6 inches long. Hills-of-snow hydrangea is useful in shrub borders, for planting near a house and for informal hedges.

Big-leaved hydrangea is the familiar blue, pink or white species that is forced into early-spring bloom by florists for sale as a house plant. Its clusters of sterile flowers are normally 4 to 8 inches across but some varieties have 15-inch clusters. Plants may blossom when only 1 foot tall; most garden plants become 3 to 6 feet tall. They have 6- to 8-inch shiny coarsely toothed leaves. All varieties are useful in borders and near a house. Big-leaved hydrangeas are unusual in that, except for white varieties, the color of the blossoms is affected by the amount of aluminum available to the plants. Aluminum is present in all soils, but its availability to plants depends on the acidity of the soil; some big-leaved hydrangeas switch from pink to blue or vice versa with a change of ½ point on their soil's pH

SEA BUCKTHORN
Hippophae rhamnoides

scale. Although most—including those recommended here —have relatively stable colors, shading is altered by acidity. Colors given for the following varieties are clearest if the soil has the pH level suggested in the how-to-grow section below. All have four-petaled flowers, except for Domotoi, which has double flowers, with many overlapping rows of petals. Domotoi and Nikko Blue have very stable blue flowers; Merritt's Beauty, red; Rose Supreme, deep pink; and Sister Therese, white. A special category of big-leaved hydrangeas is called lace cap because the flat 4- to 8-inch flower clusters are composed of fertile central blossoms surrounded by a "lace" of large flat sterile blossoms. Blue Wave and Mariesii, both with blue flowers, are excellent plants of this type. Another lace cap hydrangea, with similar blue flower clusters 2 to 4 inches across, is *H. macrophylla serrata acuminata*.

The most widely grown of all hydrangeas is called peegee hydrangea, a name coined from the botanical *paniculata grandiflora*. Young plants may grow 3 to 5 feet in a single season, eventually reaching 15 to 20 feet if unpruned. They may be pruned to grow as a single-stemmed small tree. Their conical flower clusters, which appear in late summer and early fall, are often 12 to 15 inches long and nearly a foot across. The sterile blossoms are creamy white when they open and gradually become pink. They can be dried for winter bouquets. Peegee hydrangeas have coarse leaves 3 to 6 inches long.

Oak-leaved hydrangea grows 3 to 6 feet tall and has 4- to 8-inch leaves shaped much like those of a red oak. They are dark green on top and silvery beneath and turn rich red or reddish purple in fall. In midsummer this species bears 4- to 6-inch conical clusters of creamy white sterile flowers and inconspicuous fertile flowers. The oak-leaved hydrangea spreads to form large clumps and is best grown alone so that it does not encroach upon other plants. It is especially attractive when it stands in front of a clump of trees at the edge of a lawn.

HOW TO GROW. Hills-of-snow hydrangea grows in Zones 4-10, big-leaved hydrangea in Zones 6-10, peegee hydrangea in Zones 4-9 and oak-leaved hydrangea in zones 5-9. All hydrangeas grow in full sun or light shade and do best in a moist but well-drained soil supplemented with peat moss, leaf mold or compost. Big-leaved hydrangeas require acid soil: pH 6.0 to 6.5 for pink flowers, pH 5.0 to 5.5 for blue ones. They do well in seaside gardens and big-leaved hydrangeas positively flourish near the shore. For hedges, plant hills-of-snow hydrangeas 2 to 3 feet apart.

To acidify the soil, use aluminum sulfate, which provides aluminum as well as lowers pH, mixed 1 pound to 7 gallons of water. Soak the ground with it after the plant starts growing in spring and repeat twice at two-week intervals as necessary to lower the pH ½ point. To raise the pH ½ point, spread ground limestone in spring or fall at a rate of 5 pounds per 100 square feet.

The time to prune hydrangeas depends on the species. Prune hills-of-snow and peegee hydrangeas in early spring before new growth starts so that the current season's growth can produce flowers. If hills-of-snow hydrangea is left unpruned—except to remove faded flower clusters for the sake of neatness—it produces great numbers of attractive but relatively small flower clusters that are light enough in weight so that the plant stems can hold them aloft. If you go to the opposite extreme and cut hills-of-snow hydrangea back to about 4 to 6 inches from the ground, it becomes about 3 feet tall before developing massive flower clusters so heavy that they often bend the stems to the ground in rainy weather. Unless extremely large flowers are desired, it is best to cut the stems back to about 2 feet

BIG-LEAVED HYDRANGEA
Hydrangea macrophylla

For climate zones and months of flowering, see page 154.   117

GOLDEN ST.-JOHN'S-WORT
Hypericum frondosum

WINTERBERRY
Ilex verticillata

from the ground; the plant will then produce an abundance of medium-sized flowers on relatively strong stems.

The largest flowers of peegee hydrangeas are produced on plants whose previous season's growth has been cut so that only two buds remain on each stem. This system also enables you to control plant size. If medium- or large-sized plants are desired, prune less severely—the largest plants will result when only the old flower heads are removed. The big-leaved and oak-leaved hydrangeas blossom from large buds formed on previous season's growth; thus any pruning, usually needed only to control height, should be done immediately after flowering.

All hydrangeas can be propagated from softwood cuttings of young growth in late spring or early summer, from semihardwood cuttings of more mature growth in mid- or late summer, or from hardwood cuttings of dormant leafless growth in fall or winter. Hills-of-snow and oak-leaved hydrangeas can also be propagated by digging up and replanting the underground branches known as suckers and by forcing a branch to grow roots by the method known as ground layering.

HYPERICUM

H. frondosum, also called *H. aureum* (golden St.-John's-wort); *H. kalmianum* (Kalm St.-John's-wort); *H. prolificum* (shrubby St.-John's-wort)

Three native North American species of St.-John's-wort are desirable shrubs for use as plantings near a house or as border shrubs because of the great quantity of glistening yellow flowers that they bear from mid- to late summer. All of them grow about 3 feet tall and have slender 1- to 3-inch leaves that cling to the stems until late in the year. The golden St.-John's-wort has flowers that are about 2 inches across, and Kalm St.-John's-wort has flowers approximately 1 inch in size. The shrubby St.-John's-wort, though its flowers are quite small—each bloom is only about ¾ inch across—bears them in great quantities (as its species name *prolificum* implies) and it blossoms for a longer period than do the other species, often continuing to produce flowers well into fall.

HOW TO GROW. Golden St.-John's-wort grows in Zones 5-9, Kalm St.-John's-wort and shrubby St.-John's-wort in Zones 4-8. All do best if they are placed in full sun and well-drained soil, but they will also tolerate light shade and will survive in places that are too hot and dry for other plants. St.-John's-worts grow rapidly but are short lived, usually lasting only five or six years. Because of their dense, compact habit of growth they rarely need pruning, but if it is necessary to cut off deadwood, do so in early spring. New plants can be started from softwood cuttings of young growth in late spring or early summer.

I

ILEX

I. laevigata (smooth winterberry), *I. verticillata* (winterberry, black alder). (Both also called deciduous holly)

The smooth winterberry and the winterberry are native deciduous hollies, very similar in their appearance, whose branches are lined with colorful ¼-inch berries from late summer into winter. Before the berries appear, tiny white male and female flowers blossom—the females have faint marks on their petals. Each plant usually bears flowers of one sex, and although only those with female blossoms have fruit, both sexes are usually necessary for berry production. An exception is a variety of the smooth winterberry—it is called simply Female—that sets fruit without pollination. The ⅓-inch leaves of the smooth winterberry turn yellow in fall; the leaves of the winterberry turn rusty brown. Both species usually become 6 feet tall and grow in a rather narrow shape with many erect branches. Winterberries are useful in shrub borders and for growing in wet places where few other shrubs survive.

HOW TO GROW. Winterberries grow in Zones 3-8 in full sun or light shade. They do well in ordinary garden soil, as well as wet and swampy soil, if it is moist, acid (pH 4.5 to 5.5) and supplemented with peat moss or leaf mold. New plants can be started from softwood cuttings of young growth in late spring or early summer, from semihardwood cuttings of more mature growth in mid- or late summer, or from hardwood cuttings of dormant leafless growth in fall or winter. The offspring of such vegetative reproduction will be the same sex as the parent plant.

INDIGO See *Indigofera*

INDIGOFERA
I. kirilowii (Kirilow indigo)

Kirilow indigo bears 6-inch spikes of small pink flowers in early summer. It has fine 5-inch-long fernlike leaves and grows about 4 feet tall. During cold winters its stems may be killed by frost, but this is not a disadvantage because the loss of the old stems causes fresh new ones to rise quickly in the spring and bear blossoms. Since it spreads by underground roots to form large clumps, this species is useful as a ground cover or as a shrub for the front of a border.

HOW TO GROW. Kirilow indigo grows in Zones 4-8 and does best in well-drained soil in full sun. Pruning is not essential, except to remove deadwood caused by winter cold. Even in mild climates some gardeners cut this shrub to the ground each fall or spring to encourage new growth. New plants can be started by cutting away and planting a rooted offshoot or from softwood cuttings of young growth in late spring or early summer.

J

JASMINE See *Jasminum*

JASMINUM
J. nudiflorum (winter jasmine)

The winter jasmine is half vine and half shrub, with long arching stems that in early spring—even in winter in the South—are lined with 1-inch bright yellow flowers. The shiny dark green leaves are composed of three slender 1-inch leaflets, and the young branches remain green throughout the winter. The plants may become 15 feet tall in the South if not pruned, but in cooler areas usually range from 3 to 8 feet in height. Sometimes tied to a trellis or wall in the manner of a climbing rose, they are most frequently grown as shrubs. The branches may be cut and easily forced into bloom indoors in midwinter.

HOW TO GROW. Winter jasmine grows in Zones 6-9 and in sheltered spots in Zone 5. It does best in full sun and well-drained soil. Since flowers form on previous season's growth, not on current growth, all pruning should be done immediately after flowering. The plants can be pruned severely without greatly reducing the number of flowers. New plants can be started from softwood cuttings of young growth in late spring or early summer, from semihardwood cuttings of more mature growth in mid- or late summer, or from hardwood cuttings of dormant leafless growth in fall or winter. They can also be propagated by forcing a branch to grow roots by the method known as ground layering.

JETBEAD See *Rhodotypos*
JEWEL BERRY See *Callicarpa*
JUDAS TREE, CHINESE See *Cercis*

For climate zones and months of flowering, see page 154.

KIRILOW INDIGO
Indigofera kirilowii

WINTER JASMINE
Jasminum nudiflorum

GLOBEFLOWER KERRIA
Kerria japonica pleniflora

K

KERRIA
K. japonica (kerria)

In its original form, kerria bears 1½-inch bright yellow flowers with a single row of five petals. The plant blooms for only one week in midspring, grows about 3 to 5 feet tall and makes a densely branched rounded shrub. But the variety *K. japonica pleniflora,* globeflower kerria, has flowers with numerous overlapping petals, so many that the blossoms look like golden balls hanging on the branches. This type grows 5 to 7 feet tall in an open and angular fashion; it withstands cold winters somewhat better than the original species, and its flowering period lasts two to three weeks. Both types send out a few flowers occasionally through summer and early fall. Their wedge-shaped coarsely toothed 1¼- to 4-inch leaves turn yellow in autumn, and the green twigs add a touch of color to a winter garden. Kerrias are suited for planting near a house, for standing alone and for growing in borders.

HOW TO GROW. Kerrias grow in Zones 4-9 and do best in light shade, although they will grow in full sun. A well-drained soil supplemented with peat moss, leaf mold or compost stimulates excellent growth, but kerrias are tough enough to grow in almost any soil. In Zones 4 and 5 it is not uncommon for the tips of twigs to be killed by winter cold; the damage will become apparent as buds begin to unfold in the spring, and the dead tips should be removed then. Major pruning, however, should be done immediately after the flowers fade, since flowers form on previous season's growth, rather than on new growth. Old main stems that are not branching freely should be cut back all the way to the ground to force the development of new growth. New plants can be started from softwood cuttings of young growth in late spring or early summer or from semihardwood cuttings in fall or winter. They can also be propagated by forcing a branch to grow roots by the method known as ground layering or by cutting away and replanting a rooted offshoot of the plant.

KOLKWITZIA
K. amabilis (beauty bush)

The late American botanist E. H. Wilson, who discovered the beauty bush in China on one of his many plant-hunting expeditions—he introduced 1,500 new plants to the Western world, more than any other plant collector—described it as the best deciduous shrub ever brought from that vast country. Anyone would be hard put to disagree with Wilson's opinion when the plant blossoms in early spring and becomes a spectacular fountain-shaped mound of yellow-throated pink flowers. The flowers themselves are only about ½-inch in diameter, but they are borne in such profuse, thick clusters that they nearly hide the plant's foliage. Clusters of feathery brown seeds follow the flowers and remain on the plant until the beginning of winter. The leaves are slender and range from 1 to 3 inches in length; gray-green to start, they turn dull red in autumn. The brown bark of the beauty bush peels off twigs and branches in big pieces, giving the bush a shaggy appearance. Beauty bushes grow to a height of 6 to 10 feet and display their beauty most effectively when they are allowed to stand by themselves.

HOW TO GROW. Beauty bushes grow in Zones 4-9 in almost any well-drained soil in full sun or light shade. They are best left unpruned. New plants can be started from softwood cuttings of young growth taken in late spring or early summer, or from semihardwood cuttings of more mature growth taken in midsummer, or from hardwood cuttings of dormant leafless growth taken in late fall or winter.

BEAUTY BUSH
Kolkwitzia amabilis

L

LAGERSTROEMIA

L. indica (crape myrtle)

Crape myrtles are the most colorful element of Southern gardens from mid- to late summer when each branch and twig on the plants is tipped with a 6- to 12-inch cluster of white, pink, red, lavender or purple-red flowers. Individual flowers are about 1½ inches across, so crinkly they look as if they were made of crepe paper. Crape myrtle leaves are oval and 1 to 2 inches long; they are bronze-colored when they first unfold in the spring and become yellow, orange or red before falling late in autumn. The smooth gray bark of old branches and stems gradually flakes off to reveal fresh pinkish bark beneath.

For years, the only crape myrtles available were massive many-stemmed shrubs, 15 to 20 feet tall, that were planted alone or trained by pruning to grow as single-trunked trees. Now there are varieties of all colors that grow only 5 to 7 feet tall. Smaller crape myrtles are ideal for planting near a house and for informal hedges. Among the recommended varieties are: Petite Embers, pink; Petite Orchid, dark orchid; Petite Pinkie, pink; Petite Red Imp, red; and Petite Snow, white. Good tall-growing varieties are: Durant Red and Gray's Red, both dark red; Watermelon Red, vivid pinkish red; Shell Pink, pink; Majestic Orchid, rich orchid; and Glendora White, snow white.

HOW TO GROW. Crape myrtles grow in Zones 7-10 and do best in full sun and in moist soil that has been well supplemented with peat moss, leaf mold or decayed sawdust. Do not buy bare-rooted plants, which are difficult to establish in the garden; instead, buy either container-grown plants or balled-and-burlaped ones, sold with their roots in their original soil ball wrapped in burlap. For hedges, plant crape myrtles about 4 or 5 feet apart. Prune in early spring before the new growth starts so that the current season's stems can produce flowers. Methods of pruning vary from the removal of deadwood only to the cutting back of plants nearly to the ground each spring. The latter method produces extremely large flowers on relatively few main stems that rarely grow more than 4 feet tall in a season. This technique has been used primarily to control the size of large-growing treelike varieties and is unnecessary with smaller new varieties; little pruning is needed to keep these at a low height. Plants can be started from softwood cuttings of young growth in late spring or early summer, from semi-hardwood cuttings of more mature growth in mid- or late summer, or from hardwood cuttings of dormant leafless growth in late fall or early winter.

LESPEDEZA

L. bicolor (shrub bush clover); *L. sieboldii,* also called *L. thunbergii, L. formosa, L. penduliflora, Desmodium penduliflora* (purple bush clover)

Bush clovers flower when few other plants do, in mid- to late summer and early fall. The individual blossoms, about ½ inch long, are shaped like sweet peas and borne in large clusters. The flowers of shrub bush clover are light purple in color and open in midsummer; those of purple bush clover are darker and appear in late summer and early fall. The leaves of both species are composed of three 1-inch leaflets. Bush clovers grow 6 to 10 feet tall if left unpruned, but are usually kept at 3 to 4 feet.

HOW TO GROW. Shrub bush clover grows in Zones 4-8, purple bush clover in Zones 5-8. Both species do best in full sun, but will grow in almost any well-drained soil. Since bush clovers look unkempt if allowed to grow very tall, cut them down to the ground early each spring before new growth starts so that the current season's stems can

CRAPE MYRTLE
Lagerstroemia indica

SHRUB BUSH CLOVER
Lespedeza bicolor

For climate zones and months of flowering, see page 154.

121

IBOLIUM PRIVET
Ligustrum ibolium

VICARY GOLDEN PRIVET
Ligustrum vicaryi

blossom. New stems will quickly shoot up, and by flower-ingtime the plants will become an attractive 3 feet in height, and will bear masses of colorful blooms. New plants can be started from softwood cuttings of young growth in late spring or early summer.

LIGUSTRUM

L. amurense (Amur privet), *L. ibolium* (Ibolium privet), *L. obtusifolium* (border privet, Ibota privet), *L. obtusi-folium regelianum* (Regel privet), *L. ovalifolium* (California privet), *L. vicaryi* (Vicary golden privet), *L. vulgare* (common privet)

Privets, generally untouched by pests and tolerant of the smoke and grime of cities, are the most widely planted of all flowering shrubs because of their great use in neatly trimmed hedges. It is unfortunate that they have been considered only for this purpose, since they have lovely arching boughs when mature and are seen to best advantage if allowed to grow normally or if pruned only to retain their innate gracefulness.

Privets are so useful for hedges because of their dense branching and their tough 1- to 3-inch leaves, which appear in early spring and remain later in the fall than those of most other shrubs. The small white flowers, usually less than ¼ inch in length, bloom in 1½- to 3-inch clusters at the ends of the stems in early summer. Some people find these blossoms unpleasantly scented. The flowers are followed by clusters of ¼-inch black berries, which are seldom eaten by birds and often cling through the winter.

Amur privet is extremely resistant to cold and is popular in Northern areas. It grows upright and may become 12 to 15 feet tall if left unpruned. Ibolium privet is a hybrid combining the glossy foliage of one parent, California privet, with the cold resistance of its other parent, border privet. Its mature height is about 12 feet. Border privet has spreading branches and makes a broad mound 8 to 10 feet tall. Its twigs and the undersides of its leaves, which turn purple in the fall, are densely covered with tiny hairs. Regel privet is one of the finest shrubs for borders and hedges because it usually grows only 4 to 5 feet tall and requires practically no maintenance. Its branches spread horizontally and overlap one another in tiers. California privet is extremely popular because of its fast growth and glossy leaves, which are dark green above and yellowish green beneath and cling until very late in the year. But many gardeners try to grow it too far north, and it suffers frost damage. It thrives close to the sea and becomes about 15 feet tall. Its variety *L. ovalifolium aureum*, yellow-edged California privet, has leaves that are widely used in floral arrangements because of the distinctive broad band of yellow that circles each one. Vicary golden privet, a hybrid resulting from the crossing of the yellow-edged privet and the common privet, has bright greenish gold leaves throughout the summer. It may become 10 to 12 feet tall and makes a strong accent plant wherever this color foliage is desired. Common privet grows about 15 feet tall. It holds its leaves until late in the fall and is notable for its great clusters of shiny black berries.

HOW TO GROW. Amur, border and Regel privets grow in Zones 3-9; Ibolium, Vicary golden and common privets grow in Zones 4-9; and California privet grows in Zones 6-9. Because there are several evergreen species that give year-round color in Zones 8-10, the deciduous privets listed here are rarely grown there. However, some of these normally deciduous privets, such as California, common and Vicary golden privets, become completely or nearly evergreen in warm areas. All grow very easily in almost any soil in full sun or light shade. For formal hedges, set plants

1 to 2 feet apart and shear twice a year: once in early spring and then again in early summer. To maintain privets in their natural shapes, restrict pruning to the removal of dead branches in the spring. New plants can be started from softwood cuttings of young growth in late spring or early summer, from semihardwood cuttings of more mature growth in mid- or late summer, or from hardwood cuttings of dormant leafless growth in late fall or early winter.

LILAC See *Syringa*
LILAC, SUMMER See *Buddleia*

LINDERA
L. benzoin, also called *Benzoin aestivale* (spicebush)

Spicebush's tiny yellow flowers brighten and perfume moist woodlands from Maine and Ontario to Florida and Texas in early spring. The 4-inch bright green leaves turn golden yellow in fall and, like the flowers and green twigs as well, are aromatic; the leaves and twigs have been used as spice and for tea. Spicebushes generally grow to a height of 8 feet. Male and female blossoms are usually borne on separate plants, and plants of both sexes must be present in order for the tiny scarlet berries to form on the female plants in early fall. The berries soon disappear, eaten by birds. Spicebushes are rarely bothered by pests and are excellent in shrub borders.

HOW TO GROW. Spicebushes grow in Zones 4-9 and do best in light shade in a moist, acid soil supplemented with leaf mold or peat moss; they grow in wet places where few other shrubs do well. Bare-rooted spicebushes are difficult to establish in the garden; buy either container-grown plants or balled-and-burlaped ones, with their roots in their original soil ball wrapped in burlap. If pruning is necessary, wait until after the flowers fade, since the blossoms appear on the previous season's growth. New plants can be started from softwood cuttings of young growth in late spring or early summer or by digging up and replanting the underground offshoots known as suckers. Spicebush is also easy to propagate by seeds; sow them as soon as they are ripe in the fall. The seeds will germinate in the spring and reach blossoming size in four or five years.

LOCUST See *Robinia*

LONICERA
L. fragrantissima (winter honeysuckle), *L. korolkowii* (blue-leaved honeysuckle), *L. maackii* (Amur honeysuckle), *L. morrowii* (Morrow honeysuckle), *L. tatarica* (Tatarian honeysuckle), *L. xylosteum* 'Clavey's Dwarf' (Clavey's Dwarf honeysuckle)

The honeysuckle family includes hundreds of shrubs and vines, but those recommended here are bushy deciduous shrubs suitable to home gardens. All are known for their attractive, often fragrant, ½- to 1-inch pink, white or red flowers and for their ⅓-inch red or yellow berries that birds relish. The 1- to 3-inch leaves appear early in spring and drop off late in autumn. Honeysuckles require little maintenance and are rarely bothered by pests; they are suitable for borders and tolerate city conditions.

Winter honeysuckle, up to 6 feet tall with a spread of about 8 feet, opens its intensely fragrant white flowers in early spring. They are followed by red berries in early summer. In Zones 5 and 6 it loses its stiff leathery leaves in winter, but in mild climates it is evergreen. Branches are easy to force into bloom indoors in midwinter.

Blue-leaved honeysuckle, a plant only for large gardens, grows 12 to 15 feet tall and has an equal spread. It bears 1-inch pink flowers in late spring, followed by orange-red ber-

SPICEBUSH
Lindera benzoin

WINTER HONEYSUCKLE
Lonicera fragrantissima

For climate zones and months of flowering, see page 154.

SIBERIAN HONEYSUCKLE
Lonicera tatarica sibirica

BAYBERRY
Myrica pensylvanica

ries in mid- to late summer, and has handsome blue-green leaves. Amur honeysuckle grows 12 to 15 feet tall in an upright shape and is very resistant to winter cold. In late spring it bears fragrant white flowers that turn yellowish as they fade. They are followed by red berries that ripen in early fall and cling until late fall. It has 2- to 3-inch slender oval leaves. Morrow honeysuckle is more suited to small gardens because it grows only 7 feet tall with an equal spread. Its white flowers, borne in late spring, turn yellowish as they mature; they are followed by dark crimson translucent fruit in midsummer. Its variety *L. morrowii xanthocarpa,* yellow-fruited Morrow honeysuckle, bears white flowers and bright yellow berries.

The upright 8- to 10-foot Tatarian honeysuckle is the most universally grown of all species. It has many varieties with white, pink or red flowers and red or yellow berries. One, Zabel's Tatarian honeysuckle, *L. tatarica zabelii,* has some of the darkest red flowers known among garden shrubs; another, the Siberian honeysuckle, *L. tatarica sibirica,* has deep pink flowers. Both have red fruit. Clavey's Dwarf honeysuckle grows 3 to 6 feet tall with an equal spread. It has small yellow flowers in spring and red berries in midsummer; it is widely grown as an informal hedge because of its low stature and dense blue-green foliage.

HOW TO GROW. Winter and blue-leaved honeysuckles grow in Zones 5-9, Amur in Zones 2-9, Morrow and Clavey's Dwarf in Zones 4-9 and Tatarian in Zones 3-9. All will grow in almost any soil. They do best in full sun. Although they tolerate light shade, they produce few flowers or berries. Bare-rooted blue-leaved honeysuckles are difficult to establish; buy only container-grown plants or balled-and-burlaped plants, those that have their roots wrapped in the original ball of soil. All others can be bought bare-rooted, balled and burlaped, or container grown. Since honeysuckles begin to grow very early in the spring, it is best to plant them in the fall. If given sufficient space to grow, honeysuckles rarely need pruning except to remove old dead branches. If planting dwarf honeysuckle as a hedge, space shrubs about 3 feet apart. New plants can be started from softwood cuttings of young growth in late spring or summer, from semihardwood cuttings of more mature growth in mid- or late summer, or from hardwood cuttings of dormant leafless growth in fall or winter.

M

MEZEREON See *Daphne*
MOCK ORANGE See *Philadelphus*

MYRICA
M. pensylvanica, also called *M. caroliniensis, M. cerifera latifolia* (bayberry)

The pleasant scent of bayberry candles comes from the wax coating on the tiny pale berries that line the branches of this shrub. The berries, more conspicuous than the greenish flowers of springtime, ripen in early fall and cling most of the winter, providing food for birds. The aromatic dark green leaves, 3 to 5 inches long, cling until late in fall.

Bayberries grow wild along coastal dunes from Newfoundland to Maryland, reaching a height of 8 to 9 feet in favored sites, but will grow just as well inland. In gardens, most bayberries grow 3 to 5 feet tall with a spread equally broad. They make handsome plants when grown near a house or in borders. The berried branches are often cut for winter decorations.

HOW TO GROW. Bayberries grow in Zones 2-8 and do best in full sun in sandy, acid (pH 4.5 to 5.5) well-drained soil. Bare-rooted plants are difficult to establish in the garden. So buy only container-grown plants or balled-and-burlaped ones, sold with their roots in the original soil ball wrapped in burlap. Only female plants bear berries, but both sexes must be present (1 male to 6 to 10 females) for fruit production; there is no difference in appearance between the sexes except when berries are present, so be sure you get both. Since the plants naturally grow compact and bushy, little or no pruning is required. New plants can be started by dividing and replanting rooted offshoots or from softwood cuttings of young growth in late spring or early summer. Plants propagated in these ways will be the same sex as their parents.

MYRTLE, CRAPE See *Lagerstroemia*

N

NANNYBERRY See *Viburnum*

O

OLEASTER See *Elaeagnus*
OLIVE, RUSSIAN See *Elaeagnus*
OSIER, DWARF PURPLE See *Salix*

P

PAEONIA
P. suffruticosa, also called *P. moutan* (tree peony)

The name tree peony must be dismissed as hyperbole, for this shrub usually grows only 3 to 6 feet tall and may spread an equal distance. But it is no exaggeration to say that the flowers of the tree peony are spectacular; they are 6 to 12 inches across, each petal seemingly made of translucent silk. Although the flowers of the original species come only in pink or white, hybridization has produced hundreds of shades of pink, red, yellow and purple. The flowers bloom in late spring and have centers filled with golden-yellow pollen-bearing stamens, around which may be petals in several different forms: single blossoms, with one ring of petals; semidoubles, with several rings of petals; or doubles, with numerous overlapping petals. The soft gray-green leaves are deeply lobed. Tree peonies are at their best standing alone where their attractiveness can be viewed from all sides and can flourish without competition from the roots of other plants.

HOW TO GROW. Tree peonies grow in Zones 5-8. They do best in light shade in well-drained soil that has been liberally supplemented with peat moss or leaf mold. Container-grown plants and balled-and-burlaped plants, those with their roots in their original soil ball wrapped in burlap, can be set into the ground at any time, but bare-rooted plants should be set out only in fall. The tree peonies sold by most nurserymen have been grafted—that is, the stem of one plant has been joined to the root of another plant that has a sturdier root system. When planting a grafted shrub, dig a hole deep enough so that the point at which the two plants are joined—called the graft union—is about 6 inches below the soil surface. Pruning is not necessary, but staking may be required to hold up stems weighted with heavy blossoms. Propagation of tree peonies is difficult and is best left to professional growers.

PEA TREE, SIBERIAN See *Caragana*
PEARLBUSH See *Exochorda*
PEONY See *Paeonia*
PEPPER BUSH, SWEET See *Clethra*

PHILADELPHUS
P. coronarius (sweet mock orange), *P. lemoinei* (Lemoine mock orange), *P. virginalis* (virginalis mock orange)

The name mock orange refers to the intensely sweet

TREE PEONY
Paeonia suffruticosa 'L'Esperance'

LEMOINE MOCK ORANGE
Philadelphus lemoinei 'Belle Etoile'

For climate zones and months of flowering, see page 154.

ORIENTAL PHOTINIA
Photinia villosa

FRANGIPANI
Plumeria rubra

orange-blossom fragrance of most types of mock oranges, including the ones listed here. This scent fills many gardens during two weeks in early summer as mock oranges bear masses of white 1- to 2½-inch flowers. The flowers are single, with one row of petals, or double, with numerous overlapping petals. The single-flowered types have prominent golden-yellow pollen-bearing stamens. Modern varieties have dull green leaves, 1 to 3 inches long, that are seldom bothered by insects or diseases. There is a wide range in mature sizes, from 3 to 9 feet, providing types suitable for almost any purpose. The sweet mock orange, perhaps the most common variety in old gardens, is native to Europe and is one of the parents of the majority of the hybrids sold today. It grows 7 to 9 feet tall and has single flowers 1 to 1½ inches across. Among the recommended varieties of Lemoine mock orange, Avalanche reaches 4 feet and has arching branches covered with masses of 1-inch single flowers; Belle Etoile grows 5 to 6 feet and has 2½-inch single flowers; Innocence grows 6 to 8 feet and has 1½-inch single flowers noted for their rich fragrance; Mont Blanc, which grows to a height of 4 feet and has 1¼-inch single flowers, is more resistant to winter cold than the other varieties. Virginalis mock orange, available in single- and double-flowering varieties, offers a big display of blossoms in early summer and may bloom intermittently throughout the summer and fall. Among the varieties of virginalis are: Miniature Snowflake, 2 to 3 feet tall, 1½-inch double flowers; Minnesota Snowflake, 6 to 8 feet tall, 2-inch double flowers and a bushy growth; Virginal, 5 to 8 feet tall, 2-inch double flowers and a rather gawky upright growth. This latter variety quickly loses its lower branches and should be grown only at the back of a shrub border, where its bare bottom sections will be hidden. When cut, the flowers of all types make excellent bouquets.

HOW TO GROW. Sweet mock oranges grow in Zones 4-9, Lemoine and virginalis hybrids in Zones 5-9. All are very easy to cultivate; they thrive in full sun or light shade in almost any soil, but do best in moist but well-drained soil supplemented with peat moss, leaf mold or compost. Prune immediately after flowering by removing the parts of the ends of the outer stems that have borne flowers. Each cut should be made just above a strong-growing bud or new shoot. New plants can be started from softwood cuttings of young growth in late spring, from semihardwood cuttings of more mature growth in midsummer, or from hardwood cuttings of leafless dormant growth in fall or winter.

PHOTINIA
P. villosa (Oriental photinia)

Oriental photinia is a handsome 10- to 15-foot shrub whose 1½- to 2-inch clusters of small white flowers bloom in late spring. In late fall, bright red berries about ½ inch in diameter appear just as the slender 1½- to 3-inch leaves, dark green all summer, turn brilliant shades of red. The berries are quickly eaten by birds. Oriental photinia makes a striking plant standing by itself and is also effective toward the back of a shrub border.

HOW TO GROW. Oriental photinia grows in Zones 4-8 and does best in well-drained soil in full sun but will tolerate light shade. Pruning is rarely required. Plants can be propagated by forcing a branch to grow roots by the method known as ground layering. New plants can also be started from softwood cuttings of young growth in late spring or early summer, from semihardwood cuttings of more mature growth in mid- or late summer, or from hardwood cuttings of dormant leafless growth in late fall or early winter.

PLUM See *Prunus*

PLUMERIA

P. rubra, also called *P. incarnata* (frangipani)

Almost every gardener living in the frost-free areas of Zone 10 always seems to find a place in his yard for a frangipani, whose 6- to 10-inch clusters of 2-inch or so pink, red, yellow or white golden-centered flowers perfume the air from spring until fall.

Frangipanis, about 15 feet high when mature, have leathery dark green shiny leaves 6 to 12 inches long that cluster toward the ends of the branches. The smallest branches of the frangipani are about an inch in thickness and are blunt-ended; when the shrubs are leafless, the branches look like fat sausages. The common name frangipani is said to be derived from the French word *franchipanier*, which means "coagulated milk" and refers to the white juices that the plants exude where injured. Because of the flowers' special fragrance and long season of bloom, frangipanis are most often used standing alone as accent shrubs.

HOW TO GROW. Frangipanis will grow only in Zone 10; they do best in sunny places but will tolerate locations with light shade. Almost any soil is suitable, and the plants will do well in seaside gardens. Pruning is not needed since frangipanis naturally grow in a handsome rounded shape. Propagate new plants from stem cuttings taken at any time.

POINCIANA See *Caesalpinia*
POMEGRANATE See *Punica*

POTENTILLA

P. arbuscula, *P. fruticosa* (both called bush cinquefoil)

Both species of bush cinquefoils are 2- to 4-foot shrubs notable for their 1-inch yellow or white flowers. They make the greatest display of blossoms in early summer, but scattered flowering sometimes continues into late fall. The gray-green 1-inch or smaller leaves are densely set on the branches, and are covered with many silky hairs. The name cinquefoil means "five leaves"; in this case it refers to the leaflets, and although five is the usual number, there may be three or seven. Bush cinquefoils are excellent near a house and in the front of shrub borders; several plants should be set in a group for emphasis. Recommended varieties of *P. fruticosa* are: Kathryn Dykes and Moonlight, pale yellow; Barreri, also known as Gold Drop, deep yellow; Mount Everest and Veitchii, white. Sutter's Gold is a fine variety of the Himalayan species *P. arbuscula*.

HOW TO GROW. Bush cinquefoils grow in Zones 2-9 except in Florida and along the Gulf Coast. They do best in full sun and will grow in almost any soil. Pruning is ordinarily not required because of the dense growth of the plants. New plants can be started from softwood cuttings of young growth in late spring or summer, by forcing a branch to grow roots by the method known as ground layering, or by cutting away and replanting rooted offshoots of the parent plant in early spring before new growth begins.

PRIVET See *Ligustrum*

PRUNUS

P. besseyi (western sand cherry); *P. cistena* (purple-leaved sand cherry); *P. glandulosa* (dwarf flowering almond); *P. maritima* (beach plum); *P. tomentosa* (Nanking or Manchu cherry); *P. triloba*, also called *P. triloba multiplex*, *P. triloba flore pleno* and *P. triloba plena* (flowering almond)

Low-growing types of cherries, plums and flowering almonds—all members of the *Prunus* genus—make handsome shrubs, sending out white or pink flowers in spring. They are usually about 1 inch or less across, but some are

BUSH CINQUEFOIL
Potentilla arbuscula 'Sutter's Gold'

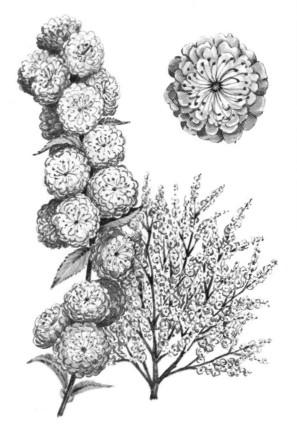

DWARF FLOWERING ALMOND
Prunus glandulosa

For climate zones and months of flowering, see page 154.

POMEGRANATE
Punica granatum

ALDER BUCKTHORN
Rhamnus frangula columnaris 'New Tallhedge'

single flowers, with one row of petals, others double, with many overlapping petals. The single-flowered ones usually bear great quantities of ¾-inch red, purple or black edible fruit in summer or early fall. It is useful for jams and pies. Birds find it irresistible, so if you want to pick it, cover the bushes with black plastic netting. The larger types of *Prunus* are suited for the backs of shrub borders, and the smaller ones are often planted near a house or in the front of borders. Branches of all can be cut in midwinter and forced to bloom indoors in early spring.

Western sand cherry may grow 7 feet tall, but one form, Hansen's bush cherry, grows only 4 feet tall. All have white flowers, followed by great quantities of ¾-inch black cherries in fall. Purple-leaved sand cherry grows 8 feet tall and has pink or white flowers followed by ½-inch purplish black cherries in fall. Dwarf flowering almond, usually 4 feet tall, lines its branches in spring with pompon-shaped pink or white double blossoms about 1 inch across. It bears no fruit. Beach plum, particularly suited for seaside locations, grows about 6 feet tall and bears clouds of tiny white flowers on bare black branches. The ½- to 1-inch purple or red fruit it bears in late summer is good for making jam. Nanking cherry, which forms a moundlike bush as much as 9 feet tall with an equal spread, has pink buds that open into white flowers before the leaves develop in the spring; ½-inch scarlet cherries follow in midsummer. Flowering almond has double pink flowers like little roses. It grows 12 to 15 feet tall and does not bear fruit.

HOW TO GROW. Western sand cherry grows in Zones 3-6, purple-leaved sand cherry in Zones 2-9, dwarf flowering almond in Zones 4-9, beach plum in Zones 3-7, Nanking cherry in Zones 2-6 and flowering almond in Zones 5-9. All need full sun and will grow in almost any well-drained soil. Western and purple-leaved sand cherries and the Nanking cherry are particularly suited to the cold winters and hot summers of the central and northern plains of the United States and Canada. Flowers and fruit are borne on branches produced the previous season. Although most types do best if not pruned, dwarf flowering almond should be pruned immediately after flowering, taking off those parts of the stems that have had blossoms—this allows lower buds to make strong new branches. Single-flowered types can be propagated by seeds sown outdoors in fall to flower in four or five years. They can also be started from softwood cuttings of young growth in late spring or early summer. Double-flowered types and Hansen's bush cherry should be propagated from softwood cuttings.

PUNICA

P. granatum (pomegranate)

The pomegranate has been grown since ancient times for its delicious fruit and its handsome red or, occasionally, creamy yellow or striped cream-and-red flowers. Pliny mentioned it, calling it *Malum punicum,* or apple of Carthage, because it was widely grown in North Africa. In this country there are single-flowered varieties, with one row of petals, as well as double-flowered ones, with numerous overlapping petals. Blossoms range from 1½ to 4 inches across and are made of thick, fleshy petals. Pomegranates come in many sizes from dwarf types about 3 feet tall to plants that may become 10 feet in height. They have slender glossy leaves, 1½ to 3 inches long, that are reddish when they unfold in the spring and turn yellow in the late fall. The double-flowered pomegranates do not bear fruit. Most single-flowering types blossom in early summer and bear 2½-inch brownish red fruit in fall. Double-flowering varieties bloom for several months in summer.

Among the recommended varieties are: Albescens, also

called Albo-Plena, 6 to 8 feet tall, with double creamy white flowers; Chico, 2 to 3 feet tall, with double orange-red flowers; dwarf pomegranate, *P. granatum nana,* 2 to 3 feet tall, with single red flowers and small 1½-inch fruit; and Wonderful, an 8- to 10-foot variety with single flowers and large fruit. Ordinary pomegranates are often grown as tall hedges or standing alone; smaller ones, useful for low hedges and plantings near a house, are also grown in containers for patio or indoor plants.

HOW TO GROW. Pomegranates grow in Zones 8-10 but bear heavy crops of fruit only in hot dry areas. They need full sun and grow in almost any soil, including slightly alkaline ones. Prune only to shape young plants or to restrain the tall growth of older ones. Such pruning should be done in early spring before new growth starts so that the current season's stems can produce flowers. When planting pomegranates for hedges, set dwarf varieties 1½ to 2 feet apart, tall-growing varieties 4 to 6 feet apart.

To duplicate named varieties in your garden, propagate from hardwood cuttings of dormant leafless growth in late fall or winter, or by digging up and planting the underground branches known as suckers. The ordinary single-flowered species can be grown easily from seeds planted in spring to flower in four or five years.

PYRUS See *Chaenomeles*

Q

QUINCE See *Chaenomeles*

R

REDBUD See *Cercis*

RHAMNUS
R. frangula (alder buckthorn)

Alder buckthorn, despite its name, is thornless. It becomes a large shrub, 12 to 18 feet tall with an equal spread. In early summer it bears tiny inconspicuous pale flowers, followed by ¼-inch berries that change from green to yellow and red, finally becoming black when fully ripe in late summer and fall. Birds devour them and, unfortunately, disseminate the seeds over a wide area so that in some sections this plant has become a weed. The 2-inch shiny dark green leaves turn yellow in the fall. A variety called New Tallhedge, *R. frangula columnaris,* grows 10 to 12 feet tall, but spreads to a width of only 4 feet. It is an excellent plant for hedges and screens because its leaves appear early in spring and do not drop until late in fall.

HOW TO GROW. Alder buckthorn grows in Zones 2-8 in almost any soil, including very wet ground, in full sun or light shade. Prune to restrict growth in early spring before new growth starts, so that the current season's stems can produce fruit. To plant a hedge of New Tallhedge alder buckthorn, plant 3- to 4-foot plants 2 to 2½ feet apart. Be sure to cut them back to 1½ to 2 feet after planting to ensure satisfactory growth.

Home propagation of New Tallhedge is prohibited since it is a patented plant, but the ordinary alder buckthorns can be started from softwood cuttings of young growth in late spring or summer, from semihardwood cuttings of more mature growth in mid- or late summer, or from hardwood cuttings of dormant leafless growth in late fall or winter. Plants can also be propagated by forcing a branch to grow roots by the method known as ground layering.

RHODODENDRON (AZALEA)
R. arborescens (sweet or smooth azalea); *R. calendulaceum* (flame azalea); *R. gandavense* (Ghent azalea); *R.*

FLAME AZALEA
Rhododendron calendulaceum

KNAP HILL HYBRID AZALEA
Rhododendron 'Knap Hill Hybrid'

For climate zones and months of flowering, see page 154.

129

MOLLIS HYBRID AZALEA
Rhododendron kosterianum hybrid

ROYAL AZALEA
Rhododendron schlippenbachii

'Knap Hill Hybrids' (Exbury, Knap Hill and Slocock Hybrid azaleas); *R. kosterianum,* also called *R. molle,* hybrids (Mollis Hybrid azalea); *R. mucronulatum* (Korean rhododendron); *R. nudiflorum* (pinxter-bloom, honeysuckle azalea); *R. roseum,* also called *R. prinophyllum* (roseshell azalea); *R. schlippenbachii* (royal azalea); *R. vaseyi* (pinkshell azalea); *R. viscosum* (swamp azalea); *R. yedoense,* also called *R. yodogawa* (Yodogawa azalea)

Azaleas are among the most colorful of all flowering shrubs, bearing 3- to 6-inch clusters of red, yellow, orange, pink, white or purple flowers in spring and early summer, and in many cases providing brilliantly hued leaves in fall. The deciduous species described here allow gardeners in Northern regions to enjoy the beauty of this genus; they are not to be confused with evergreen azaleas that are widely grown from Zone 6 south. Many nursery catalogues list azaleas separately from the related plants commonly called rhododendrons, but both belong to a single genus, *Rhododendron.* Azaleas will serve most garden uses admirably, and they also can be grown in open woodlands in light shade where, with proper initial soil preparation, they are often able to take care of themselves indefinitely.

Sweet azalea grows 4 to 6 feet tall and bears clusters of very fragrant 2-inch white or rose-tinged flowers in midsummer. Its leaves turn a deep glossy red in autumn. The flame azalea is one of the most brightly colored of native North American shrubs, bearing large clusters of yellow, orange or scarlet 2-inch flowers in early summer. Plants usually become 4 to 6 feet tall.

Ghent azaleas are hybrids developed in Belgium about 150 years ago. Their single flowers, with one ring of petals, or double flowers, with numerous overlapping petals, are 1½ to 2 inches across and come in white and in shades of yellow, orange, pink and red. Among the recommended varieties are: Bouquet de Flore, bright pink; Daviesi, white; Pallas, orange red, and Narcissiflora, double yellow. All of these varieties have yellow blotches on their lower petals and blossom in late spring.

Knap Hill Hybrids are exceptional hybrids developed at an English nursery of that name, but the term is also applied to the superb Exbury Hybrids, sometimes called de Rothschild Hybrids, bred at the de Rothschild estate in Exbury, Hampshire, England, as well as the Slocock Hybrids grown at the Slocock nursery in England. All these plants have individual flowers as large as 3 inches across, in great clusters of up to 18 flowers to a head. Basic colors are yellow, pink, red and white, but nearly every flower has at least two colors. The shrubs blossom in early summer, and the foliage usually turns yellow, orange or red in fall. Plants grow about 4 to 5 feet tall. Exbury and Knap Hill Strains are the ones usually offered by nurserymen in this country. Among the recommended Exbury Hybrids and their basic colors are: Berry Rose, rose pink; Firefly, red; Gibraltar, brilliant orange; Sun Chariot, yellow; and White Swan, white. Excellent Knap Hill Hybrids are: Bullfinch, deep red; Flamingo, pink; Golden Oriole, yellow; and White Throat, double white.

Mollis Hybrid azaleas bear large clusters of 2- to 3-inch flowers in late spring. The colors include many shades of yellow, orange and pink as well as white. Plants usually grow about 5 feet tall. Among the fine varieties are: Christopher Wren, yellow; Consul Ceresole, rose pink; Koster's Brilliant, orange red; and Snowdrift, white.

Korean rhododendron grows 4 to 6 feet tall and opens its rosy purple flowers so early in spring that they are sometimes nipped by frost. The flowers are only about 1½ inches across, but they appear in very large numbers. Cornell Pink is an especially fine variety, with clear pink flowers unadulterated by the magenta that is present in the blossoms of the original species.

Pinxter-bloom, 4 to 6 feet tall, is a hardy native species that bears faintly scented pale pink or white flowers 1½ inches in diameter in late spring. Roseshell azalea is quite similar to pinxter-bloom, except that its 2-inch flowers are a deep rose pink and are more fragrant. The plants usually grow 7 feet tall.

Royal azalea is so lovely that man can hardly hope to improve upon its soft pink flowers. They are 3 inches across, and freckled on the upper petals. The leaves of royal azaleas turn shades of yellow, orange and red in fall. Shrubs usually grow 6 to 8 feet tall.

Pinkshell azalea, 5 to 8 feet tall, bears 1½-inch pink flowers in late spring. Its leaves turn red in autumn. Swamp azalea, 6 to 12 feet tall, has very fragrant 1½- to 2-inch white, pink-tinged flowers in early to midsummer. The leaves turn orange or bronzy red in the fall.

Yodogawa azalea has 2-inch double reddish purple flowers in late spring. Plants rarely grow more than 3 feet tall, but may spread to 6 feet in diameter. The variety *R. yedoense poukhanense,* Korean Yodogawa azalea, has single flowers and is a bit more resistant to winter cold than the double-flowered type. The leaves of both turn purplish in the fall in Northern gardens, but remain nearly evergreen in milder climates.

HOW TO GROW. Sweet, Ghent, royal and Yodogawa azaleas and the Korean rhododendron grow in Zones 4-8; flame, Knap Hill and Mollis Hybrids, and Yodogawa azaleas in Zones 5-8; and pinxter-bloom, roseshell, pinkshell and swamp azaleas in Zones 3-8. All are alike in their need for moist, acid soil (pH 4.5 to 5.5) that has been well supplemented with peat moss or leaf mold. Azaleas will grow in full sun or light shade, but light shade is preferable in hot areas. Pruning is almost never required. New plants can be started from softwood cuttings of young growth in early spring or summer, or by forcing a branch to grow roots by the method known as ground layering. If you are willing to experiment and wait for blossoms, you can also produce a great many new plants very economically from seeds. Seedlings usually require four to six years to produce flowers; most will be handsome, but they will not necessarily look like those of the parent plants.

RHODOTYPOS
R. scandens, also called *R. kerrioides* (jetbead)

Jetbead has an unusually long flowering season, opening its first blossoms in late spring and continuing to flower sporadically until midsummer. The 1- to 2-inch blossoms are followed by clusters of shiny black ¼-inch seeds that cling to the plants throughout the winter. The 2- to 3-inch light green leaves remain on the shrub until late in the fall. The jetbead grows 3 to 5 feet tall and has arching branches that bend close to the ground. It makes a good plant for the front of a border.

HOW TO GROW. Jetbead grows in Zones 5-8 in full sun or light shade. Although it will endure a wide variety of soils, it does best in one well supplemented with peat moss or leaf mold. Jetbeads can be left unpruned, but if the bushes become straggly, cut a few of the oldest main stems to the ground each spring. This drastic pruning sacrifices some flowers and fruit but encourages the plants to send up many new stems. New plants can be started from cuttings taken at any of several seasons: from softwood cuttings of young growth in late spring or early summer, from semihardwood cuttings of more mature growth in mid- or late summer, or from hardwood cuttings of dormant leafless growth in late fall or winter.

PINKSHELL AZALEA
Rhododendron vaseyi

JETBEAD
Rhodotypos scandens

For climate zones and months of flowering, see page 154.

SHINING SUMAC
Rhus copallina

ROSE ACACIA
Robinia hispida

RHUS

R. aromatica, also called *R. canadensis* (fragrant sumac); *R. copallina* (shining sumac); *R. glabra* (smooth sumac); *R. typhina* (staghorn sumac)

Sumacs are most effective in autumn when spirelike clusters of fuzzy red fruit adorn the ends of the branches that are brilliant with orange or deep red leaves. The fruit is preceded by flowers, but they are usually barely noticeable because the greenish color blends in with the foliage. The plants sometimes have both male and female flowers, but usually they are either all male or all female. Both sexes are necessary for fruit production, but only the female plants bear berries. Sumacs spread by underground roots to form large, moundlike bushes. They grow wild in many parts of the United States and Canada in sandy well-drained places where the soil is poor, and it is in such places and in semiwild settings that they are most useful.

Fragrant sumac has three-leaflet aromatic leaves, each leaflet being 1½ to 3 inches long. This species grows 2 to 6 feet tall and bears small clusters of red berries in late summer. It makes an easily maintained ground cover for large areas. Shining sumac has 4- to 6-inch spikes of bright red berries that cling through the fall and winter. The featherlike leaves have 9 to 21 leaflets, each 2 to 3 inches long, with unique midribs webbed like a duck's foot. This species usually grows 3 to 6 feet tall. Smooth sumac bears bright red berries in fall and winter. It grows 6 to 15 feet tall. The 12- to 18-inch featherlike leaves are composed of many 2- to 4-inch leaflets. The cut-leaved variety of smooth sumac, *R. glabra laciniata,* has very deeply lobed leaves. Staghorn sumac, so called because its branches are covered with a fuzz similar to that on young deer's antlers, grows unusually large; it becomes 10 to 30 feet tall and looks best at the back of a border or in a semiwild setting. This species has feather-shaped leaves 12 to 24 inches long composed of 13 or more 2- to 4-inch leaflets. It bears 4- to 8-inch spikes of fruit in fall and winter. The varieties *R. typhina dissecta,* the shred-leaved staghorn sumac, and *R. typhina laciniata,* the cut-leaved staghorn sumac, have leaves that are deeply lobed.

HOW TO GROW. Fragrant sumac grows in Zones 3-9, shining sumac in Zones 4-9, smooth sumac in Zones 2-8 and staghorn sumac in Zones 3-8. All of these sumacs do best in full sun and well-drained, quite dry soil. To encourage development of more stems, cut a few of the oldest stems down to ground level in early spring each year. Sumacs are easily propagated in a number of ways. New plants can be started by digging up and replanting the underground branches known as suckers, by forcing a branch to grow roots by the method known as ground layering, from softwood cuttings of new growth taken in late spring or early summer, from semihardwood cuttings of more mature growth in mid- or late summer, and from hardwood cuttings of dormant leafless growth in late fall or winter. Root cuttings can also be planted in fall or spring.

RHUS COTINUS See *Cotinus*

ROBINIA

R. hispida (rose acacia, moss locust)

The rose acacia produces pendant clusters of 1¼-inch unscented pink flowers in late spring and early summer. The clusters, about 2½ inches long, contain 5 to 10 closely set blossoms and appear when the foliage is fully developed. Individual leaves are 6 to 10 inches long and are made up of 7 to 13 leaflets, each about an inch long. Occasionally, short red-bristled seed pods follow the flowers in late summer.

The stems of the rose acacia are covered with a moss of red bristles, which gives the shrub one of its common names, moss locust. The variety *R. hispida macrophylla*, smooth rose acacia, has fewer bristles, the leaves are larger and the flowers are a deeper pink.

Rose acacias are unusual in that they can be grown in two distinct ways: as 3- to 4-foot shrubs that spread by means of underground offshoots, or suckers, and cover large areas, or as small "trees," in which case they are grafted to the tops of upright stems of the black locust, *R. pseudoacacia*. When grown on their own roots, they are most useful in semiwild settings such as banks, where they serve as ground covers, requiring little maintenance. They can also be grown in clusters provided they are pruned regularly to restrain their spreading.

HOW TO GROW. Rose acacias grow in Zones 5-9 and do best in full sun and well-drained soil. The stems of rose acacia are very brittle and, for that reason, those that have been grafted should be planted in places that are sheltered from the wind. Remove any unwanted suckers at ground level at any time. All other pruning, however, should be done after the flowers have faded, since the flowers form on the previous season's growth, not on new growth. New plants can be started from softwood cuttings of young growth in late spring or early summer, from root cuttings or by division of the suckers.

ROSA
R. alba incarnata (Great Maiden's Blush rose), *R. centifolia* (cabbage or Provence rose), *R. harisonii* (Harison's Yellow rose), *R. hugonis* (Father Hugo's rose, Golden Rose of China), *R. rugosa* (Japanese rose)

Although technically all rose bushes are shrubs—because, like other shrubs, they have many woody stems originating below or close to the surface of the ground —only some are treated as such. They are ones that are so much more frost resistant than other types of roses and require so much less pampering that they can hold their own in borders with other shrubs, blossoming year after year. Their flowers provide a mass of color in early summer and are followed by fruit called hips, which in some cases become bright red or orange in late summer and fall. Such roses are highly desirable beside a fence or wall, in borders or as individual ornaments.

Among the many excellent roses useful as shrubs—some are described as "shrub roses" by nurserymen—are the five recommended here; all are outstanding for their beauty, vigor and resistance to frost. Great Maiden's Blush rose grows 4 to 8 feet tall and in early summer bears clusters of moderately fragrant 2- to 3-inch lushly petaled, or double, pink flowers; in summer and fall 3/4-inch scarlet hips appear. Cabbage or Provence rose grows 3 to 6 feet tall and in early summer has moderately fragrant 1- to 4-inch double pink flowers, borne singly or in clusters, each flower having up to 100 overlapping petals; the seed hips are inconspicuous. Harison's Yellow rose grows 5 to 8 feet tall and in spring or early summer bears fragrant 1½- to 2-inch semidouble bright yellow flowers; its brownish black seed hips are not very noticeable. Father Hugo's rose is very distinctive; its long arching main stems grow 6 to 8 feet tall and are lined in late spring with nonfragrant 2-inch single yellow flowers, each with one row of petals; the seed hips are inconspicuous, but the small fernlike leaves turn reddish orange in fall. Japanese rose is a handsome 5- to 6-foot species whose clusters of fragrant 2½- to 3½-inch single purplish red flowers bloom in early summer and occasionally in fall; the flowers are set off against crinkly dark green leaves that turn orange in fall, just as the

CABBAGE ROSE
Rosa centifolia

FATHER HUGO'S ROSE
Rosa hugonis

For climate zones and months of flowering, see page 154.

133

highly decorative orange-red hips, about 1 inch across, appear. The Japanese rose comes in several varieties, with single or double pink, white or red flowers.

HOW TO GROW. Japanese rose grows in Zones 2-10, but Great Maiden's Blush rose and Harison's Yellow rose grow only in Zones 4-10, and cabbage and Father Hugo's roses only in Zones 5-10. All do best in full sun in well-drained soil that has been liberally supplemented with peat moss, leaf mold or compost. Prune as lightly as possible—part of the appeal of these roses is the natural grace of the plants themselves. Remove deadwood in early spring and, after flowering, cut back any branches that have become too tall. New plants can be started in a number of ways: by forcing a branch to grow roots by the method known as ground layering; from softwood cuttings of young growth in late spring or early summer; from semihardwood cuttings of more mature growth in mid- or late summer; from hardwood cuttings of dormant leafless growth in late fall or winter; or in early spring by division of the underground offshoots, or suckers, that spring up around old plants.

ROSE OF CHINA, GOLDEN See *Rosa*
ROSE OF SHARON See *Hibiscus*

S

ST.-JOHN'S-WORT See *Hypericum*

SALIX

S. caprea (goat willow, French pussy willow); *S. discolor* (pussy willow); *S. gracilistyla* (rose gold pussy willow); *S. purpurea gracilis,* also called *S. purpurea nana* (dwarf purple osier, dwarf blue-leaved arctic willow)

Pussy willows are grown primarily for their catkins —early spring flowers that consist of white or silvery pink scaly clusters—which line the stems before the leaves open. Male and female catkins are borne on separate plants. Male plants bear more colorful catkins, and it is this type that is sold by nurserymen. Pussy willows are often planted as single shrubs standing alone or combined with other kinds of plants in borders. Their branches may easily be forced for indoor bloom in winter.

Goat willow, a European species, may grow to a height of 15 to 20 feet. Its fat silvery pink catkins reach a length of 1½ inches each and, when fully mature, are studded with golden-yellow pollen-bearing stamens. During the summer the shrubs have 3- to 6-inch dark green leaves that are silvery beneath. The pussy willow native to the U.S. usually grows 8 to 10 feet tall. It has slender pearl-white catkins, each about 1 inch long. This species has very slender reddish brown twigs; its bright green leaves are 2 to 4 inches long. The rose gold pussy willow rarely grows over 6 to 10 feet tall and has 1¼-inch catkins that are rosy pink with prominent yellow pollen-bearing stamens. It has 2- to 4-inch gray-green leaves. Dwarf purple osier is grown not for its flowers, but for the thickly set 1- to 1½-inch blue-green leaves that line its many slender branches. Unpruned, it makes a mound about 3 feet tall, but it stands shearing well and can easily be kept as a single low plant or as a formal hedge 12 to 24 inches tall.

HOW TO GROW. Goat willow and dwarf purple osier grow in Zones 4-9, pussy willow in Zones 2-9 and rose gold pussy willow in Zones 5-9. However, none grow in Florida or along the Gulf Coast. All do best in full sun and a moist soil well supplemented with peat moss, leaf mold or compost. All can be allowed to grow unpruned, and all except for the dwarf purple osier, which is naturally bushy and is grown for its foliage, can also be cut back to within 4 to 6 inches of the ground each year or two. Flowers form on

JAPANESE ROSE
Rosa rugosa

the previous season's growth, not on new growth, so do not prune until after the flowers have faded. Because pussy willows are fast-growing shrubs—they may grow up to 6 feet in a year—this severe pruning results in the longest stems and the largest possible catkins. To grow dwarf purple osier as a hedge, set plants 18 to 24 inches apart. Pussy willows are exceedingly easy to multiply. They root so easily that stems of almost any size can simply be stuck into moist soil in the spring, and they will take hold within a few weeks. New plants can also be grown from softwood cuttings of young growth in late spring or early summer, from semihardwood cuttings of more mature growth in mid- or late summer, or from hardwood cuttings of dormant leafless growth in late fall or early winter.

SAMBUCUS

S. caerulea, also called *S. glauca* (blue elder or elderberry); *S. canadensis* (American or sweet elder, elderberry)

Elders, long cherished as the source of raw material for a native American wine, jam and pie, bear 5- to 10-inch clusters of tiny creamy white flowers in early to midsummer, followed by blue-black or red berries in late summer and early fall. The berries are favorites of birds, so pick them promptly if you want them. The flower heads are also used in wine making. Elders have coarse fern-shaped leaves, each with five to nine leaflets. They may grow 3 or more feet a year if tips are not pruned, and form bold mounds of foliage 6 to 15 feet tall with an equal spread so they are not recommended for small gardens.

Blue elder usually grows about 15 feet tall. Its berries are black, but a whitish waxy covering called bloom (common on many fruits and berries) makes them appear blue. American elder usually grows 8 to 12 feet tall and has blue-black berries. Golden elder, *S. canadensis aurea,* has bright yellow leaves throughout the summer and bears red berries. Cut-leaved elderberry, *S. canadensis laciniata,* also known as *S. canadensis dissectum,* has delicate, fernlike leaves and blue-black berries.

HOW TO GROW. Blue elder grows in Zones 5-9 on the West Coast, American elder in Zones 3-9 east of the Rockies. Both grow best in full sun in moist soil generously supplemented with peat moss or leaf mold. Plants can be left unpruned or, if they become too large, can be pruned as heavily as desired without being injured. Prune in early spring before new growth starts so that the current season's growth can produce flowers and fruit. New plants can be started from softwood cuttings of young growth in late spring or early summer, from semihardwood cuttings of more mature growth in mid- or late summer, or from hardwood cuttings of dormant leafless growth in late fall or winter. Plants can also be propagated from root cuttings taken in spring or fall.

SAPPHIREBERRY See *Symplocos*
SERVICEBERRY See *Amelanchier*
SILVERBERRY See *Elaeagnus*
SMOKE TREE See *Cotinus*
SNOWBALL See *Viburnum*
SNOWBERRY See *Symphoricarpos*

SORBARIA

S. aitchisonii, also called *S. angustifolia, Spiraea aitchisonii* (Kashmir false spirea); *S. sorbifolia,* also called *S. grandiflora, Spiraea sorbifolia* (Ural false spirea)

False spireas are grown for their immense spires of late-blooming tiny white flowers, held high above mounds of coarse fernlike foliage that unfolds very early in spring. Individual leaves are about 15 inches long with 13 to 25 leaf-

GOAT WILLOW
Salix caprea

AMERICAN ELDER
Sambucus canadensis

For climate zones and months of flowering, see page 154.

URAL FALSE SPIREA
Sorbaria sorbifolia

BUMALDA SPIREA
Spiraea bumalda 'Anthony Waterer'

lets. Kashmir false spirea has flower clusters as much as 18 inches long at the ends of red-barked stems in late summer. The plants may become 10 feet tall and are most useful in large gardens. Ural false spirea has 5- to 10-inch spikes of flowers in midsummer and usually grows about 6 feet tall. It spreads rapidly by underground branches, or suckers, and should be placed where it will not encroach upon other plants. Both types are well suited to a semi-wild setting, where they can take care of themselves.

HOW TO GROW. Kashmir false spirea grows in Zones 6-8, Ural false spirea in Zones 2-8. Both grow in almost any soil and tolerate light shade although they do best in full sun in a moist soil supplemented with peat moss or leaf mold. To induce strong, productive new stems to sprout, cut back each old stem so that only two buds of the previous season's growth remain. Prune in early spring before new growth starts so the current season's growth can produce flowers. Cut faded flowers to improve the plants' appearance. New plants can be started from softwood cuttings of young growth in late spring or early summer, from semihardwood cuttings of more mature growth in mid- or late summer, from hardwood cuttings of dormant leafless growth in late fall or winter, or from suckers.

SPICEBUSH See *Lindera*
SPINDLE TREE See *Euonymus*

SPIRAEA

S. arguta (garland spirea); *S. billardii* (Billard spirea); *S. bumalda* (Bumalda spirea); *S. cantoniensis,* also called *S. reevesiana* (Reeve's spirea); *S. japonica* (Japanese spirea); *S. nipponica* 'Snowbound' (boxwood spirea); *S. prunifolia,* also called *S. prunifolia plena* (bridal wreath, shoe-button spirea); *S. thunbergii* (Thunberg spirea); *S. vanhouttei* (Vanhoutte spirea)

Spireas' contribution to gardens consists almost entirely of a massive display of tiny white, pink or red flowers. Most are hybrids that provide such a range of size, shape and color they serve almost any purpose.

Garland spirea grows 4 to 6 feet tall, producing slender arching stems that are covered with tiny white flowers just as the leaves unfold in midspring. The dwarf variety of garland spirea, *S. arguta compacta,* has dense branches and grows about 4 feet tall. Billard spirea grows 4 to 6 feet tall and equally broad. It has bright reddish flowers in 6- to 8-inch spikes in mid- to late summer. Bumalda spirea has two varieties of special interest: Anthony Waterer, about 2 feet tall, and Frobel, 3 to 3½ feet tall. Both bear pink flowers in flat-topped clusters up to 6 inches across in midsummer; the slender leaves are pinkish as they unfold. Reeve's spirea grows 4 to 6 feet tall and has clusters of white double flowers in late spring. Its dark green leaves unfurl as the flowers fade and take on reddish tints in fall. Among the varieties of Japanese spirea, alpine, *S. japonica alpina,* grows only 12 inches tall and has flat-topped clusters of tiny light pink flowers in midsummer. The Mikado variety, *S. japonica atrosanguinea,* has similarly formed, but deep crimson flowers at the same time; it grows 4 feet tall. Boxwood spirea is a handsome type that makes a dense mound 2½ to 3 feet tall. The name alludes to the small blue-green leaves, which look like the leaves of boxwood; they appear in early summer and cling until late fall. At the same time as the leaves appear, clusters of white flowers line the slender canes. Bridal wreath grows 5 to 8 feet tall and is unique among spireas not only for its ⅜-inch white buttonlike double flowers that line the branches before the leaves appear, but also for colorful leaves. They are shiny dark green in the summer, but turn to brilliant shades of orange and red in the fall. Thunberg spirea grows 3 to 5 feet tall and has many tiny starlike white flowers in midspring. It is usually the first spirea to blossom, opening its flowers before its leaves. The slender foliage of this type turns yellow or orange in the fall.

Vanhoutte spirea grows about 6 feet tall; the long arching stems are lined in late spring with so many clusters of white flowers that they hide the foliage. The most widely grown spirea, this type remains a favorite because of its ease of culture and great beauty.

HOW TO GROW. Garland, Billard, boxwood, bridal wreath, Thunberg and Vanhoutte spireas grow in Zones 4-10, Bumalda and Japanese spireas in Zones 5-10 and Reeve's spirea in Zones 6-10. All do best in full sun, but tolerate light shade. Almost any soil is suitable. The following spireas produce flowers on the previous season's growth, not on new growth, and should be pruned immediately after flowering: garland, Reeve's, boxwood, bridal wreath, Thunberg and Vanhoutte. Billard, Bumalda and Japanese spireas blossom on the current season's growth and should be pruned in early spring before new growth starts so that the current season's stems can produce flowers. Many of the spireas recommended here are hybrids and should be propagated from softwood cuttings of young growth in late spring or early summer, from semihardwood cuttings of more mature growth in mid- or late summer, or from hardwood cuttings of dormant leafless growth in late fall or early winter. Because Billard, Bumalda and Japanese spireas spread by underground roots, they may also be grown by cutting away and replanting a rooted offshoot.

SPIREA, FALSE See *Sorbaria*

STEPHANANDRA

S. incisa, also called *S. flexuosa* (cut-leaved stephanandra)

Although stephanandras bear clouds of tiny white blossoms at the tips of their branches in early summer, they are not usually grown for their flowers, but rather for their dense, bright green deeply lobed foliage and their graceful arching shape. Plants usually reach a height of 4 to 5 feet with an equal or greater spread, and are thickly clothed with exceptionally colorful ¾- to 2½-inch-long leaves. They are tinged with red when they appear in the spring, and even in the summer those growing from the tips of new branches may show bronze hues. In the fall they change to shades of red purple or red orange. The leaves drop to reveal the attractive zigzagging of the shrubs' bright cinnamon-brown branches. This unusual foliage, thick and fine-textured, makes stephanandras popular for borders and informal hedges. The dwarf cut-leaved stephanandra, *S. incisa crispa,* is especially suitable for planting near a house, at the forefront of borders, in low hedges and even as a ground cover. It usually grows about 2 feet tall, but spreads to 3 or 4 feet, the tips of its arching branches taking root wherever they meet moist soil.

HOW TO GROW. Stephanandras grow in Zones 5-8 and do best in full sun and moist soil that has been well supplemented with peat moss or leaf mold, but will tolerate light shade and endure almost any soil. For hedges, set tall-growing stephanandras 3 feet apart, the dwarf variety 2 feet apart. In windswept locations, the tips of the stems sometimes suffer frost damage and should be pruned in early spring. To encourage branching and dense growth, some of the oldest stems as well as the weak ones should be cut to ground level each spring. Do all pruning before new growth starts so that the current season's stems can produce flowers. New plants can be started by forcing a branch to grow roots by the method known as ground layering, or

BRIDAL WREATH
Spiraea prunifolia

VANHOUTTE SPIREA
Spiraea vanhouttei

For climate zones and months of flowering, see page 154.

137

DWARF CUT-LEAVED STEPHANANDRA
Stephanandra incisa crispa

SHOWY STEWARTIA
Stewartia ovata grandiflora

by cutting away and replanting a rooted offshoot or division of the plant. New plants can also be started from softwood cuttings of young growth in late spring or early summer, from semihardwood cuttings of more mature growth in mid- or late summer, or from hardwood cuttings of dormant leafless growth in late fall or early winter.

STEWARTIA

S. malacodendron (Virginia stewartia); *S. ovata,* also called *S. pentagyna* (mountain stewartia); *S. ovata grandiflora* (showy stewartia)

Stewartias are handsome 10- to 15-foot shrubs valued for their exquisite white single flowers, each with one row of petals. The blossoms appear in midsummer. The 2- to 5-inch leaves are deep green during the summer and take on brilliant shades of scarlet and orange in the fall. Old plants branch in an open pattern that reveals the trunks, whose dark brown bark flakes off to expose green inner bark. Mountain stewartia has cuplike flowers 2 to 3 inches across with yellow pollen-bearing stamens. Showy and Virginia stewartias have blossoms up to 4 inches across with centers accented by purple stamens.

HOW TO GROW. Virginia stewartia grows in Zones 7-9, showy and mountain stewartias in Zones 5-9. All do best where they have full sun most of the day, but shade during the hottest hours. They need a moist acid soil (pH 4.5 to 5.5) supplemented with peat moss or leaf mold. Planting should be done in the spring. Do not buy large old plants or bare-rooted ones, for both are difficult to establish in the garden. You are more likely to be successful with young plants (4 to 5 feet tall), bought container grown or balled and burlaped—that is, sold with their roots in the original soil ball wrapped in burlap. Pruning is almost never required. New plants can be started by forcing a branch to grow roots by the method known as ground layering, from softwood cuttings of young growth taken in late spring or from root cuttings.

STRAWBERRY BUSH See *Euonymus*
SUMAC See *Rhus*
SUMMER SWEET See *Clethra*
SWEET SHRUB See *Calycanthus*
SWEETLEAF, ASIATIC See *Symplocos*

SYMPHORICARPOS

S. albus laevigatus (snowberry); *S. chenaultii* (Chenault coralberry); *S. orbiculatus,* also called *S. vulgaris* (Indian currant, coralberry)

Named for the colors of their fruit, these shrubs are valued for their ability to grow in shade as well as sun. They produce heavy crops of conspicuous berries in summer and fall. All types are useful in informal hedges. Snowberry grows 3 to 6 feet tall, with arching stems set with 1- to 1½-inch deep green leaves. In early summer the ends of twigs produce tiny pink flowers, followed by clusters of ½-inch snow-white waxy berries that cling until late fall. Many nurserymen who stock the variety *S. albus laevigatus* list it as *S. albus* or *S. racemosus,* synonyms for the basic species, which is less desirable and seldom sold. Chenault coralberry, 3 feet high, has fall-ripening ¼-inch berries that are mostly pink, but white on their shaded sides. Its arching stems are lined with tiny pink blossoms in midsummer. The fruit and the ½- to 1-inch leaves cling until late fall. Chenault coralberry's variety Hancock grows 2 feet tall, but spreads several feet, making it an excellent ground cover. Indian currant grows 6 feet tall; it has ½- to 2-inch leaves and arching stems tipped with tiny yellowish white blossoms in midsummer; ¼-inch purplish red berries ripen in early fall. This species is often used to control erosion on slopes because its matted root system holds soil in place.

HOW TO GROW. Snowberries grow in Zones 3-9, Chenault and Hancock coralberries in Zones 4-9 and Indian currants in Zones 2-9. All of them do well in full sun or light shade and will stand rather dry soil if necessary. All except the snowberry spread rapidly by means of underground roots. To shape plants or to remove dead branches, prune them in early spring before new growth starts so that the current season's growth can produce flowers. For hedges, set plants 2 to 2½ feet apart. New plants are best started by cutting away and replanting a rooted offshoot of the plant. They can also be started from softwood cuttings of young growth in late spring or early summer, from semihardwood cuttings of more mature growth in mid- or late summer, or from hardwood cuttings of dormant leafless growth in late fall or winter.

SYMPLOCOS
S. paniculata (sapphireberry, Asiatic sweetleaf)

Sapphireberry is well named, for sapphire blue is the color of its ¼-inch berries, which ripen in late fall. Fruit of such an unusual color makes this shrub a spectacular garden accent, but a short-lived one—birds are extremely fond of the berries and quickly strip them off the branches. Sapphireberry usually grows 10 to 15 feet tall and forms a wide-branching shrub that may have a diameter equal to its height. It puts out dark green leaves in late spring, and at the same time bears many 1½-inch clusters of tiny fuzzy white flowers that are very fragrant. Sapphireberries are attractive either set at the back of a shrub border or when they stand alone.

HOW TO GROW. Sapphireberries grow in Zones 5-8. They do well in full sun or light shade, and grow best in acid soil (pH 4.5 to 5.5). Pruning is rarely needed. New plants can be started from softwood cuttings of young growth in late spring or early summer, or by forcing a branch to grow roots by the method known as ground layering.

SYRINGA
S. chinensis, also called *S. rothomagensis* (Chinese or Rouen lilac); *S. josikaea* 'Sylvia' (Sylvia Hungarian lilac); *S. meyeri,* also called *S. palibiniana* (Meyer's lilac); *S. microphylla superba* (daphne lilac); *S. persica* (Persian lilac); *S. prestoniae* (Preston lilac); *S. velutina* 'Miss Kim' (Miss Kim Korean lilac); *S. villosa* (late lilac); *S. vulgaris* (common lilac, French lilac)

Lilacs do not have attractive fruit, and their foliage, with few exceptions, does not turn an appealing color in fall; all they offer is flowers—magnificent ones. For many generations the only lilacs in most gardens were the briefly blooming tall bushes of the common purple species and its white-flowered variety. But beginning in 1876, breeding programs in France led to great improvements on the common lilac—many-petaled blossoms, large clusters and a wide range of colors. The welcome given these new varieties, known as French lilacs, encouraged plant breeders to hybridize lilacs from various parts of the world and also to introduce species from the Orient that have blooming seasons several weeks longer than that of the common lilacs. Today lilacs can be white, pink, yellow or almost any shade of blue and purple. They bloom through much of the spring, and the bushes vary enormously in size: some types are 3 feet tall at maturity and others reach a height of 20 feet or more. The tall ones are attractive as large plants standing by themselves and serve as excellent shrubs for windbreaks and screens; plants of intermediate size make delightful informal hedges and are the mainstay of

SNOWBERRY
Symphoricarpos albus laevigatus

SAPPHIREBERRY
Symplocos paniculata

For climate zones and months of flowering, see page 154.

PERSIAN LILAC
Syringa persica

COMMON LILAC
Syringa vulgaris 'Moonglow'

many shrub borders; low-growing types are useful in low informal hedges and are often planted near a house.

Chinese or Rouen lilac is a hybrid that grows 10 to 15 feet tall and bears 6-inch clusters of very fragrant light purple flowers in mid- to late spring. Sylvia Hungarian lilac grows 10 to 12 feet tall and bears 4- to 6-inch clusters of fragrant pink flowers in late spring. Meyer's lilac grows 4 to 6 feet tall and has 4-inch clusters of fragrant violet flowers in mid- to late spring. This species, unlike most lilacs, which do not flower until they are four or five years old, blossoms freely even as a very small plant two or three years of age. Daphne lilac becomes about 6 feet tall and spreads 10 to 12 feet across; in mid- to late spring its branches carry great quantities of fragrant pink flowers in 2½-inch clusters. It may also put forth a few flowers in the fall. Persian lilac grows 5 to 6 feet tall and has gracefully arching stems, which in mid- to late spring are laden with clusters of very fragrant purple flowers, each cluster only 2 to 3 inches long but set in larger groups on the stems. Many of the plants sold under this name are actually the similar but larger-growing Chinese lilac. Preston lilacs are dense upright shrubs that grow 6 to 8 feet tall and bear mildly fragrant flowers in clusters 6 to 8 inches long in late spring. Among the many fine varieties are: Donald Wyman, very deep pink; Isabella, medium pink; and James MacFarlane, deep pink. Miss Kim Korean lilac grows in a mound about 3 feet tall and 3 feet across. It has 3-inch clusters of deep purple buds, which open to fragrant icy blue flowers in late spring. Late lilac grows 8 to 10 feet tall with an equal spread, sending out 5- to 10-inch clusters of rosy purple flowers in late spring. Its fragrance is similar to that of privets and is not as appealing as that of most lilacs. The common lilac grows 8 to 15 feet tall and has 6- to 8-inch clusters of exceedingly fragrant purple or white flowers. While the original species has single blossoms, with one row of petals, many of its varieties have double blossoms, with numerous overlapping petals. Of the hundreds of varieties of a wide range of colors now available, the following are considered to be among the finest of all: *white*—Vestale, single; Mme. Lemoine, double; *pink*—Moonglow, single; Esther Staley, single; Katherine Havemeyer, double; *violet*—Cavour, single; Violetta, double; *blue*—Decaisne, single; President Grevy, double; *purple*—Marengo, single; President Carnot, double; Ludwig Spaeth, single; Adelaide Dunbar, double; *magenta*—Congo, single; Charles Joly, double; and *pale yellow*—Primrose, single. In Zones 8 and 9 where varieties of the common lilac are difficult to grow, Angel White (single, white) and Lavender Lady (single, lavender) are particularly satisfactory.

HOW TO GROW. Chinese, Meyer's, Persian and Preston lilacs grow in Zones 5-9, Sylvia Hungarian lilac in Zones 2-9, daphne lilac in Zones 5-7, Miss Kim Korean lilac in Zones 4-9, late lilac in Zones 2-7 and common lilac in Zones 3-7. None, however, grow in Florida or along the Gulf Coast. All lilacs do best in full sun, but they will tolerate very light shade. The best soil is one close to neutral, with a pH of 7.0; it should be supplemented with peat moss or leaf mold. For hedges, plant lilacs 2 to 4 feet apart, depending on the ultimate height of the plant.

To have blossoms every year, cut out old flower heads as soon as the blossoms fade. This is also the time to thin out the weak main stems arising from the soil and to take out very old stems that are no longer blossoming freely. The goal should be to have stems of all ages coming along, younger ones to produce strong new growth, older ones to bear flowers. Overgrown lilacs can be cut to within 4 inches of the ground. In three or four years they will make fine free-flowering shrubs again. Lilacs can be propagated easily by digging up and replanting underground branches, or suckers, from around the edge of plants producing them. New plants can also be propagated from softwood cuttings of young growth in late spring or early summer, from semihardwood cuttings of more mature growth in mid- or late summer, or from hardwood cuttings of dormant leafless growth in late fall or early winter.

T

TAMARISK See *Tamarix*

TAMARIX
T. hispida (Kashgar tamarisk), *T. odessana* (Odessa tamarisk), *T. parviflora* (small-flowered tamarisk), *T. pentandra* (five-stamened tamarisk)

Most species of tamarisks grow wild in the sandy saline soil of the Mediterranean, Caspian and Black Sea coasts, unharmed by salty winds that would injure less tolerant plants, and they are ideal for planting by the seashore, in desert regions or in windy places as well as in ordinary gardens. Their long feathery branches, veiled in a mist of pink blossoms, make an unforgettable garden picture. The fluffy flowers, which attract many bees, are about ⅛ inch across, tightly packed in pencil-shaped spikes grouped in large clusters at the ends of branches. The unusual foliage texture is created by ¼-inch scalelike leaves that cling close to the stems.

Two varieties of the Kashgar tamarisk are excellent garden plants: Pink Cascade grows about 6 feet tall; Summer Glow has darker pink flowers and reaches a height of 8 feet. Both blossom in late summer and early fall and have silvery blue-green foliage. Odessa tamarisk grows 6 feet tall and flowers in mid- to late summer. Small-flowered tamarisk grows 12 to 15 feet tall and flowers in late spring and early summer. Five-stamened tamarisk grows 12 to 15 feet tall and blooms in mid- to late summer. Its variety *T. pentandra rubra* has deeper pink flowers.

HOW TO GROW. Kashgar tamarisk grows in Zones 6-10, Odessa and small-flowered tamarisks in Zones 4-10 and five-stamened tamarisk in Zones 2-10. All do best in full sun and well-drained soil. Their roots are coarse and sparse; set bare-rooted plants out in early spring and cut the tops back to about 6 to 12 inches from the ground. Container-grown plants can be set out at any time without cutting back. Balled-and-burlaped plants, those with their original soil ball wrapped in burlap, are not usually satisfactory because tamarisks do not have enough roots to hold the soil ball together. Kashgar, Odessa and five-stamened tamarisks should be pruned back severely in early spring before new growth starts, leaving only 2- to 3-inch stubs of the previous season's growth so that the current season's growth can produce many stems and an abundance of flowers. Small-flowered tamarisk blossoms on the previous season's growth, not on new growth, and should be pruned immediately after they bloom; cut off the outer ends of the stems that produced flowers. New plants can be started from softwood cuttings of young growth in late spring or early summer, from semihardwood cuttings of more mature growth in mid- or late summer, or from hardwood cuttings of dormant leafless growth in late fall or early winter.

V

VACCINIUM
V. corymbosum (high-bush blueberry)

Blueberries are most familiar as fruit, but the bushes the berries grow on are very attractive, usually growing 5 to 6 feet tall with an equal spread. In late spring, just before the leaves unfold, they bear small clusters of ¼-inch

FIVE-STAMENED TAMARISK
Tamarix pentandra

For climate zones and months of flowering, see page 154.

HIGH-BUSH BLUEBERRY
Vaccinium corymbosum

FRAGRANT SNOWBALL
Viburnum carlcephalum

bell-shaped white flowers. The berries ripen in midsummer and may be as large as an inch across on some cultivated varieties. During the summer the plants are thickly covered with shiny dark green leaves about 1½ to 2 inches long; in the fall the leaves turn brilliant orange and scarlet. In winter the bare twigs are red. Blueberry bushes are suitable for shrub borders, but are more often grown as individual plants, standing by themselves or—to get large crops of fruit and capitalize on their dramatic fall colors—as informal hedges. Most of the many excellent varieties now available will produce some fruit if they are planted alone, but much heavier crops are generally produced if two or more varieties are used, enabling bees to cross-pollinate from one variety to another.

Birds are extremely fond of blueberries. To save some for yourself, cover the bushes when berries start to ripen with black plastic netting, which is unobtrusive; it is sold by garden centers.

HOW TO GROW. High-bush blueberries grow in Zones 3-8. They do best in full sun, but will tolerate very light shade. They must have a moist acid soil (pH 4.5 to 5.5) liberally supplemented with peat moss, leaf mold or decayed sawdust. Since their roots are very fine and close to the surface, they should be protected from heat and drought by a permanent 2- to 3-inch soil covering, or mulch, of wood chips, ground bark, pine needles or sawdust. Pruning is not essential except to remove deadwood, but regular spring pruning of the oldest canes and weak branches increases the crops of berries. For hedges, plant high-bush blueberries 4 to 6 feet apart.

New plants can be started from softwood cuttings of young growth in late spring or early summer, from semi-hardwood cuttings or more mature growth in mid- or late summer, or from hardwood cuttings of dormant leafless growth in late fall or early winter.

VIBURNUM
V. burkwoodii (Burkwood viburnum); *V. carlcephalum* (fragrant snowball); *V. carlesii* (Korean spice viburnum); *V. cassinoides* (withe rod); *V. dentatum* (arrowwood); *V. dilatatum* (linden viburnum); *V. lantana* (wayfaring tree); *V. lentago* (nannyberry); *V. opulus* (European cranberry bush); *V. plicatum,* also called *V. tomentosum plicatum, V. tomentosum sterile* (Japanese snowball); *V. prunifolium* (black haw); *V. sieboldii* (Siebold viburnum); *V. trilobum,* also called *V. americanum* (American cranberry bush). (All also called viburnum)

Viburnums are such a varied and important genus of flowering, fruit-bearing shrubs that few generalizations apply to all of them. Various types grow from 2 to over 20 feet in height, and are thus valuable for many garden uses such as shrub borders, informal hedges, screen plantings, plantings near a house or as single plants that are grown to stand by themselves.

Like hydrangeas *(page 116),* viburnums have two kinds of blossoms—sterile flowers, incapable of producing berries, and fertile ones, which can produce berries. Unlike hydrangeas, the fertile flowers are usually as attractive as the sterile ones. Viburnums offer an added attraction—the handsome fruit of fertile flowers is appealing to birds and that of some species makes delicious jellies and jams. Flowers are usually white or pink and many are delightfully fragrant. The foliage of most viburnums turns some shade of red in the fall.

Burkwood viburnum grows 4 to 6 feet tall and bears 2½- to 3½-inch round clusters of very fragrant pink or white star-shaped fertile flowers in late spring. Its berries change from red to black as they ripen in late summer; the glossy 1½- to 4-inch leaves are dark green above and whitish underneath during the summer and become dark red in the fall.

Fragrant snowball, a plant that looks best standing by itself, grows 6 to 7 feet tall and bears ball-shaped 4- to 5-inch clusters of sweetly fragrant white star-shaped fertile flowers in late spring. Berries change from red to black as they ripen in midsummer. The fragrant snowball's toothed 3- to 4-inch leaves turn red in the fall. Korean spice viburnum is a 3- to 5-foot species that bears 1½- to 3-inch clusters of fragrant pink star-shaped fertile flowers in midspring. It has 2- to 3½-inch toothed leaves that turn purplish red in the fall. Its variety *V. carlesii compactum* grows to a dense bush 2½ to 3½ feet tall.

Withe rod, whose canes were once the weapons of stern schoolmasters, grows 5 to 6 feet tall and has 3- to 4-inch flat-topped clusters of masses of tiny creamy white fertile flowers in early summer. Its berries change from green to pink, then from red to blue before becoming black when they ripen in late summer. Its 1½- to 4½-inch leaves turn bright red in the fall.

It is easy to see why Indians used the stems of arrowwood as shafts for their arrows. Mature plants may send curving branches 10 to 15 feet high, but always have many straight young stems coming up from ground level. This species has 2-inch clusters of tiny creamy white fertile flowers in early summer, followed by dark blue berries in the early fall. Its shiny nearly round 1½- to 3-inch leaves are coarsely toothed and become red in the fall.

Linden viburnum grows 6 to 9 feet tall and bears 3- to 5-inch flat clusters of pure white fertile flowers in early summer. The flowers are followed by bright red berries in early fall, when the broad 2- to 5-inch leaves begin to turn rusty red. The variety *V. dilatatum xanthocarpum* is distinguished by yellow fruit.

Wayfaring tree grows 10 to 15 feet tall and has 2- to 4-inch flat clusters of tiny white fertile flowers in midspring, followed by berries that turn from red to black in early fall and cling to the shrub through part of the winter. The 2- to 5-inch round gray-green leaves turn red in the fall. Nannyberry may grow as a large shrub or small tree to a height of 15 to 20 feet or more. Its long arching branches bear 3- to 4½-inch clusters of tiny white fertile flowers in late spring, followed by ½-inch black berries in early fall. The slender glossy 2- to 4-inch leaves turn shades of red and orange in the fall.

European cranberry bush is resistant to the smoke and grime of cities. It grows 8 to 12 feet tall and has 2- to 3-inch clusters of tiny white fertile flowers ringed by a circle of ¾-inch flat sterile flowers, which open in late spring. In early fall the fertile flowers are followed by translucent red berries, which remain on the shrub through most of the winter. The berries resemble cranberries but are so tart that even birds do not eat them. There are a number of varieties of the European cranberry bush, all with three-lobed leaves that turn red in the fall.

V. opulus compactum grows only 5 to 6 feet tall and has heavy crops of fruit. Dwarf European cranberry bush, *V. opulus nana*, which does not bear flowers or fruit, grows about 2 to 2½ feet tall and has very dense foliage, making it an especially good low hedge. European snowball, *V. opulus roseum*, also called *V. opulus sterile*, is so named because it has 3-inch ball-shaped clusters of sterile white flowers in late spring, but has no fruit. It is very susceptible to attack by aphids. Yellow-fruited European cranberry bush, *V. opulus xanthocarpum*, has bright yellow berries.

Japanese snowball grows 5 to 7 feet tall and bears 2- to 3-inch ball-shaped clusters of sterile white flowers in late

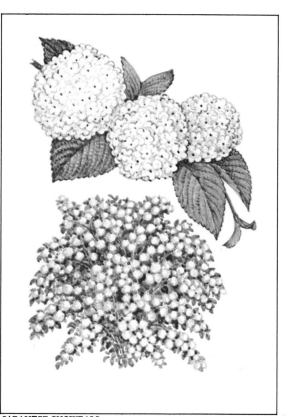

JAPANESE SNOWBALL
Viburnum plicatum

MARIE'S DOUBLEFILE VIBURNUM
Viburnum plicatum tomentosum mariesii

For climate zones and months of flowering, see page 154.

spring. The 2- to 4-inch leaves are whitish beneath and turn purplish red in the fall. Its variety, called doublefile viburnum, *V. plicatum tomentosum,* has broadly spreading horizontal branches, which in late spring are lined with a double row of flat-topped white flower clusters 3 to 4 inches wide. Each cluster of this variety is composed of a center of tiny fertile flowers surrounded by 1- to 1½-inch flat sterile blossoms. Another variety, Marie's doublefile viburnum, *V. plicatum tomentosum mariesii,* is similar except that its sterile flowers are more numerous and larger, reaching up to 2 inches across. The ordinary species does not bear fruit, but all varieties do: colorful berries that turn from red to black as they ripen in midsummer.

Black haw grows 10 to 15 feet tall and has 2- to 4-inch flat clusters of tiny white fertile flowers in midspring. The ½-inch blue-black berries, which ripen in early fall, are good for jam and jelly. The dark green 1½- to 3-inch leaves turn wine red in the fall. Siebold viburnum, a plant that is very attractive standing by itself, usually grows 6 to 10 feet tall. Its 3- to 4-inch clusters of tiny creamy white fertile flowers appear in late spring and are followed by fruit that, beginning in midsummer, changes from green to pink, then from red to dark blue and finally ripe black in early fall. The coarsely toothed dark green shiny leaves, 2 to 5 inches long, take on a rich red color in the fall.

American cranberry bush grows 8 to 12 feet tall and has 2- to 3-inch clusters of tiny white fertile flowers surrounded by a ring of ¾-inch sterile flowers in late spring. The blossoms are followed by bright red berries that resemble cranberries and ripen in early fall when the leaves turn red. The berries cling most of the winter—they are too tart for birds, but make delicious jams. The variety *V. trilobum compactum* grows 4 to 5 feet tall.

HOW TO GROW. Burkwood viburnum, fragrant snowball and linden viburnum grow in Zones 5-9; Korean spice viburnum, Siebold viburnum and Japanese snowball grow in Zones 4-9; withe rod, arrowwood, nannyberry and American cranberry bush grow in Zones 2-9; wayfaring tree, European cranberry bush and black haw grow in Zones 3-9. All do best in full sun, but will tolerate light shade. Nearly any well-drained garden soil is suitable. For informal hedges 3 to 8 feet tall, plant them 2½ to 4 feet apart. Korean spice and Burkwood viburnums and fragrant snowballs are sometimes grown as grafted plants—that is, their stems are grafted to the roots of stronger-growing species. Do not buy such grafted plants since the stronger species tend to sprout and overwhelm the desired variety. Bare-rooted Japanese snowballs and fragrant and Korean spice viburnums are difficult to establish. Buy only plants that are balled and burlaped—that is, sold with their roots in their original soil ball wrapped in burlap—or container-grown plants; set them in the garden in spring. The other viburnums can be purchased either bare-rooted, balled and burlaped or container grown and may be planted at any time without difficulty. To preserve the natural graceful shape of viburnums, limit pruning to the removal of any dead branches. New plants can be started from softwood cuttings of young growth in late spring or early summer, from semihardwood cuttings of more mature growth in mid- or late summer, or from hardwood cuttings of dormant leafless growth in late fall or early winter.

VITEX
V. agnus-castus (chaste tree)

The leaves and flowers of the chaste tree were beloved by the ancients for a supposed ability to "cool the heat of lust," and presumably that is why the tree was widely grown in England in the 16th Century. It has gray-green

AMERICAN CRANBERRY BUSH
Viburnum trilobum

leaves and blooms in midsummer and early fall, bearing tiny blue or white flowers in dense spikes, 6 to 8 inches long. Leaves and flowers have a strong and pleasant aroma.

The chaste tree puts out new growth so late in the spring that an inexperienced gardener may think that it is dead. As a matter of fact, this plant often does die to the ground over the winter in Zone 6, but quickly sprouts new blossoming stems. Plants that have died back or have been cut to the ground usually become 3 to 5 feet tall by the time they blossom; in mild climates, where they do not suffer winter damage, the plants may become 20 feet or more tall with an equal spread.

HOW TO GROW. Chaste trees grow in Zones 6-10 and do best in full sun in well-drained soil. They grow faster in hot weather. Pruning consists of cutting out any winter-killed branches in spring. If desired, plants can be cut to within 6 inches of the ground early each spring before new growth starts. New plants can be started from softwood cuttings of young growth in late spring or early summer, from semihardwood cuttings of more mature growth in mid- or late summer, or from hardwood cuttings of dormant leafless growth in late fall or early winter. In Zones 6 and 7 new plants grown from softwood or semihardwood cuttings must be kept from freezing during their first winter by placing them in a cold frame (*page 86*).

W

WAYFARING TREE See *Viburnum*

WEIGELA

W. florida, also called *W. rosea, W. amabilis, Diervilla florida* (old-fashioned weigela); *W.* hybrids (hybrid weigela)

When weigelas are at their peak in late spring, they are among the most colorful of all shrubs. Each stem is lined with clusters of tubular wide-mouthed flowers an inch or more across. But at any season their arching branches make them graceful bushy plants, and they grow rapidly and have many stems, all of which bear enormous numbers of flowers. The leaves are usually green, but in some varieties are purplish green or edged with creamy white. Old-fashioned weigela bears pink flowers and grows 9 to 10 feet tall if left unpruned, but modern hybrids offer many colors from white through pink to very dark red and rarely exceed 5 to 6 feet. Excellent hybrids are: Candida and Bristol Snowflake, both white; Styriaca, purplish pink; Eva Rathke, bright red; Bristol Ruby and Vanicek (also called Newport Red and Rhode Island Red), both of which have red flowers. Weigelas are excellent in shrub borders and are notably resistant to pests.

HOW TO GROW. Weigelas grow in Zones 5-9 and do best in full sun but will tolerate light shade. They will grow in almost any soil. Remove dead tips in the spring. Since flowers generally form on the previous season's growth, rather than on new growth, do not prune weigelas until after the flowers have faded. Occasionally, a few blossoms will appear late in the summer on the current season's growth. New plants can be started from softwood cuttings of young growth in late spring or early summer, from semihardwood cuttings of more mature growth in mid- or late summer, or from hardwood cuttings of dormant leafless growth in late fall or winter.

WILLOW See *Salix*
WINTER HAZEL See *Corylopsis*
WINTERBERRY See *Ilex*
WITCH HAZEL See *Hamamelis*
WITHE ROD See *Viburnum*
WOLF WILLOW See *Elaeagnus*

CHASTE TREE
Vitex agnus-castus

WEIGELA
Weigela 'Vanicek'

For climate zones and months of flowering, see page 154.

Appendix

Characteristics of 274 flowering shrubs

The dots below indicate which characteristics apply to each shrub.

Shrub	Under 3 feet	3 to 6 feet	Over 6 feet	White	Yellow-orange	Pink-red	Blue-purple	Under 1 inch	1 to 2 inches	Over 2 inches	Spring	Summer	Fall	Informal hedge	Formal hedge	Ground cover	Decorative fruit	Notable fragrance	Notable foliage*	Moist to wet	Dry	Acid	Sun	Shade
ABELIOPHYLLUM DISTICHUM (Korean abelialeaf)		●		●				●			●						●	●	●				●	●
ACANTHOPANAX SIEBOLDIANUS (five-leaved aralia)		●													●		●	●	●				●	●
AESCULUS PARVIFLORA (bottle-brush buckeye)		●	●	●					●			●						●	●				●	
AMELANCHIER STOLONIFERA (running serviceberry)	●	●		●				●			●						●		●				●	
ARONIA ARBUTIFOLIA (red chokeberry)		●	●	●		●		●			●						●		●				●	●
ARONIA ARBUTIFOLIA BRILLIANTISSIMA (brilliant chokeberry)		●	●	●				●			●						●		●				●	●
ARONIA MELANOCARPA (black chokeberry)	●			●				●			●						●		●				●	●
ARONIA PRUNIFOLIA (purple chokeberry)		●	●	●				●			●						●		●				●	●
BERBERIS KOREANA (Korean barberry)		●			●			●			●			●	●		●		●				●	
BERBERIS MENTORENSIS (Mentor barberry)		●	●		●			●			●			●	●		●		●				●	
BERBERIS THUNBERGII (Japanese barberry)		●	●		●			●			●			●	●		●		●				●	
BERBERIS THUNBERGII ATROPURPUREA (red-leaved Japanese barberry)		●	●		●			●			●			●	●		●		●				●	
BERBERIS THUNBERGII ERECTA (truehedge columnberry)		●	●		●			●			●			●	●		●		●				●	
BERBERIS THUNBERGII MINOR (box barberry)	●	●			●			●			●			●	●		●		●				●	
BUDDLEIA ALTERNIFOLIA (fountain butterfly bush)		●				●	●		●			●		●	●			●					●	
BUDDLEIA DAVIDII (orange-eyed butterfly bush)		●	●			●	●		●			●	●					●					●	
CAESALPINIA PULCHERRIMA (Barbados pride)		●	●		●	●				●		●							●		●		●	●
CALLICARPA DICHOTOMA (purple beauty-berry)	●							●				●				●	●		●				●	●
CALLICARPA GIRALDIANA (Girald beauty-berry)	●											●				●	●		●				●	●
CALLICARPA JAPONICA (Japanese beauty-berry)	●											●					●		●				●	●
CALYCANTHUS FLORIDUS (sweet shrub)		●				●			●		●						●	●	●				●	●
CARAGANA ARBORESCENS (Siberian pea tree)			●		●				●		●			●	●				●		●		●	
CARAGANA ARBORESCENS LORBERGII (Lorberg's pea tree)		●			●				●		●			●	●				●		●		●	
CARAGANA ARBORESCENS PENDULA (weeping Siberian pea tree)		●			●				●		●			●	●				●		●		●	
CARYOPTERIS CLANDONENSIS (bluebeard)	●						●	●					●						●				●	
CARYOPTERIS CLANDONENSIS 'HEAVENLY BLUE' (bluebeard)	●						●	●					●										●	
CERCIS CHINENSIS (Chinese redbud)		●	●			●		●			●								●					●
CHAENOMELES HYBRIDS (hybrid flowering quince)	●	●		●		●			●		●			●	●		●		●				●	
CHAENOMELES JAPONICA (Japanese quince)	●					●				●	●						●		●				●	
CHAENOMELES JAPONICA ALPINA (alpine Japanese quince)	●					●			●		●						●		●				●	
CHAENOMELES SPECIOSA (flowering quince)		●		●		●				●	●			●	●		●		●				●	
CLETHRA ALNIFOLIA (summer sweet)		●		●				●				●						●		●		●	●	●
CLETHRA ALNIFOLIA ROSEA (pink summer sweet)		●				●		●				●						●		●		●	●	●
COLUTEA ARBORESCENS (bladder senna)		●	●		●			●			●	●	●		●		●						●	
COMPTONIA PEREGRINA (sweet fern)	●	●														●		●	●		●	●	●	●
CORNUS ALBA (Tatarian dogwood)		●	●	●				●			●						●		●				●	●
CORNUS ALBA ARGENTEO-MARGINATA (silver-edged dogwood)		●	●	●				●			●						●		●				●	●
CORNUS ALBA SIBIRICA (Siberian dogwood)		●	●	●				●			●						●		●				●	●
CORNUS ALBA SPAETHII (yellow-edged dogwood)		●	●	●				●			●						●		●				●	●
CORNUS MAS (cornelian cherry)		●			●			●			●						●						●	●
CORNUS MAS AUREO-ELEGANTISSIMA (cornelian cherry)		●			●			●			●						●		●				●	●
CORNUS MAS FLAVA (yellow-fruited cornelian cherry)		●			●			●			●						●						●	●
CORNUS SERICEA (red osier dogwood)		●	●	●				●			●						●			●			●	●
CORNUS SERICEA FLAVIRAMEA (yellow-twigged dogwood)		●	●	●				●			●						●			●			●	●
CORNUS SERICEA KELSEYI (Kelsey dogwood)	●			●				●			●						●			●			●	●
CORYLOPSIS GLABRESCENS (fragrant winter hazel)		●			●			●			●							●	●			●	●	●
CORYLOPSIS PAUCIFLORA (buttercup winter hazel)		●			●			●			●							●	●			●	●	●
CORYLOPSIS SPICATA (spike winter hazel)	●	●			●			●			●							●	●			●	●	●

* Plants listed may have distinctively shaped or colored leaves, or leaves that turn notable colors in fall, or both.

** Characteristics apply only to varieties recommended in the encyclopedia entry.

	PLANT HEIGHT			FLOWER COLOR				BLOSSOM SIZE			FLOWER SEASONS			SPECIAL USES			OTHER TRAITS			SOIL NEEDS			LIGHT	
	Under 3 feet	3 to 6 feet	Over 6 feet	White	Yellow-orange	Pink-red	Blue-purple	Under 1 inch	1 to 2 inches	Over 2 inches	Spring	Summer	Fall	Informal hedge	Formal hedge	Ground cover	Decorative fruit	Notable fragrance	Notable foliage *	Moist to wet	Dry	Acid	Sun	Shade
CORYLUS AVELLANA AUREA (golden-leaved hazelnut)		●				●		●	●								●		●		●		●	●
CORYLUS AVELLANA CONTORTA (curly hazelnut)		●				●		●	●								●		●		●		●	●
CORYLUS MAXIMA PURPUREA (purple-leaved hazelnut)		●				●		●	●								●		●		●		●	●
COTINUS COGGYGRIA (smoke tree)		●			●	●	●					●					●		●				●	
COTINUS COGGYGRIA 'NOTCUTT' (Notcutt smoke tree)		●				●	●					●					●		●				●	
COTINUS OBOVATUS (American smoke tree)		●				●	●					●					●		●				●	
COTONEASTER ADPRESSA PRAECOX (early cotoneaster)	●					●		●			●					●	●		●		●		●	
COTONEASTER APICULATA (cranberry cotoneaster)	●					●		●			●					●	●		●		●		●	
COTONEASTER DIELSIANA (Diel's cotoneaster)		●				●		●			●					●	●		●		●		●	
COTONEASTER DIVARICATA (spreading cotoneaster)		●				●		●			●					●	●		●		●		●	
COTONEASTER MULTIFLORA (many-flowered cotoneaster)		●	●	●				●			●						●		●		●		●	
COTONEASTER RACEMIFLORA SOONGORICA (Sungari cotoneaster)		●	●	●				●			●						●		●		●		●	
CYTISUS HYBRIDS (hybrid broom)	●	●	●	●	●	●	●		●							●							●	
CYTISUS KEWENSIS (Kew broom)	●				●				●		●				●								●	
CYTISUS NIGRICANS (spike broom)		●			●				●			●											●	
CYTISUS PRAECOX (Warminster broom)		●			●			●			●												●	
CYTISUS PRAECOX ALBUS (white Warminster broom)		●		●				●			●												●	
CYTISUS PURPUREUS (purple broom)	●					●	●	●			●												●	
CYTISUS SCOPARIUS (Scotch broom)		●			●			●			●												●	
DAPHNE GENKWA (lilac daphne)	●					●	●	●			●							●	●				●	●
DAPHNE MEZEREUM (February daphne)	●					●		●			●							●	●				●	●
DAPHNE MEZEREUM ALBUM (white February daphne)	●			●				●			●							●	●				●	●
DEUTZIA GRACILIS (slender deutzia)	●	●		●				●			●				●					●	●		●	●
DEUTZIA GRACILIS ROSEA (pink slender deutzia)	●	●				●		●			●				●					●	●		●	●
DEUTZIA LEMOINEI (Lemoine deutzia)		●	●	●				●			●									●	●		●	●
DEUTZIA ROSEA EXIMIA (pinkchoice deutzia)		●				●		●			●									●	●		●	●
DEUTZIA ROSEA 'PINK POMPON' (Pink Pompon deutzia)		●				●		●			●									●	●		●	●
DEUTZIA SCABRA CANDIDISSIMA (snowflake deutzia)		●	●	●								●								●	●		●	●
DEUTZIA SCABRA 'PRIDE OF ROCHESTER' (fuzzy deutzia)		●	●	●				●				●								●	●		●	●
ELAEAGNUS ANGUSTIFOLIA (Russian olive)		●			●			●				●				●	●	●	●		●		●	
ELAEAGNUS ARGENTEA (silverberry)		●			●				●			●					●	●	●				●	
ELAEAGNUS MULTIFLORA (cherry elaeagnus)		●			●				●			●					●	●	●				●	
ELAEAGNUS UMBELLATA (autumn elaeagnus)		●			●				●			●					●	●	●				●	
ENKIANTHUS CAMPANULATUS (redvein enkianthus)		●	●			●		●			●							●	●			●	●	●
ENKIANTHUS CAMPANULATUS ALBIFLORUS (white redvein enkianthus)		●	●	●				●			●							●	●			●	●	●
ENKIANTHUS PERULATUS (white enkianthus)		●		●				●			●							●	●			●	●	●
ERYTHRINA BIDWILLII (Bidwill's coral tree)		●				●			●		●							●	●				●	●
EUONYMUS ALATUS (winged euonymus)		●															●		●				●	●
EUONYMUS ALATUS COMPACTUS (dwarf winged euonymus)	●														●		●		●				●	●
EUONYMUS AMERICANUS (strawberry bush)		●															●		●				●	●
EUONYMUS EUROPAEUS ALBUS (white European spindle tree)		●															●		●				●	●
EUONYMUS EUROPAEUS ALDENHAMENSIS (Aldenham spindle tree)		●															●		●				●	●
EUONYMUS EUROPAEUS INTERMEDIUS (intermediate spindle tree)	●														●		●		●				●	●
EUONYMUS HAMILTONIANUS YEDOENSIS (Yeddo euonymus)		●															●		●				●	●
EXOCHORDA GIRALDII WILSONII (Wilson pearlbush)		●	●	●					●		●									●	●		●	
EXOCHORDA MACRANTHA 'THE BRIDE' (The Bride pearlbush)	●			●					●		●									●	●		●	
EXOCHORDA RACEMOSA (common pearlbush)		●	●	●					●		●									●	●		●	
FORSYTHIA 'ARNOLD DWARF' (Arnold Dwarf forsythia)	●															●			●	●	●		●	●

** COTINUS COGGYGRIA

147

	PLANT HEIGHT			FLOWER COLOR				BLOSSOM SIZE			FLOWER SEASONS			SPECIAL USES			OTHER TRAITS			SOIL NEEDS			LIGHT	
	Under 3 feet	3 to 6 feet	Over 6 feet	White	Yellow-orange	Pink-red	Blue-purple	Under 1 inch	1 to 2 inches	Over 2 inches	Spring	Summer	Fall	Informal hedge	Formal hedge	Ground cover	Decorative fruit	Notable fragrance	Notable foliage *	Moist to wet	Dry	Acid	Sun	Shade
FORSYTHIA 'ARNOLD GIANT' (Arnold Giant forsythia)		●			●				●		●			●					●	●			●	●
** FORSYTHIA INTERMEDIA (border forsythia)		●			●				●		●			●					●	●			●	●
FORSYTHIA INTERMEDIA 'BEATRIX FARRAND' (border forsythia)		●			●				●	●	●			●					●	●			●	●
FORSYTHIA OVATA (Korean forsythia)		●																	●	●			●	●
FORSYTHIA SUSPENSA FORTUNEI (Fortune's weeping forsythia)		●																	●	●			●	●
FORSYTHIA SUSPENSA SIEBOLDII (Siebold's weeping forsythia)	●																		●	●			●	●
FORSYTHIA VIRIDISSIMA 'BROXENSIS' (green-stemmed forsythia)	●				●			●			●					●			●	●	●		●	●
FOTHERGILLA GARDENII (dwarf fothergilla)	●		●					●			●							●	●			●	●	
FOTHERGILLA MAJOR (large fothergilla)		●	●					●			●							●	●			●	●	
FOTHERGILLA MONTICOLA (Alabama fothergilla)	●		●					●			●							●	●			●	●	
FRANKLINIA ALATAMAHA (franklinia)		●	●	●					●				●				●	●	●			●	●	●
FUCHSIA MAGELLANICA (Magellan fuchsia)	●					●	●	●				●	●						●	●			●	●
HAMAMELIS 'ARNOLD PROMISE' (Arnold Promise witch hazel)		●			●				●		●							●	●				●	●
HAMAMELIS MOLLIS (Chinese witch hazel)		●			●				●		●							●	●				●	●
HAMAMELIS VERNALIS (vernal witch hazel)		●			●				●		●							●	●				●	●
HAMAMELIS VIRGINIANA (common witch hazel)		●			●				●				●					●	●				●	●
HIBISCUS SYRIACUS (rose of Sharon)		●	●	●		●	●			●		●	●							●			●	●
HIBISCUS SYRIACUS 'BLUE BIRD' (Blue Bird rose of Sharon)		●					●			●		●	●							●			●	●
HIPPOPHAE RHAMNOIDES (sea buckthorn)		●			●						●					●				●	●		●	
HYDRANGEA ARBORESCENS GRANDIFLORA (hills-of-snow hydrangea)	●		●	●						●		●	●							●			●	●
HYDRANGEA MACROPHYLLA (big-leaved hydrangea)	●		●	●		●	●			●		●								●	●		●	●
HYDRANGEA MACROPHYLLA SERRATA ACUMINATA (lace cap hydrangea)	●			●		●	●			●		●								●			●	●
HYDRANGEA PANICULATA GRANDIFLORA (peegee hydrangea)	●	●	●	●		●				●		●	●							●			●	●
HYDRANGEA QUERCIFOLIA (oak-leaved hydrangea)		●		●						●		●							●	●			●	●
HYPERICUM FRONDOSUM (golden St.-John's-wort)	●				●				●			●							●				●	●
HYPERICUM KALMIANUM (Kalm St.-John's-wort)	●				●				●			●											●	●
HYPERICUM PROLIFICUM (shrubby St.-John's-wort)	●				●		●					●	●										●	●
ILEX LAEVIGATA (smooth winterberry)		●	●					●				●					●			●			●	●
ILEX VERTICILLATA (winterberry)		●	●					●				●					●		●	●			●	●
INDIGOFERA KIRILOWII (Kirilow indigo)		●				●		●				●				●					●		●	●
JASMINUM NUDIFLORUM (winter jasmine)	●	●	●		●				●		●										●		●	
KERRIA JAPONICA (kerria)		●			●				●		●	●	●						●	●	●		●	●
KERRIA JAPONICA PLENIFLORA (globeflower kerria)	●	●			●				●		●	●	●						●	●	●		●	●
KOLKWITZIA AMABILIS (beauty bush)		●				●		●			●						●				●		●	●
LAGERSTROEMIA INDICA (crape myrtle)	●	●	●	●		●	●			●		●		●					●		●		●	●
LESPEDEZA BICOLOR (shrub bush clover)	●	●				●	●	●				●	●							●	●		●	●
LESPEDEZA SIEBOLDII (purple bush clover)	●	●				●	●	●				●	●							●	●		●	●
LIGUSTRUM AMURENSE (Amur privet)		●	●	●				●				●		●	●		●			●	●		●	●
LIGUSTRUM IBOLIUM (Ibolium privet)		●	●	●				●				●		●	●		●			●	●		●	●
LIGUSTRUM OBTUSIFOLIUM (border privet)		●	●	●				●				●		●	●		●			●	●		●	●
LIGUSTRUM OBTUSIFOLIUM REGELIANUM (Regel privet)	●		●	●				●				●		●	●		●			●	●		●	●
LIGUSTRUM OVALIFOLIUM (California privet)		●	●	●				●				●		●	●		●			●	●		●	●
LIGUSTRUM OVALIFOLIUM AUREUM (yellow-edged California privet)		●	●	●				●				●		●	●		●		●	●	●		●	●
LIGUSTRUM VICARYI (Vicary golden privet)		●	●	●				●				●		●	●		●		●	●	●		●	●
LIGUSTRUM VULGARE (common privet)		●	●	●				●				●		●	●		●			●	●		●	●
LINDERA BENZOIN (spicebush)		●	●		●			●			●						●	●	●	●		●	●	●
LONICERA FRAGRANTISSIMA (winter honeysuckle)		●	●	●				●			●						●	●		●	●		●	●
LONICERA KOROLKOWII (blue-leaved honeysuckle)			●			●		●			●						●		●	●	●		●	●

Plants listed may have distinctively shaped or colored leaves, or leaves that turn notable colors in fall, or both.

**Characteristics apply only to varieties recommended in the encyclopedia entry.*

	PLANT HEIGHT			FLOWER COLOR				BLOSSOM SIZE			FLOWER SEASONS			SPECIAL USES			OTHER TRAITS			SOIL NEEDS			LIGHT	
	Under 3 feet	3 to 6 feet	Over 6 feet	White	Yellow-orange	Pink-red	Blue-purple	Under 1 inch	1 to 2 inches	Over 2 inches	Spring	Summer	Fall	Informal hedge	Formal hedge	Ground cover	Decorative fruit	Notable fragrance	Notable foliage *	Moist to wet	Dry	Acid	Sun	Shade
LONICERA MAACKII (Amur honeysuckle)		•	•				•		•		•			•			•	•		•	•		•	•
LONICERA MORROWII (Morrow honeysuckle)		•	•				•		•		•			•			•	•		•	•		•	•
LONICERA MORROWII XANTHOCARPA (yellow-fruited Morrow honeysuckle)		•	•				•		•		•			•			•	•		•	•		•	•
LONICERA TATARICA (Tatarian honeysuckle)		•	•			•		•			•			•			•	•		•	•		•	•
LONICERA TATARICA SIBIRICA (Siberian honeysuckle)		•				•		•			•			•			•	•		•	•		•	•
LONICERA TATARICA ZABELII (Zabel's Tatarian honeysuckle)		•				•		•			•			•			•	•		•	•		•	•
LONICERA XYLOSTEUM 'CLAVEY'S DWARF' (honeysuckle)	•					•		•			•			•		•	•	•	•		•	•		•	•
MYRICA PENSYLVANICA (bayberry)		•	•											•	•	•	•		•	•	•	•	•	
PAEONIA SUFFRUTICOSA (tree peony)		•		•	•	•	•			•	•						•	•	•				•	
PHILADELPHUS CORONARIUS (sweet mock orange)		•	•	•					•			•						•			•	•	•	
PHILADELPHUS LEMOINEI 'BELLE ETOILE' (Lemoine mock orange)		•		•					•			•						•			•	•	•	
PHILADELPHUS LEMOINEI HYBRIDS (Lemoine mock orange)		•	•	•				•	•	•		•						•			•	•	•	
PHILADELPHUS VIRGINALIS (virginalis mock orange)	•	•	•	•					•			•						•			•	•	•	
PHOTINIA VILLOSA (Oriental photinia)		•	•					•			•						•		•				•	•
PLUMERIA RUBRA (frangipani)		•	•	•	•	•			•		•	•	•					•			•	•	•	•
POTENTILLA ARBUSCULA (bush cinquefoil)	•	•		•	•			•				•	•								•	•	•	
POTENTILLA ARBUSCULA 'SUTTER'S GOLD' (bush cinquefoil)	•	•			•			•				•	•								•	•	•	
POTENTILLA FRUTICOSA (bush cinquefoil)	•	•		•	•			•				•	•								•	•	•	
PRUNUS BESSEYI (western sand cherry)		•	•	•				•			•						•				•	•	•	
PRUNUS CISTENA (purple-leaved sand cherry)		•	•			•		•			•						•		•	•	•		•	
PRUNUS GLANDULOSA (dwarf flowering almond)		•		•		•		•			•									•	•		•	
PRUNUS MARITIMA (beach plum)		•			•			•			•						•			•	•		•	
PRUNUS TOMENTOSA (Nanking cherry)		•	•		•			•			•						•			•	•		•	
PRUNUS TRILOBA (flowering almond)		•				•		•			•						•		•	•	•		•	
PUNICA GRANATUM (pomegranate)	•	•	•	•	•	•			•	•		•	•				•		•	•	•		•	
PUNICA GRANATUM NANA (dwarf pomegranate)	•					•					•	•								•	•		•	
RHAMNUS FRANGULA (alder buckthorn)		•															•		•	•	•		•	•
RHAMNUS FRANGULA COLUMNARIS 'NEW TALLHEDGE' (New Tallhedge alder buckthorn)		•												•	•		•		•	•	•		•	•
RHODODENDRON ARBORESCENS (sweet azalea)		•		•		•			•			•					•	•	•			•	•	•
RHODODENDRON CALENDULACEUM (flame azalea)		•			•	•			•			•						•			•	•	•	•
RHODODENDRON 'EXBURY HYBRIDS' (Exbury Hybrid azalea)		•		•	•	•				•		•					•	•	•			•	•	•
RHODODENDRON GANDAVENSE (Ghent azalea)		•	•	•	•	•			•		•								•			•	•	•
RHODODENDRON 'KNAP HILL HYBRIDS' (Knap Hill Hybrid azalea)		•		•	•	•			•	•							•	•	•			•	•	•
RHODODENDRON KOSTERIANUM HYBRIDS (Mollis Hybrid azalea)		•		•	•	•			•	•									•			•	•	•
RHODODENDRON MUCRONULATUM (Korean rhododendron)		•			•	•		•			•								•			•	•	•
RHODODENDRON NUDIFLORUM (pinxter-bloom)		•		•		•			•			•							•			•	•	•
RHODODENDRON ROSEUM (roseshell azalea)		•				•			•			•						•				•	•	•
RHODODENDRON SCHLIPPENBACHII (royal azalea)		•				•			•	•		•							•	•			•	•
RHODODENDRON VASEYI (pinkshell azalea)		•	•			•			•			•							•	•			•	•
RHODODENDRON VISCOSUM (swamp azalea)		•	•	•					•			•					•		•	•	•		•	•
RHODODENDRON YEDOENSE (Yodogawa azalea)	•					•			•		•								•	•	•		•	•
RHODODENDRON YEDOENSE POUKHANENSE (Korean Yodogawa azalea)	•					•			•		•								•	•	•		•	•
RHODOTYPOS SCANDENS (jetbead)		•		•					•	•		•	•				•		•	•	•		•	•
RHUS AROMATICA (fragrant sumac)	•	•														•	•	•	•		•		•	
RHUS COPALLINA (shining sumac)		•														•	•		•		•		•	
RHUS GLABRA (smooth sumac)			•														•		•	•			•	
RHUS GLABRA LACINIATA (cut-leaved smooth sumac)			•														•		•	•			•	
RHUS TYPHINA (staghorn sumac)			•														•		•	•			•	

CHARACTERISTICS OF FLOWERING SHRUBS: CONTINUED

	PLANT HEIGHT			FLOWER COLOR				BLOSSOM SIZE			FLOWER SEASONS			SPECIAL USES			OTHER TRAITS			SOIL NEEDS			LIGHT	
	Under 3 feet	3 to 6 feet	Over 6 feet	White	Yellow-orange	Pink-red	Blue-purple	Under 1 inch	1 to 2 inches	Over 2 inches	Spring	Summer	Fall	Informal hedge	Formal hedge	Ground cover	Decorative fruit	Notable fragrance	Notable foliage *	Moist to wet	Dry	Acid	Sun	Shade
RHUS TYPHINA DISSECTA (shred-leaved staghorn sumac)		●															●		●		●		●	
RHUS TYPHINA LACINIATA (cut-leaved staghorn sumac)		●															●		●		●		●	
ROBINIA HISPIDA (rose acacia)		●				●		●			●	●				●							●	
ROBINIA HISPIDA MACROPHYLLA (smooth rose acacia)		●				●		●			●	●				●							●	
ROSA ALBA INCARNATA (Great Maiden's Blush rose)		●	●			●			●		●						●	●					●	
ROSA CENTIFOLIA (cabbage rose)		●				●			●		●							●					●	
ROSA HARISONII (Harison's Yellow rose)		●	●		●			●			●							●					●	
ROSA HUGONIS (Father Hugo's rose)		●			●			●			●								●				●	
ROSA RUGOSA (Japanese rose)		●		●		●			●		●	●	●				●	●	●				●	
SALIX CAPREA (goat willow)		●				●		●										●	●	●				
SALIX DISCOLOR (pussy willow)		●	●				●	●											●	●				
SALIX GRACILISTYLA (rose gold pussy willow)		●				●		●											●	●				
SALIX PURPUREA GRACILIS (dwarf purple osier)	●														●				●	●			●	
SAMBUCUS CAERULEA (blue elder)		●	●	●								●					●		●	●			●	
SAMBUCUS CANADENSIS (American elder)		●	●	●								●					●						●	
SAMBUCUS CANADENSIS AUREA (golden elder)		●	●	●								●					●		●	●			●	
SAMBUCUS CANADENSIS LACINIATA (cut-leaved elderberry)		●	●	●								●					●		●	●			●	
SORBARIA AITCHISONII (Kashmir false spirea)		●	●				●					●							●				●	●
SORBARIA SORBIFOLIA (Ural false spirea)		●		●			●					●							●				●	●
SPIRAEA ARGUTA (garland spirea)		●		●				●			●			●				●	●				●	●
SPIRAEA ARGUTA COMPACTA (dwarf garland spirea)		●		●				●			●			●				●	●				●	●
SPIRAEA BILLARDII (Billard spirea)		●				●		●				●						●	●				●	●
SPIRAEA BUMALDA 'ANTHONY WATERER' (Bumalda spirea)	●					●		●				●						●	●	●			●	●
SPIRAEA BUMALDA 'FROBEL' (Frobel Bumalda spirea)		●				●		●				●						●	●	●			●	●
SPIRAEA CANTONIENSIS (Reeve's spirea)		●	●					●			●			●				●	●	●			●	●
SPIRAEA JAPONICA ALPINA (alpine Japanese spirea)	●					●		●				●						●	●	●			●	●
SPIRAEA JAPONICA ATROSANGUINEA (Mikado spirea)		●				●		●				●						●	●	●			●	●
SPIRAEA NIPPONICA 'SNOWBOUND' (Snowbound boxwood spirea)	●		●					●			●	●						●	●				●	●
SPIRAEA PRUNIFOLIA (bridal wreath)		●	●	●				●			●							●	●	●			●	●
SPIRAEA THUNBERGII (Thunberg spirea)		●		●				●			●							●	●	●	●		●	●
SPIRAEA VANHOUTTEI (Vanhoutte spirea)		●	●	●				●			●							●	●	●			●	●
STEPHANANDRA INCISA (cut-leaved stephanandra)		●		●								●		●				●	●	●	●		●	●
STEPHANANDRA INCISA CRISPA (dwarf cut-leaved stephanandra)	●		●					●				●	●		●			●	●	●	●		●	●
STEWARTIA MALACODENDRON (Virginia stewartia)		●	●	●						●		●							●	●		●	●	●
STEWARTIA OVATA (mountain stewartia)		●	●	●						●		●							●			●	●	●
STEWARTIA OVATA GRANDIFLORA (showy stewartia)		●	●	●						●		●							●			●	●	●
SYMPHORICARPOS ALBUS LAEVIGATUS (snowberry)		●				●		●				●	●			●			●	●	●		●	●
SYMPHORICARPOS CHENAULTII (Chenault coralberry)	●					●		●				●	●	●		●			●	●	●		●	●
SYMPHORICARPOS ORBICULATUS (Indian currant)		●			●			●				●	●			●			●	●	●		●	●
SYMPLOCOS PANICULATA (sapphireberry)		●	●	●				●			●						●	●				●	●	●
SYRINGA CHINENSIS (Chinese lilac)		●				●	●	●			●								●				●	●
SYRINGA JOSIKAEA 'SYLVIA' (Sylvia Hungarian lilac)		●			●		●	●			●								●				●	●
SYRINGA MEYERI (Meyer's lilac)	●					●	●	●			●								●				●	●
SYRINGA MICROPHYLLA SUPERBA (daphne lilac)		●				●		●			●	●	●						●				●	●
SYRINGA PERSICA (Persian lilac)		●				●	●	●			●								●				●	●
** SYRINGA PRESTONIAE (Preston lilac)		●			●			●			●								●				●	●
SYRINGA VELUTINA 'MISS KIM' (Miss Kim Korean lilac)	●					●	●	●			●		●						●				●	●
SYRINGA VILLOSA (late lilac)		●				●	●	●			●								●				●	●

* Plants listed may have distinctively shaped or colored leaves, or leaves that turn notable colors in fall, or both.

** Characteristics apply only to varieties recommended in the encyclopedia entry.

	PLANT HEIGHT			FLOWER COLOR				BLOSSOM SIZE			FLOWER SEASONS			SPECIAL USES			OTHER TRAITS			SOIL NEEDS			LIGHT	
	Under 3 feet	3 to 6 feet	Over 6 feet	White	Yellow-orange	Pink-red	Blue-purple	Under 1 inch	1 to 2 inches	Over 2 inches	Spring	Summer	Fall	Informal hedge	Formal hedge	Ground cover	Decorative fruit	Notable fragrance	Notable foliage	Moist to wet *	Dry	Acid	Sun	Shade
SYRINGA VULGARIS (common lilac)		●	●	●	●	●	●		●		●							●					●	●
SYRINGA VULGARIS 'MOONGLOW' (Moonglow common lilac)		●		●		●			●		●							●					●	●
** TAMARIX HISPIDA (Kashgar tamarisk)	●	●				●			●			●	●						●				●	
TAMARIX ODESSANA (Odessa tamarisk)		●				●			●			●							●				●	
TAMARIX PARVIFLORA (small-flowered tamarisk)		●				●			●		●	●							●				●	
TAMARIX PENTANDRA (five-stamened tamarisk)		●				●			●			●							●				●	
TAMARIX PENTANDRA RUBRA (five-stamened tamarisk)		●				●			●			●							●				●	
VACCINIUM CORYMBOSUM (high-bush blueberry)		●	●	●				●					●				●		●	●		●	●	●
VIBURNUM BURKWOODII (Burkwood viburnum)		●	●	●					●		●			●			●	●	●	●			●	●
VIBURNUM CARLCEPHALUM (fragrant snowball)		●	●	●					●		●			●			●	●	●	●			●	●
VIBURNUM CARLESII (Korean spice viburnum)		●		●					●		●			●			●	●	●	●			●	●
VIBURNUM CARLESII COMPACTUM (Korean spice viburnum)	●	●		●					●		●			●			●	●	●	●			●	●
VIBURNUM CASSINOIDES (withe rod)		●		●					●			●		●			●		●	●			●	●
VIBURNUM DENTATUM (arrowwood)		●	●	●					●			●		●			●		●	●			●	●
VIBURNUM DILATATUM (linden viburnum)		●	●	●					●			●		●			●		●	●			●	●
VIBURNUM DILATATUM XANTHOCARPUM (linden viburnum)		●	●	●					●			●					●		●	●			●	●
VIBURNUM LANTANA (wayfaring tree)		●	●	●					●		●			●			●		●	●			●	●
VIBURNUM LENTAGO (nannyberry)		●	●	●					●		●			●			●		●	●			●	●
VIBURNUM OPULUS (European cranberry bush)		●	●	●					●		●			●			●		●	●			●	●
VIBURNUM OPULUS COMPACTUM (European cranberry bush)	●		●	●					●		●			●			●		●	●			●	●
VIBURNUM OPULUS NANA (dwarf European cranberry bush)	●															●			●	●			●	●
VIBURNUM OPULUS ROSEUM (European snowball)		●	●	●					●		●								●	●			●	●
VIBURNUM OPULUS XANTHOCARPUM (yellow-fruited European cranberry bush)		●	●	●					●		●						●		●	●			●	●
VIBURNUM PLICATUM (Japanese snowball)	●	●	●	●					●		●			●			●		●	●			●	●
VIBURNUM PLICATUM TOMENTOSUM (doublefile viburnum)	●	●	●	●		●	●		●		●			●			●		●	●			●	●
VIBURNUM PLICATUM TOMENTOSUM MARIESII (Marie's doublefile viburnum)	●	●	●	●						●	●			●			●		●	●			●	●
VIBURNUM PRUNIFOLIUM (black haw)		●	●	●					●		●						●		●	●			●	●
VIBURNUM SIEBOLDII (Siebold viburnum)		●	●	●					●		●						●		●	●			●	●
VIBURNUM TRILOBUM (American cranberry bush)		●	●	●					●		●			●			●		●	●			●	●
VIBURNUM TRILOBUM COMPACTUM (American cranberry bush)	●	●	●	●					●		●						●		●	●			●	●
VITEX AGNUS-CASTUS (chaste tree)	●	●	●			●	●	●				●	●					●	●				●	
WEIGELA FLORIDA (old-fashioned weigela)		●			●	●			●		●									●			●	●
WEIGELA HYBRIDS (hybrid weigela)		●			●	●			●		●									●			●	●
WEIGELA 'VANICEK' (Vanicek weigela)		●				●			●		●									●			●	●

A guide to pests and diseases

In the right soil and climate, shrubs are vigorous enough to withstand most pests and diseases. Even so, trouble can strike occasionally and prompt action is imperative to keep infestations under control.

Generally the best protection is prevention. Keeping shrubs healthy increases their resistance. Cleaning the garden eliminates the weeds and debris in which many pests breed. Pruning removes the weak or damaged branches most vulnerable to attack. You can also call on birds and beneficial insects for help,

PEST	DESCRIPTION	METHODS OF CONTROL
	APHIDS These tiny pear-shaped plant lice make massed attacks on stems, leaves and buds, piercing tissues with their needled beaks and sucking out the juices. The first sign of infestation may be curled leaves. Later, you will see the so-called honeydew that aphids excrete on foliage and there may be a cover of black sooty mold on the afflicted parts of the plant. If aphids are left unchecked, they stunt growth, deforming the shrub. They also may carry virus diseases and fire-blight bacteria. VULNERABLE SHRUBS: BROOM, BUSH CINQUEFOIL, CRAPE MYRTLE, ELDER, FLOWERING QUINCE, ROSE ACACIA, SPIREA, VIBURNUM	Watch for aphids in early spring and knock them off plants with a stream of water from a garden hose before colonies build up. If they persist, spray with pyrethrum, rotenone or malathion.
	LILAC BORERS Borers cannot be seen as they eat away inside stems, but telltale sawdust around the holes and on the ground indicates their presence. The kind that attacks lilacs is the larva of a wasplike moth that lays its eggs at the base of main stems or on bark wounds in late spring. The borers hatch in summer, lie dormant in winter and eat again in spring. They grow about an inch long before pushing through the bark in late spring or summer to become moths. Severely infested branches wilt and eventually break off or die. VULNERABLE SHRUBS: LILAC AND, OCCASIONALLY, PRIVET	In early spring, inject into the holes a borer-killing preparation sold at garden centers or probe the holes with flexible wire to kill the borers; then trim bark wounds smooth and paint with tree-wound dressing. When moths appear, spray the bark with methoxychlor to prevent them from laying eggs.
	SCALES Scales are seldom more than $\frac{1}{8}$ inch long, but propagate so rapidly they quickly encrust a branch. In many species, like the San Jose scale (illustrated), the tiny, wingless young soon develop flat, waxy shells, which they shed as they grow; in other species they remain soft-bodied. Adult males are winged insects; the wingless females do the most damage, settling on leaves and stems to suck the sap. The bark around scales turns red; scales also produce honeydew. Affected shrubs yellow, lose foliage and may die. VULNERABLE SHRUBS: CORALBERRY, DAPHNE, EUONYMUS, LILAC	Spray dormant infested plants in early spring with lime-sulfur solution or dormant oil spray. (Do not use lime sulfur where it will fall on painted surfaces; it will discolor them.) During the growing season, spray with malathion or diazinon in both mid- and late spring. Prune out badly encrusted branches.
	CATERPILLARS Shrubs may fall prey to many kinds of leaf-eating caterpillars at any time during the growing season, but especially in spring when the eastern tent caterpillar (illustrated) hatches. Among such insect forms with a special taste for shrubs are the familiar cankerworm or inchworm and the gypsy moth's larvae—as well as hickory horned devils, which grow up to 5 inches long and are the largest caterpillars native to North America. Any of these leaf eaters can tatter foliage, and repeated attacks can kill plants. VULNERABLE SHRUBS: ELDER, HAZELNUT, LILAC, PRIVET, SUMAC	Apply dormant oil spray in early spring to smother unhatched eggs deposited on twigs or in the bark. If caterpillars appear, spray the foliage in spring and again in midsummer with malathion or carbaryl. If tent caterpillars strike, crumple their nests into newspapers and destroy them.

for pests have natural enemies—house wrens and catbirds feed on caterpillars, ladybug beetles destroy aphids, scales and mealy bugs.

Some shrubs profit from a "dormant oil" spray, which is prepared by mixing water with a highly refined horticultural grade of petroleum oil and is applied in the plant's dormant stage before the buds open in spring. Although the oil itself is not poisonous, it is effective in smothering insect eggs, preventing them from hatching. Spray on a mild, dry, sunny day when temperatures are between 45° and 85° F.

Chemical sprays should be used only for the plants and pests specified, and only in the season and dosage recommended on their labels. Never spray chemicals when it is windy; do not smoke while spraying and wash your hands afterward before eating or drinking. The chemicals that are suggested by their common names in the chart below are widely available in convenient sizes and under various brand names at garden supply stores.

DISEASE	DESCRIPTION	METHODS OF CONTROL
	FUNGUS LEAF SPOT The most common of all plant diseases, fungus leaf spot generally strikes during rainy or humid periods. Thousands of types of fungi may cause the spots, and the size, shape and color vary according to the fungus involved. The spots are clearly outlined at first but grow together into large blotches and finally kill the foliage. Often the spots are dotted with black spores from which these fungi multiply, and occasionally the centers of the spots will fall out, leaving holes. VULNERABLE SHRUBS: AZALEA, BEAUTY-BERRY, BROOM, BUTTONBUSH, COTONEASTER, DAPHNE, EUONYMUS, HYDRANGEA, SUMAC, VIBURNUM	Spray infected plants with captan, ferbam, folpet, maneb or zineb at the beginning of the growing season and repeat every two weeks until the plants bloom. Cut off and burn infected foliage. When watering shrubs, avoid splashing the leaves.
	FIRE BLIGHT As the name suggests, this bacterial disease makes blossoms and leaves shrivel and blacken suddenly as if they had been seared by fire. The bacteria attack in early spring—often carried by insects, rain, wind or even garden tools—and progress down the shoots into the bark where they form dark sunken cracks or cankers. In summer, the bacteria become dormant in the cankers, to return the following spring. VULNERABLE SHRUBS: CHOKEBERRY, COTONEASTER, FLOWERING ALMOND, FLOWERING QUINCE, PHOTINIA, SERVICEBERRY	Apply an antibiotic chemical spray such as streptomycin sulfate at four or five-day intervals during the blossoming period. Prune diseased branches when dry to stop the spread of bacteria, cutting 4 to 6 inches beyond the infected areas. Disinfect tools between cuts by dipping them in 70 per cent alcohol.
	CROWN GALLS The swollen growths known as crown galls occur on the crown of the plant near the soil line. They are rounded and rough-surfaced, and may be hard or spongy. Crown galls eventually become several inches in diameter and cause the plant to weaken and die. Most are caused by soil bacteria that enter the crown through wounds caused by spading, hoeing or grafting. VULNERABLE SHRUBS: EUONYMUS, FLOWERING QUINCE, FORSYTHIA, HAZELNUT, ROSE, RUSSIAN OLIVE, WEIGELA	Inspect nursery plants carefully before buying and reject any with suspicious bumps at the soil line. In the garden, dig up and burn infected shrubs and place new plants in a different location (the bacteria may live in the soil for several years). Avoid injuring shrubs when planting, cultivating or mowing lawns.
	POWDERY MILDEW This common fungus disease coats foliage with a white or gray mealy powder that generally is more unattractive than fatal, although it can wither and kill leaves or shrivel buds before they open. Powdery mildew attacks first in damp shaded spots or in crowded corners where air circulation is poor. It is most prevalent in late summer and early fall, when cool humid nights follow warm dry days. VULNERABLE SHRUBS: CRAPE MYRTLE, ELDER, EUONYMUS, HONEYSUCKLE, HYDRANGEA, LILAC, SERVICEBERRY, VIBURNUM	Spray shrubs at 10-day intervals, starting when mildew is first noticed, with dinocap, sulfur or folpet. Avoid late-afternoon sprinkling. Prune overgrown shrubs and remove superfluous plants if necessary to allow air to circulate freely.

Where and when flowering shrubs bloom

Although a few shrubs such as flowering quince can be grown almost anywhere in North America, the majority thrive only in particular regions. Most lilacs, for instance, do best in cold areas, while crape myrtles prefer Southern climates. To guide you to plants that flourish where you live, the preceding encyclopedia entries list growing zones numbered to correspond to the climate map below, which divides the U.S. and Canada into 10 regions according to depth of winter cold. The en- tries also give the seasons when flowers blossom, fruits ripen and leaves turn color, as well as when shrubs should be pruned and propagated. The actual times of the seasons vary from zone to zone; the golden burst of forsythia blossoms, for example, starts around February in Zone 9 but does not reach Zones 4 and 5 until March or April. The table at bottom lists the approximate dates for spring, summer and fall in each zone (except Zone 1, where flowering shrubs are not grown).

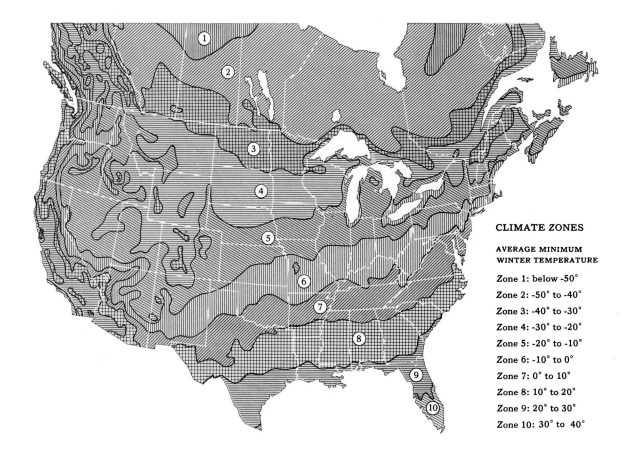

CLIMATE ZONES

AVERAGE MINIMUM WINTER TEMPERATURE

Zone 1: below -50°
Zone 2: -50° to -40°
Zone 3: -40° to -30°
Zone 4: -30° to -20°
Zone 5: -20° to -10°
Zone 6: -10° to 0°
Zone 7: 0° to 10°
Zone 8: 10° to 20°
Zone 9: 20° to 30°
Zone 10: 30° to 40°

FLOWERING SEASONS IN YOUR ZONE

ZONE	SPRING	SUMMER	FALL	ZONE
1	(flowering shrubs not grown)			1
2	Mid-April to mid-June	Mid-June through July	August to mid-September	2
3	Early April to mid-June	Mid-June through July	August to mid-September	3
4	Late March to mid-June	Mid-June to mid-August	Mid-August to mid-October	4
5	Mid-March through May	June through August	September to mid-October	5
6	Mid-March through May	June through August	September through October	6
7	Early March through May	June through August	September to mid-November	7
8	Mid-February to mid-May	Mid-May to mid-September	Mid-September to mid-November	8
9	Mid-January to mid-April	Mid-April through September	October to mid-December	9
10	January through March	April through September	October through December	10

Picture credits

The sources for the illustrations that appear in this book are shown below. Credits for the pictures from left to right are separated by semicolons, from top to bottom by dashes. Cover—Ruth McVaugh Allen. 4—Keith Martin courtesy James Underwood Crockett; Leonard Wolfe. 6—Humphrey Sutton. 11—Illustration by Allianora Rosse—U.S.D.A. 12 —Illustration by Allianora Rosse—Courtesy Daniel J. Foley. 13—Illustration by Allianora Rosse—J. F. Rock courtesy Arnold Arboretum, Harvard University. 14—Illustration by Allianora Rosse—U.S.D.A. 19,20—Clarence E. Lewis. 21—Clarence E. Lewis except bottom left P. Bruns courtesy Arnold Arboretum, Harvard University. 22—Clarence E. Lewis except bottom right Ruth McVaugh Allen. 23 —Dr. E. R. Degginger; Clarence E. Lewis—C. W. Cares; Ruth McVaugh Allen; Clarence E. Lewis. 24—Michael Irwin except bottom right Clarence E. Lewis. 25—Michael Irwin; Isabel Zucker—Clarence E. Lewis. 26—Clarence E. Lewis. 27—Clarence E. Lewis except bottom left Grant Heilman. 28—Robert T. Panuska. 29—Clarence E. Lewis except top right Ruth McVaugh Allen and bottom center James Underwood Crockett. 30—Clarence E. Lewis; Ruth McVaugh Allen—Thase Daniel; Clarence E. Lewis. 31—Clarence E. Lewis except top right Thase Daniel. 32—Dr. E. R. Degginger. 33—René Delbuguet except bottom right Brian Seed. 34 —Grant Heilman. 43—Brian Seed. 44—Thomas W. Martin from Rapho-Guillumette—Thase Daniel; Mrs. Moreton R. Bates. 47—Brian Seed. 49,53,54,56,57,59,61—Drawings by Vincent Lewis. 65—Molly Adams. 66,67—Drawings by Adolph E. Brotman; Molly Adams. 68,69—Drawing by Adolph E. Brotman; Eduardo Frias. 70,71—Drawing by Adolph E. Brotman; John Yates. 72,73—J. P. Porter; Drawing by Adolph E. Brotman. 74 through 79—Drawings by Adolph E. Brotman; Photographs by Michael Irwin. 80—Harry Smith courtesy Exbury Gardens Ltd. 82,84,87,89,90—Drawings by Vincent Lewis. 92 through 145—Illustrations by Allianora Rosse. 152,153—Drawings by Davis Meltzer. 154—Map by Adolph E. Brotman.

Acknowledgments

For their help in the preparation of this book, the editors wish to thank the following: American Association of Nurserymen, Inc., Washington, D.C.; Charles Fiore Nurseries, Inc., Prairie View, Ill.; Corliss Brothers, Inc., Ipswich, Mass.; Dr. John L. Creech, Agricultural Research Service, U.S. Department of Agriculture, Beltsville, Md.; Mrs. Edith Crockett, Librarian, The Horticultural Society of New York, New York City; Alfred J. Fordham, Arnold Arboretum, Harvard University; Miss Marie Giasi, Librarian, Brooklyn Botanic Garden, Brooklyn, N.Y.; Charles R. Harrison, Horticulturist, Palmerston North, New Zealand; Miss Dorothea Harrison, Concord, Mass.; Dr. Richard Henley, Department of Horticulture, University of Kentucky, Lexington, Ky.; H. J. Kastl, County Agent, Nassau County Extension Association, Mineola, N.Y.; Thomas P. McElroy Jr., Ornithologist, West Palm Beach, Fla.; Joseph S. Merritt, Joseph S. Merritt, Inc., Dundalk, Md.; Morris Arboretum, Philadelphia, Pa.; A. B. Morse Company, Barrington, Ill.; The Mount Vernon Ladies' Association, Mount Vernon, Va.; The New York Botanical Garden Library, Bronx Park, N.Y.; Dr. Neil G. Odenwald, Louisiana Cooperative Extension Service, Louisiana State University A&M College, University Station, La.; The Ralph Waldo Emerson Association, Cambridge, Mass.; Dr. Thomas J. Sheehan, Department of Ornamental Horticulture, University of Florida, Gainesville, Fla.; George H. Spalding, Botanical Information Consultant, Los Angeles State and County Arboretum, Los Angeles, Calif.; Theodore S. Swanson, Swanson's Land of Flowers, Seattle, Wash.; Dr. Donald Wyman, Horticulturist Emeritus, Arnold Arboretum, Harvard University.

Bibliography

Arbib, Robert and Tony Soper, *The Hungry Bird Book*. Taplinger Publishing Company, 1965.

Bailey, L. H., *The Standard Cyclopedia of Horticulture*. The Macmillan Company, 1942.

Brooklyn Botanic Garden, *Handbook on Flowering Shrubs*. Brooklyn Botanic Garden, 1964.

Chittenden, Fred J., *The Royal Horticultural Society Dictionary of Gardening*. Clarendon Press, 1956.

Coats, Alice M., *Garden Shrubs and Their Histories*. E. P. Dutton and Company, Inc., 1964.

Coats, Alice M., *The Plant Hunters*. McGraw-Hill Book Company, 1969.

Cox, E.H.M., *Plant Hunting in China*. The Scientific Book Guild, 1945.

Davison, Verne E., *Attracting Birds: From the Praries to the Atlantic*. Thomas Y. Crowell Company, 1967.

Dustan, Alice L., *Landscaping Your Own Home*. The Macmillan Company, 1955.

Farrington, Edward I., *Ernest H. Wilson, Plant Hunter*. The Stratford Company, 1931.

Faust, Joan Lee, *The New York Times Book of Trees and Shrubs*. Alfred A. Knopf, Inc., 1964.

Free, Montague, *Plant Pruning in Pictures*. Doubleday and Company, Inc., 1961.

Hartmann, Hudson T. and Dale E. Kester, *Plant Propagation, Principles and Practices*. Prentice-Hall, Inc., 1968.

Ireys, Alice Recknagel, *How to Plan and Plant Your Own Property*. M. Barrows and Company, Inc., 1967.

Kingdon-Ward, Frank, *Pilgrimage for Plants*. Taplinger Publishing Company, 1960.

Lee, Frederic P., *The Azalea Book*. D. Van Nostrand Company, Inc., 1965.

McElroy, Thomas P., Jr., *The New Handbook of Attracting Birds*. Alfred A. Knopf, Inc., 1960.

McKenny, Margaret, *Birds in the Garden and How to Attract Them*. Grosset and Dunlap, Inc., 1939.

Pirone, Pascal P., *Diseases and Pests of Ornamental Plants*. The Ronald Press Company, 1970.

Rockwell, F. F., *10,000 Garden Questions Answered by 20 Experts*. Doubleday and Company, Inc., 1959.

Shurtleff, Malcolm C., *How to Control Plant Diseases in Home and Garden*. Iowa State University Press, 1966.

Taylor, Norman, *The Guide to Garden Shrubs and Trees*. Houghton Mifflin Company, 1965.

Taylor, Norman, *Norman Taylor's Encyclopedia of Gardening*. Houghton Mifflin Company, 1961.

Terres, John K., *Songbirds in Your Garden*. Thomas Y. Crowell Company, 1953.

Westcott, Cynthia, *The Gardener's Bug Book*. Doubleday and Company, Inc., 1964.

Whittle, Tyler, *The Plant Hunters*. Chilton Book Company,

Wyman, Donald, *Shrubs and Vines for American Gardens*. The Macmillan Company, 1969.

Zucker, Isabel, *Flowering Shrubs*. D. Van Nostrand Company, Inc., 1966.

Index

Numerals in italics indicate an illustration of the subject mentioned

abelialeaf, 20. *See also Abeliophyllum*
Abeliophyllum, 94, chart 146. *See also* Abelialeaf
Acacia rose, 22, 88, *chart* 152. *See also Robinia*
Acanthopanax, 94, chart 146. *See also* Aralia
Accents, doorway, 10
Acid-loving shrubs, fertilizer for, 42, 52
Acidity, 41, 42-48, 50; adjusting, 42, 48
Aesculus, 94-95, chart 146. *See also* Bottle-brush buckeye
Air: circulation of, and disease prevention, 40, *chart* 153; in rooting medium, 85; for roots, 49
Alder, black. *See Ilex*
Alder, witch. *See Fothergilla*
Alder buckthorn, 16. *See also Rhamnus*
Alkalinity, 42-48; correction of, 42-48
Allspice, Carolina. *See Calycanthus*
Almond, flowering, 22, *chart* 153. *See also Prunus*
Althea, shrub. *See Hibiscus*
Amelanchier, 95, chart 146. *See also* Serviceberry
Ammonium sulfate, 52, 91
Angelica shrub. *See Acanthopanax*
Annuals, 17
Aphids, *chart 152,* 153
Aralia, 9, 16, 30. *See also Acanthopanax*
Arboretums, 10, 13
Architecture, and landscaping, 68
Aronia, 95-96, chart 146. *See also* Chokeberry
Arrowwood, 28, *29, chart* 45. *See also Viburnum*
Azalea, 10, 13, 18, *23,* 39, 53, *65, 70-71, 80,* 81; to attract birds, 42, 43, *chart* 45; climate preferences of, 8-9; diseases of, *chart* 153; Exbury, 17, *80,* 81, 90; flower season of, 22, 24, 30, *chart* 45; Mollis, *23, 70-71,* 90; planting, 40, 41-42; preparation of soil for, 41-42; propagation of, from cuttings, 86; propagation of, from seed, 82, 88-91; removing seeds of, 63, 90; soil requirements of, 9, 42, 91. *See also Rhododendron*

backgrounds, 15, 17, *66-67,* 73
Bacteria, *chart* 152, *chart* 153
Balled-and-burlaped plants, 38, 39-40
Barbados pride. *See Caesalpinia*
Barberry, 7, 9, 15, *32,* 39, 58, 60; berries of, 28, *32,* 63; and black stem rust, 58; box, 70; flower season of, 22; fruit seasons of, 22, 28, 32, 63; for hedges, 16, 58; Japanese, 7, 9, 18, 22, *32,* 60, 63; Korean, *32;*

Mentor, 16, 58; propagation of, from stem cuttings, 85; truehedge columnberry, 16, 64. *See also Berberis*
Bare-rooted plants, 3̈8, 39-40; planting, *49*
Bark, colorful, 9, 18, *33,* 64
Bartram, John, 91
Bartram, William, 91
Bayberry: to attract birds, *chart* 45; candles, 36; climate preferences of, 8-9; fruit of, 28, 32, 36, *chart* 45, 63; fruit seasons of, 28, 32, *chart* 45; soil requirements of, 42. *See also Myrica*
Beach plum, 9. *See also Prunus*
Beauty bush, 9, 24, 46, 53. *See also Kolkwitzia*
Beauty-berry, 30, *31, chart* 153. *See also Callicarpa*
Beetles, ladybug, 153
Benzoin. See Lindera
*Berberis, 96-*97, *chart* 146. *See also* Barberry; Truehedge columnberry
Berries, 7, 10, *28, 29, 30, 31, 32, 33, 44, 47;* to attract birds, 42, *44, chart* 45-46, *47;* colorful, 9, 63; for indoor arrangements, 63, seasons of, 24, 28, 29, 30, 31, 32, 33, *chart* 45-46. *See also* Fruit
Birds, 42, *44, chart* 45-46, *47;* attracting, 7, 17, 42-47, 63; and pests, 42, 152-153
Black stem rust, 58
Bladder senna. *See Colutea*
Blooming periods, 24
Blossom size, *chart* 146-151
Bluebeard, 26, 57. *See also Caryopteris*
Blueberry, 10, 18; bark of, 32; birds attracted by, 18, *chart* 45; climate preferences of, 8-9; fruit of, 18, 28, 30, *chart* 45, 63; fruit season of, 28, 30, *chart* 45, 63; soil requirements of, 42. *See also Vaccinium*
Bone meal, 42, 52
Borders, 16-17; as background, 16, 17; as boundary markers, 16, 17; defined, 16; as foreground, 16; planning, 16-17; as privacy screens, 16, 17; as windbreaks, 16
Borers, lilac, *chart* 152
Botanical gardens, 36
Bottle-brush buckeye, 8, 24, 88. *See also Aesculus*
Bougainvillea, *74-75*
Boundaries, 10, 16, *66-67*
Bouquets, 7. *See also* Cut flowers; Forcing
Bridal wreath, 9, 20, 30. *See also Spiraea*
Broken branches, pruning, *54*
Broom, 9, 15, 39; bark of, 32; diseases of, *chart* 153; flower season of, 22, 24; pests of, *chart* 152; propagation of, from stem cuttings, 86; soil requirements of, 9, 41-42. *See also Cytisus*
Buckeye, bottle-brush, 8, 24, 88. *See also Aesculus*
Buckthorn, alder, 16. *See also Rhamnus*

Buckthorn, sea, 30, 32. *See also Hippophae*
Buddleia, 12, 97-98, *chart* 146. *See also* Butterfly bush
Buddleja. See Buddleia
Buds, 38, 87
Bulbs, 17
Burning bush. *See Euonymus*
Butterfly bush: to attract birds, *chart* 46; climate preferences of, 9, 57; dieback of, 57; flower season of, 22, 26, *chart* 46; propagation of, from stem cuttings, 85, 86; pruning, 57; rejuvenation of, 57. *See also Buddleia*
Buttonbush, 26, *chart* 153

Caesalpinia, *98, chart* 146
Calendar of color, 18, 20-23
Callicarpa, 98-99, chart 146. *See also* Beauty-berry
Callus tissue, 87
Calycanthus, 99, chart 146. *See also* Sweet shrub
Candles, bayberry, 36
Cankers, 38, 153
Cankerworm, *chart* 152
Captan, 91, *chart* 153
*Caragana, 99-*100, *chart* 146. *See also* Pea tree
Carbaryl, *chart* 152
Caryopteris, 100, chart 146. *See also* Bluebeard
Cassia, 10
Caterpillars, *chart* 152, 153
*Cercis, 100-*101, *chart* 146. *See also* Redbud
Chaenomeles, 101, chart 146. *See also* Quince
Characteristics, 15, *chart* 146-151
Chaste tree, 26, *27,* 57. *See also Vitex*
Chaulmoogra tree, 13
Chemical spray, 153
Cherry. *See Prunus*
Cherry, cornelian, 20, *21,* 26, 28, 63. *See also Cornus*
Chokeberry, 8-9, 22, 28, 30, 32, *33, chart* 153. *See also Aronia*
Choosing shrubs, 10, 35-37, 64-79; for boundaries, 66; criteria for, 64; for hedges, 16; for highlighting, 78; near house, 10-15, 68; for paths, 70; rules for, 35-37; for screens, 73, 76; for terraces, 74
Cinnamon, 10
Cinquefoil, 17, *24,* 68, *78-79, chart* 152. *See also Potentilla*
Clethra, 39, *101-*102, *chart* 146. *See also* Summer sweet
Climate, 7, 8, 9, 14, 16, 152; areas, 18, 20-33; and choosing plants, 8, 36; and cuttings, 83; and flower seasons, *chart* 154; zones, *map* 154
Clover, bush, 26. *See also Lespedeza*
Cold frame, 84, 86, 91
Color, 9, 17, 57-58, 64; calendar of, 18-33; flower, *chart* 146-151
Colutea, 102, chart 146
*Comptonia, 102-*103, *chart* 146. *See also* Sweet fern
Container-grown plants, 38, 39-40

Control, pest and disease, 152-153, *chart* 152-153
Coral tree. *See Erythrina*
Coralberry, 30, *chart* 46, *chart* 152. *See also Symphoricarpos*
Cornelian cherry, 20, *21*, 26, 28, 63. *See also Cornus*
Cornus, 103-104, *chart* 146. *See also* Cornelian cherry; Dogwood
Corylopsis, 104, *chart* 146. *See also* Winter hazel
Corylus, 104-105, *chart* 147. *See also* Hazelnut
Cotinus, 105, *chart* 147. *See also* Smoke tree
Cotoneaster, 9, 15, 43, 47, 68, 105-106, *chart* 147; to attract birds, 42, *43, chart* 45, *47;* cranberry, 28, 30; diseases of, *chart* 153; fruit season of, 28, 30, *chart* 45; propagation of, by layering, 88; propagation of, from stem cuttings, 85, 86
Cottonseed meal, 42, 52
Cow manure, 42
Crab apple, Sargent, 42, *43, 44, chart* 45
Cranberry bush, 8-9, 28, *29,* 30, 32, 63, 64. *See also Viburnum*
Cranberry cotoneaster, 68. *See also Cotoneaster*
Crape myrtle, 9, 26, 35, 55, *chart* 152, *chart* 153, 154. *See also Lagerstroemia*
Creech, John L., *14*
Criteria, for choosing shrubs, 64
Crossbreeding, 9, 17
Crown galls, *chart* 153
Currant, Indian. *See Symphoricarpos*
Cut flowers: berries and foliage, 63; drying, 63; forcing, 60-62; searing stems of, 62-63; in season, 62-63
Cutting back, 51, 88
Cuttings, root, 88
Cuttings, stem, 83-88; and climate zones, 83; hardwood, 83, 86-88, *87;* semihardwood, 83-86; softwood, 83-86, *84*
Cydonia. See Chaenomeles
Cytisus, 39, 106-107, chart 147. *See also* Broom

daffodils, 17
Damping off, 91
Daphne, 9, 15, 20, 24, 63, 70, 92, 93, 107-108, chart 147, *chart* 152, *chart* 153
Day lily, 17
DeBary, Heinrich Anton, 59
Density, 58, 59-60, 64, 72-73
Department of Agriculture, U.S., 10, 11, 13, 14
De Rothschild, Lionel, 17, 81
Desmodium. See Lespedeza
Deutzia, 9, 17, 22, 24, 37, 56, 108, 109, chart 147
Diazinon, *chart* 152
Diervilla. See Weigela
Dinocap, *chart* 153
Diseases, 17, 38, 40, 54, 152-153, *chart 153*
Division, *82,* 83
Dogwood, 8, *23, 33;* to attract birds,

chart 45-46; flowering season of, *22, 23;* fruit season, 24, *chart* 45-46; Kelsey, 32; propagation of, by division, 83; pruning, 32, 57-58; red osier, *chart* 46; red-stemmed, 32, *33,* 57-58; Siberian, 7, 33, *chart* 45-46, 83; Tatarian, 22, 24, 32; Westonbirt, 18, *23;* in winter, 7, 32, *33;* yellow-twigged, 32, *33,* 57-58. *See also Cornus*
Dolomite limestone, 48
Dormant oil spray, *chart* 152, 153
Dormant plants, 38, 39, 88
Dowsing, 85
Drying, for winter arrangements, 63

elaeagnus, 24, 30, 63, *109, chart* 147. *See also* Russian olive
Elder, 24, *25,* 28, 45-46, *chart* 152, *chart* 153. *See also Sambucus*
Elderberry. *See Sambucus*
Enkianthus, 22, 30, 40, 42, 86, 109-110, chart 147
Erythrina, 110, chart 147
Euonymus, 11, 30, 31, 39, 110-111, chart 147; diseases of, *chart* 153; fruit season of, 30, *31;* for hedges, 16, 66, 73; pests of, *chart* 152; propagation of, from stem cuttings, 86; winged, 16, 30, *31,* 66, 73. *See also* Spindle tree; Strawberry bush
Evergreens, 8, 68, 73, *78*
Exochorda, 111-112, chart 147. *See also* Pearlbush

fall: berries in, 18, 24, *28, 29, 30, 31;* colorful foliage in, 7, 10, 18, *28;* early, 28, 29; flowers in, 17; late, 30, 31
False spirea, *24,* 60, 63, *78-79. See also Sorbaria*
Ferbam, *chart* 153
Fern, sweet, 9. *See also Comptonia*
Ferns, 42, *43*
Fertilizer: for acid-loving shrubs, 42, 52; addition of at plantingtime, 42; applying to established shrubs, 51-52; bone meal as, 42, 52; chemical, 52; cottonseed meal as, 42, 52; cow manure as, 42; fast-acting, 52; ingredients of, 52; slow-acting, 52; types of, 52
Field-grown plants, 39
Filbert. *See Corylus*
Fire blight, *chart* 152, *chart 153*
Flower color, 15, 64, *chart* 146-151
Flower fence, Barbados. *See Caesalpinia*
Flower season, 17, *chart* 45-46, *chart* 146-151; fall, 17; spring, 18, *19, 20, 21, 22, 23;* summer, 18, *24, 25, 26, 27;* in various climate zones, *chart* 154
Flowers, 7, 9, 10; on informal hedges, 15; nectar-rich, to attract birds, 42, *chart* 45-46; production of, 10, 55-56, 57; pruning for larger, 55-56; pruning for more, 55
Focal points, 64, *65, 78-79*
Foliage: colorful, in fall, 7, 9, 17, 18, *28, 29, 30, 31;* for indoor display,

63; notable, *chart* 146-151; texture of, 17
Folpet, 91, *chart* 153
Forcing, 60-62, *61,* 84
Foreground plantings, 17
Forsythia, 9, 12, 15, 18, 20, 21, 55, 64, 66-67, 89, 112-113, chart 147-148; for boundary line, *66-67;* climate preferences of, 9, 154; flower season of, 20, 21; forcing, 60, 84; Korean green-stemmed, 32; propagation of, 84, 86, 88
Forsythia, white. *See Abeliophyllum*
Fothergilla, 22, 30, 112, 113, *chart* 148
Fragrance, 70, *chart* 146-151
Frangipani, 62. *See also Plumeria*
Franklinia, 26, 91, 92, 93, 113-114, chart 148
Fruit: to attract birds, 42, 44, *chart* 45-46, 47; decorative, 9, 15, 63, *chart* 146-151; for indoor display, 63; season, 24, *28, 29, 30, 31, 32, 33, chart* 45-46; in winter, 18, *32,* 33
Fuchsia, 24, 46, 114, chart 148
Fungicide, 91
Fungus diseases, 38, 58, 91, *chart* 153
Fungus leaf spot, *chart 153*

galls, crown, *chart 153*
Glory bower, 26, 28
Goat willow, 18, *19,* 20. *See also Salix*
Golden bell. *See Forsythia*
Gordonia. See Franklinia
Groundsel bush, 9
Growth rate, 7-8
Gumi. *See Elaeagnus*
Gypsy moth larvae, *chart* 152

hamamelis, *114-115, chart* 148. *See also* Witch hazel
Hand pruning shears, *53,* 63
Hardiness, 8, 9, 35, 36, 40
Haw, black, *chart* 45-46. *See also Viburnum*
Hazelnut, *chart* 152, *chart* 153. *See also Corylus*
Hedges, 15, *72-73;* choice of plants for, 10, 15-16, 64, 73, *chart* 146-151; formal, 15, 16, 58, 59-60, *chart* 146-151; informal, 15-16, 58, 60, *chart* 146-151; initial pruning of, 59-60; planting, *58-59;* purposes of, 15, 73; shearing, 16, 54, 58, 60
Heeling in, 48
Height, 8, 16, 17, *chart* 146-151
Hemlocks, 73
Hibiscus, 115-116, chart 148. *See also* Rose of Sharon
Hickory horned devil, *chart* 152
Hippophae, 116, chart 148. *See also* Buckthorn, sea
Holly. *See Ilex*
Honeydew, 152
Honeysuckle, 9, 10, 32, 36-37, 40, 42, 43; to attract birds, 42, *43, chart* 45-46; flower seasons of, 20, 22; fruit seasons of, 24, 26. *See also Lonicera*
Horned devil, hickory, *chart* 152
Horse chestnut. *See Aesculus*
Hortensia. *See Hydrangea*
Humidity, and diseases, *chart* 153

Hybrids, 9, 89-90
Hydrangea, 6, 7, 9, 12, 25, 68-69, 74-75, 116-118, 117, chart 148; big-leaved, *6, 7,* 55; changeable color of, 50; as cut flower, 62; diseases of, *chart* 153; drying for arrangements, 63; flower season of, 24, *25,* 26; oak-leaved, *25, 30,* 82, 83; peegee, 55, 63; propagation of, by division, 82, 83; propagation of, by stem cuttings, 85; pruning, 55
Hypericum, 118, chart 148. *See also* St.-John's-wort

Ilex, 118-119, chart 148. *See also* Winterberry
Inchworm, *chart* 152
Indigo, 24. *See also Indigofera*
Indigofera, 119, chart 148. *See also* Indigo
Insects, 38, 42, 55; beneficial, 152
Iron, 48
Iron sulfate, 48

Jasmine, 9, 20, 32, 36. *See also Jasminum*
Jasminum, 119, chart 148. *See also* Jasmine
Jetbead, 22, 32. *See also Rhodotypos*
Jewel berry. *See Callicarpa*
Judas tree, Chinese. *See Cercis*

Kerria, 10, 22, 32, 70, 83, 120, chart 148
Knife, pruning, *53*
Kolkwitzia, 120, chart 148. *See also* Beauty bush

Ladybug beetles, 153
Lagerstroemia, 121, chart 148. *See also* Crape myrtle
Landscaping, 10-15, 35, 40, *64-79*
Larvae, gypsy moth, *chart* 152
Layering, 88, *90*
Lead plant, 24
Leaf joints, *87*
Leaf nodes, 38
Leaf spot, fungus, *chart 153*
Leaves, 28, *29, 30, 31,* 38, 52, 63, 64. *See also* Foliage
Lespedeza, 121-122, chart 148. *See also* Clover, bush
Lice, plant, *chart* 152
Life span, of shrubs, 8, 36-37
Light requirements, 9, 16-17, 35, 70-71, *chart* 146-151
Ligustrum, 122-123, chart 148. *See also* Privet
Lilac, 8, *11,* 18, 22, 35, 39, *72-73,* 81; climate preferences of, 9, 154; diseases of, *chart* 153; flower season of, *22;* as hedge, *72-73;* life span of, 8, 36-37; pests of, *chart* 152; propagation of, by division, 81, 82, 83; propagation of, from cuttings, 86; pruning, 55, 63. *See also Syringa*
Lilac, summer. *See Buddleia*
Lilac borers, *chart 152*
"Lilac of the South," 35

Lime-sulfur solution, *chart* 152
Limestone, 48, 59
Lindera, 123, chart 148. *See also* Spicebush
Location, 10-15, 35, 48
Locust. *See Robinia*
Lonicera, 123-124, chart 148-149. *See also* Honeysuckle
Lopping shears, *53*

Malathion, *chart* 152
Maneb, *chart* 153
Marigolds, 17
Mealy bugs, 38, 153
Methoxychlor, *chart* 152
Meyer, Frank, *11*
Mezereon. *See Daphne*
Microclimates, 36
Mildew, 40, *chart 153*
Mites, 38
Mock orange, 9, *24,* 35, 36-37, 56. *See also Philadelphus*
Moisture, 9, 49, 91
Mold, black sooty, *chart* 152
Moths, of lilac borers, *chart* 152
Mulching, 52; to conserve moisture, 52, 91; depth, 52; to maintain soil temperature, 52, 91; materials for, 52; to prevent weeds, 52; to protect feeding roots, 52
Myrica, 124-125, chart 149. *See also* Bayberry
Myrtle, crape, 9, 26, 35, 55, *chart* 152, *chart* 153, 154. *See also Lagerstroemia*

Nannyberry, 30, *44, chart* 45-46, 76. *See also Viburnum*
Naphthaleneacetic acid, 85
Native plants, 16-17
Nectar, 42
Nitrogen, 52
Nodes, 83, 84
Noise barrier, 73
Nursery bed, 88, 89, 91

Oleaster. *See Elaeagnus*
Olive, Russian, *chart* 153. *See also Elaeagnus*
Organic matter: as mulch, 49, 52, 91; in topsoil, 41; as soil conditioner, 41, 59. *See also* Peat moss
Osier, dwarf purple, 70. *See also Salix*
Outdoor living room, 74
Overfeeding, 51-52

Paeonia, 125, chart 149. *See also* Peony
Paths, 64, *70-71*
Patio plantings, *74-75*
Pea tree, 22, 35, 76. *See also Caragana*
Pearlbush, 22. *See also Exochorda*
Peat moss, 85, 86, 90-91; acidity of, 48; as mulch, 52; as soil conditioner, 41, 49, 91
Peony, tree, *13, 22. See also Paeonia*

Pepper bush, sweet. *See Clethra*
Perennials, 17
Perlite, 85
Pests, 17, 38, 54, 55, 152-153, *chart 152*
Petunias, 17
pH scale, 42, 59
Philadelphus, 125-126, chart 149. *See also* Mock orange
Phlox, garden, 17
Phosphorus, 52
Photinia, 22, 30, *126, chart* 149, *chart* 153
Pinxter-bloom, 45. *See also Rhododendron*
Planning, 16-17
Plant hunters, 10-14, 91
Plant lice, *chart 152*
Planting, 41-51; balled and burlaped shrubs, 50-51; bare-rooted shrubs, *49,* 50, 51; container-grown shrubs, 50-51; depth, 49-50, 82; double-row hedge, 58, *59;* hardwood cuttings, *87;* hedges, 58; new plants, 86, 91; root cuttings, 88, *89;* soil condition and, 40; suckers, 82
Plum, 9. *See also Prunus*
Plumeria, 126, 127, chart 149. *See also* Frangipani
Poinciana. See Caesalpinia
Pollination, 62
Polluted air, tolerance of, 9
Pomegranate. *See Punica*
Pond, highlighting, *78-79*
Potassium, 52
Potentilla, 127, chart 149. *See also* Cinquefoil
Powdery mildew, *chart 153*
Privet, *33,* 76-77; Amur, 16, 32, *33,* 63, 73; border, 76-77; fruit season of, 32, *33,* 63; as hedge, 15, 16, 73; pests of, *chart* 152; as screen, 16, 73, *76-77;* in winter, 32, *33, 63. See also Ligustrum*
Propagation, 81-91; by division, *82,* 83; from hardwood cuttings, 83, 86-88, *87;* by layering, 88, *90;* from root cuttings, 88, *89;* from seed, 82, 88-91; from softwood cuttings, 83-86, *84;* from stem cuttings, 83-88; vegetative reproduction, 82-88
Pruning: of bare-root shrubs, 49, 51; early spring, *54;* and flowering habit, 55, 56; frequency of, 52-53; hard, for larger blossoms, 56; hedges, 15, 16, 58, 59-60; initial, 49, 51, 59-60, *87,* 88; maintenance, *54-55;* for more blossoms, 55-56, 57; plants from hardwood cuttings, 88; preventive, 54, 55-56, *chart* 152-153; to rejuvenate old shrubs, 56-*57;* remedial, *54-55;* removing flowers, *56,* 63; severe, *57;* shrubs with colored stems, 57-58; time for, 54, 55, 56; tools, *53-54;* winter-killed stems, 57
Pruning knife, *53*
Pruning saw, *53,* 54, 57
Pruning shears, hand, *53,* 86
Prunus, 127-128, chart 149. *See also* Almond, flowering; Beach plum
Punica, 128-129, chart 149
Pussy willow, 9; forcing, 60, 84;

propagation of, from stem cuttings, 84, 86. See also Salix
Pyrethrum, chart 152
Pyrus japonica. See Chaenomeles

quince: climate preferences of, 9, 154; diseases of, chart 153; flower season of, 20, 21; flowering, 10, 20, 21; 60; forcing, 60; life span of, 8; pests of, chart 152; propagation of, from cuttings, 86; propagation of, by layering, 88; pruning, 55; as showpiece, 10. See also Chaenomeles

redbud, 8, 22, 30, 53. See also Cercis
Rejuvenation, complete, 56-57
Reproduction: from seed, 82, 88-91; vegetative, 82-88
Retaining wall, 74-75
Rhamnus, 128, 129, chart 149. See also Alder buckthorn
Rhododendron, 20, 21, 129-131, chart 149. See also Azalea; Pinxter-bloom
Rhodotypos, 131, chart 149. See also Jetbead
Rhus, 132, chart 149-150. See also Sumac
Rhus cotinus. See Cotinus
Robinia, 132, chart 150. See also Rose acacia
Rock Joseph, 13
Root cuttings, 88, 89
Rooting hormone, 84, 85, 90
Rooting medium, 84, 85, 90
Rosa, 58, 133-134, chart 150. See also Rose
Rose, 9, 14, 22, 23, 66-67; to attract birds, chart 46; cabbage, 24; diseases of, chart 153; Father Hugo's, 22, 23; on fence, 66-67; flower season of, 23, 24; fruit season of, 28, 30, chart 46; as hedge, 58; Japanese, 9, 14, 24, 28, 30, chart 46; multiflora, 58. See also Rosa
Rose acacia, 22, 88, chart 152. See also Robinia
Rose of Sharon, 9, 26, 27, 36-37, 55. See also Hibiscus
Rotenone, chart 152
Russian olive, chart 153. See also Elaeagnus
Rust, black stem, 58

St.-John's-wort, 24, 68. See also Hypericum
Salix, 18, 19, 134-135, chart 150. See also Goat willow; Osier; Pussy willow
Sambucus, 135, chart 150. See also Elder
Sapphireberry, 30, 45. See also Symplocos
Saw, pruning, 53, 54
Scale, of plantings, 66, 70, 76
Scales, 55, chart 152, 153

Screens: borders as, 17; choice of shrubs for, 10, 64, 73; to conceal eyesores, 72-73; hedges as, 15; privacy, 64, 72-73; spot, 76-77; from traffic, 66-67, 72; as windbreaks, 64. See also Hedges
Sea buckthorn. See Hippophae
Searing stems, 62-63
Seaside conditions, 7, 9
Seasons: in climate zones, chart 154; flower, chart 146-151; of particular attractiveness, 18, 20-33; of shrubs to attract birds, chart 45-46; for propagation, 81, 82, 83, 86, 87, 88, 90
Seed: production of, 56, 63; propagation from, 82, 88-91
Semihardwood cuttings, 83-86
Senna, bladder. See Colutea
Serviceberry, 8-9, 26, 28, 42, chart 46, 88, chart 153. See also Amelanchier
Shade trees, 74-75
Shape, choice of 9, 10-15, 16, 64
Shearing, 16, 60. See also Pruning
Shears: hand pruning, 53; hedge, 15, 53, 54; lopping, 53
Silverberry. See Elaeagnus
Size, choice of, 9, 10-15, 16, 35, 64
Smoke tree, 24, 34, 35, 76. See also Cotinus
Snowball, 22, 30. See also Viburnum
Snowberry, 9, 28, 29, chart 46. See also Symphoricarpos
Softwood cuttings, 83-86, 84
Soil: adjustment of pH of, 42-48; conditioning, 41; drainage, 41; effect of organic matter on, 41; needs, 9, 16, 42, 91, chart 146-151; for new azalea plants, 91; porosity of, 41; preparation of, 49, 59; and resistance to pests and diseases, 152; subsoil, 41; testing, 42; texture of, 41; topsoil, 41
Sorbaria, 135-136, chart 150. See also Spirea, false
Spacing, 40-41, 58
Sphagnum moss, 85, 91
Spicebush, 9, 20, 21, 28, 30. See also Lindera
Spider mites, 38
Spindle tree, 28, 39. See also Euonymus
Spiraea, 136-137, chart 150. See also Bridal wreath; Spirea
Spiraea aitchisonii. See Sorbaria
Spiraea sorbifolia. See Sorbaria
Spirea, 9, 15, 17, 22, 23, 24, 25, 60, 64, 66, 70, 78-79; dwarf garland, 66; flower season of, 22, 23, 24, 25; Froebel, 37; pests of, chart 152; propagation of, from stem cuttings, 85; rate of growth of, 37, 89. See also Spiraea
Spirea, false, 24, 63. See also Sorbaria
Spring: early, 20-21; flowers in, 7, 10, 18; late, 17, 22-23
Spruces, 73
Standard, 8
Stem cuttings, 83-88; hardwood, 83, 86-88; semihardwood, 83-86; softwood, 83-86

Stems, colorful, 7, 32, 33, 57-58
Stephanandra, 24, 28, 70, 84, 137-138, chart 150
Stewartia, 24, 30, 40, 138, chart 150
Strawberry bush, 28, 30, 92, 93. See also Euonymus
Streptomycin sulfate, chart 153
Suckers, 82, 83
Sulfur: fungicide, chart 153; soil amendment, 48, 59
Sumac, 8-9, 26, 27, 28, 29; to attract birds, chart 45-46; diseases of, chart 153; drying for arrangements, 63; in fall, 28, 29; flower season of, 26, 27; fruit seasons of, 26, 32, chart 45-46, 63; pests of, chart 152; propagation of, by division, 83; propagation of, from root cuttings, 88. See also Rhus
Summer: early, 17, 24-25; flowers in, 7, 17, 18; fruit in, 10; late, 26-27
Summer lilac. See Buddleia
Summer sweet, 8-9, 26, 39, 42. See also Clethra
Sweet fern, 9. See also Comptonia
Sweet pepper bush. See Clethra
Sweet shrub, 9, 22, 53, 88. See also Calycanthus
Sweetleaf, Asiatic. See Symplocos
Symphoricarpos, 138-139, chart 150. See also Coralberry; Snowberry
Symplocos, 139, chart 150. See also Sapphireberry
Syringa, 11, 39, 139-141, 140, chart 150. See also Lilac

tamarisk, 24, 26. See also Tamarix
Tamarix, 39, 141, chart 151. See also Tamarisk
Tent caterpillar, eastern, chart 152
Terrace plantings, 74-75
Textures, 17, 64, 73
Thiram, 91
Tree-wound dressing, chart 152
Trees, shade, 8, 74-75
Truehedge columnberry, 16, 64. See also Berberis.
Tubs, moveable, 68, 74

uses, 9-10, 10-15, 39, chart 146-151

Vaccinium, 141-142, chart 151. See also Blueberry
Vegetative reproduction, 82-88
Vermiculite, 85
Viburnum, 11, 15, 22, 30, 31, 142-144, chart 151; diseases of, chart 153; doublefile, 22, 26; in fall, 30, 31; flower season of, 22; fruit season of, 26, 63; Korean spice, 70; linden, 63; pests of, chart 152; propagation of, from cuttings, 86; spring-flowering, 53. See also Arrowwood;

Cranberry bush; Haw, black; Nannyberry; Snowball; Withe rod
Virus diseases, *chart* 152
Vitex, 144-*145, chart* 151, *See also* Chaste tree

Watering, 49, 50, 51, 59, 91, *chart* 152
Wayfaring tree. *See Viburnum*
Weigela, 22, *24,* 42, *43, chart* 45, 56, *145, chart* 151, *chart* 153
Wilson, Ernest, *12*
Willow: goat, 18, *19,* 20; pussy, 9, 60, 84. *See also Salix*
Willow, wolf. *See Elaeagnus*
Windbreaks, 10, 15, 64, 73. *See also* Screens
Winter, 32-33; bark, *33;* berries in, *32, 33*
Winter hazel, 20, 60. *See also Corylopsis*

Winterberry, *28, 44, chart* 45-46. *See also Ilex*
Witch alder. *See Fothergilla*
Witch hazel, 8-9, *20,* 30, 60, 61, 85. *See also Hamamelis*
Withe rod, 7. *See also Viburnum*
Wolf willow. *See Elaeagnus*

Zineb, *chart* 153
Zinnias, 17